THE KHILAFAT MOVEMENT

Qazi Mohammad Adeel Abbasi

Translated from Urdu by Arif Ansari

Acknowledgement
National Council for Promotion of Urdu Language
Ministry of Education, Department of Higher Education
Government of India

INDIA · SINGAPORE · MALAYSIA

Details of the original Urdu book:

Tehreek-e-Khilafat by Qazi Mohammad Adeel Abbasi
© National Council for the Promotion of Urdu Language, New Delhi
1st Edition published in 1978
4th Edition published in 2013 by the National Council for the Promotion of Urdu Language
ISBN: 978-81-7587-388-9
Publisher: Director, National Council for the Promotion of Urdu Language, Farogh Urdu Bhavan, FC-33/9 Institutional Area, Jasola, New Delhi, 110025. Tel: 49539000 Fax: 49539099
Sales Department: West Block-8, RK Puram, New Delhi-110025. Tel: 26109746 Fax: 26108159
E-mail: urducouncil@gmail.com
Website: www.urducouncil.nic.in

To my late life-partner
Najmun Nisa Begum

Table of Contents

Translator's Note

"A caliphate or khilafat (Arabic: خِلَافَة) is an institution or public office governing a territory under Islamic rule. The person who holds this office carries the title of caliph and is considered a politico-religious successor to the Islamic prophet Muhammad and a leader of the entire Muslim world (Ummah). Historically, the caliphates were polities based on Islam that developed into multi-ethnic trans-national empires." (Source: https://en.wikipedia.org/wiki/Caliphate)

"The Khilafat movement or the Caliphate movement, also known as the Indian Muslim movement (1919-24), was a pan-Islamist political protest campaign launched by Muslims of British India lead by Shaukat Ali, Maulana Mohammad Ali Jauhar, Hakim Ajmal Khan, and Abul Kalam Azad to restore the caliph of the Ottoman Caliphate, who was considered the leader of the Muslims, as an effective political authority. It was a protest against the sanctions placed on the caliph and the Ottoman Empire after the First World War by the Treaty of Sevres." (Source: https://en.wikipedia.org/wiki/Khilafat_Movement)

In this translation, the word 'caliphate' is used for the institution or public office as described above, while its Arabic equivalent 'khilafat' is used exclusively in the context of its namesake movement in the Indian subcontinent.

This book is a translation of the Urdu book *Tahreek-e-Khilafat* written by Qazi Mohammad Adeel Abbasi (March 31, 1898 - March 22, 1980).

Qazi Mohammad Adeel Abbasi's account of the Khilafat Movement is not just a front row view but an account from the trenches of the movement. As mentioned in the preface of *Tahreek-e-Khilafat*, Adeel Abbasi left home at a very young age to join the non-cooperation movement led by Mahatma Gandhi and was imprisoned by the British for his involvement. Adeel Abbasi actively participated in the Khilafat Movement as it evolved alongside the non-cooperation movement under Gandhiji's leadership. Adeel Abbasi made significant contributions to Urdu journalism and literature. At a very young age, he became the Chief Editor of the daily *Zamindar*, a leading nationalist Urdu paper published from Lahore. His book *Iqbal ka Falsafa-e-Hayat-o-Shayari* ("Iqbal's Philosophy of Life and Poetry") was hailed by literary critics as a landmark treatment of the poet. He also wrote an acclaimed book in English titled "Aspects of Society and Politics," the book release event for which was presided by then Prime Minister of India, Mrs. Indira Gandhi.

I dedicate this translation to the memory of my father, Abul Mafakhir Muhammad Anwar Ansari (1922-1978). He was born and brought up in Firangi Mahal, the Lucknow family that was deeply involved in the Khilafat Movement. A photograph of him sporting a Turkish cap as a teenager and his later politics suggest that he was a proponent of this movement, although the movement was long over by the time he came of age.

I would like to express my sincere gratitude and appreciation to Mr. Mohammad Arshad Abbasi, not only for entrusting me with the translation of his father's book but also for his diligent review of the translation draft and for highlighting its errors and omissions. This greatly improved the quality of this book and boosted my confidence in the veracity of the translation. I would also like to thank Asna Ansari for editing the first draft and Sahil Ansari for designing the cover.

Arif Ansari
Bethesda, Maryland, USA
June 2022

Foreword

The fundamental difference between human beings and animals is the capacity for speech and consciousness. These two God-given capabilities have not only given humans the noblest status of all creatures but also acquainted them with those mysteries of symbols and codes of the universe which could take his mental and spiritual advancement to lofty heights. Awareness of the hidden factors of life and universe is what is known as knowledge. Knowledge has two basic branches: intrinsic and extrinsic. Intrinsic knowledge has been concerned with the inner world of humans and its civilization and catharsis. In addition to Holy Prophets, the efforts made by pious elders, true Sufis and saints, and thoughtful poets to embellish and beautify the intrinsic are different links in the same chain of knowledge. Extrinsic knowledge is concerned with the external world of humans and its formation and construction. History and philosophy, politics and economics, sociology and science, etc. are such areas of knowledge. Whether knowledge is internal or external, language has played a foundational role in its protection and promotion. Whether it is the spoken word or written word, language has been the most effective means of transferring knowledge from one generation to another. The written word is older than the spoken word. That is why man discovered the art of writing and when the art of printing was invented, the life of the word and its sphere of influence increased further.

Books are a repository of words and for that reason they are the main source of various science and arts. The main objective of the National Council for the Promotion of Urdu Language is to publish good Urdu books and make them available at the lowest price possible to those interested in knowledge and literature. Urdu is a language that is understood, spoken, and read throughout India. In fact, those who understand, speak, and read Urdu are spread throughout the world. It is an effort of the Council to prepare syllabus and non-syllabus textbooks in this language that is dear to so many, which would be popular among all kinds of readers, and to publish them in the best of styles. To achieve this objective, along with the publication of original books on various kinds of subjects, the Council has also paid attention to the publication of critiques and translation of standard books from other languages.

It is a cause of great satisfaction for Taraqqi Urdu Bureau and, since its inception, the National Council for the Promotion of Urdu Language, that Urdu readers have been very receptive to the various books on arts and sciences they have published. Under an editing program, the Council has started a scheme of printing books of fundamental importance. This book is a part of this scheme, which I hope will fill an important academic need.

I would also request that academics write to us if they see anything incorrect in this book so that the errors that remain can be removed in the next publication.

Dr. Khwaja Muhammad Ikramuddin
Director, National Council for the Promotion of Urdu Language
New Delhi

Preface

When it was suggested to me that I write a series of articles on the "Khilafat Movement" in a weekly journal, I readily agreed and, as an introduction, even wrote a few parts under the title "A Cursory Glance at the History of Turkey." The thought was that after that, I would just write offhand. I was under the impression that I would have no difficulty since I had participated in that movement and heard many eye-witness accounts. But I became busy with other things and when I suddenly remembered one day that I needed to fulfill that commitment and started collecting my thoughts and studying books, I realized how difficult the task was.

The purpose of lifting a pen to write about the Khilafat Movement was to examine the whys and wherefores of the graceful elegance of ancient times and the sunrise of the modern age. In a far-flung place like Basti, neither books nor journals were available for such a study, nor did I have the time to set out on a journey to look for them. That is why I had to settle for whatever little was available to me there.

As far as the history of the Khilafat Movement is concerned, it has been observed that authors and compilers often gave it only a perfunctory treatment, and those who did write did not include the history of all its relevant years. To study and research this topic, archival newspaper articles were needed, but, with the exception of some material from the journals *Mashriq* and *Zamindar* (Lahore), which were secure with a dear friend of mine, no archival material could be found from *Hamdam* (Lucknow), *Siyasat* (Amritsar), *Madina* (Bijnor), or *Bande Mataram* (Lahore). When I made an inquiry at Aligarh Muslim University, I was informed that newspaper archives had been destroyed. Albeit, many people have written about the life of Gandhiji, and that was very helpful since Gandhiji's life from 1918 to 1925 is woven into the thread of the Khilafat Movement.

The concept of Islamic Khilafat, or Caliphate, is as old as Islam itself, but it is a forgotten lesson today. Perhaps its reminder, to some people, is not only irrelevant but inappropriate in the light of the demands of present times. But there are two points of significance in this regard. First, it is imperative for those who have faith in every aspect of Islam to keep fresh in our minds those scars on the chests that, despite being steps in the right direction in principle, fell prey to being excluded. Whether they are acted upon or not, it is very much necessary to keep them in our minds as a matter of belief. Another aspect of the Khilafat movement that is worth mentioning is that it laid the foundation for the independence for our country and sowed the seeds of Hindu-Muslim unity. For the first time, India got out from under the indignity of taking pride in being Britain's peasantry and with newfound self-respect and self-reliance, its citizens learned not to be ashamed to call themselves Indians. The Khilafat Movement was a beacon of light that lit up India's conscience, and in that light saw and found itself.

It is true that the life and soul of the Khilafat Movement was Mahatma Gandhi, but in the same way it is also true that the Khilafat Movement gave Gandhiji the tools to unite India and set it on the path toward complete independence. That is why those who are interested in the history of the Indian Independence movement should also study the Khilafat Movement.

It should be kept in the forefront of the mind that my intention is to talk about the Khilafat Movement within India, and the Greco-Turkish War and the abolition of the Caliphate are mentioned in this context. Other affairs from outside India have been found worthy of only cursory treatment, and have been mentioned because they relate to the Independence movement and the Khilafat Movement within India, or because they influenced the state of affairs of Turkey. This was a heavy load to bear, but I persevered and carried it through. If this can serve as a first version and I am able to inspire some resolute person to take this to a second version, I would consider it a success.

I am thankful to Hakim Abul Kalam *Saheb* of Gorakhpur, Janab Wahid *Saheb*, Owner, Wahid Library Gorakhpur, Syed Mohammad Laeen *Saheb* Advocate, Lucknow, Janab Sabahuddin Abdul Rahman *Saheb*, Darul Musannifeen Azamgarh, Maqbool Ahmad *Saheb*, Principal Khair Inter College Basti, Maulana Abdul Hameed *Saheb*, Secretary Ahl-e-Hadees Conference, and all those who gathered books, procured newspapers and journals, and gave me encouragement. Particular mention should be made of dear Hamid Ali *Saheb*, Municipal Commissioner Gorakhpur, for his assistance. In his extensive personal library, I found many editions of *Mashriq* and a few rare editions of *Zamindar* in bound form and a number of books, without which this book could not have been completed and for which I am deeply indebted to him.

I have dedicated this book to my late life partner.

I got married to Najmun Nisa Bibi on April 21, 1918. At the time, I was 18 or 19 and she was 16 or 17. In 1920, after receiving the BA degree, I enrolled at the University of Allahabad, and after the Nagpur Congress, I joined the non-cooperation movement. After quitting studies, when I returned home, I found a storm of anger and despair. I was under all kinds of pressure to quit this movement. I was very doleful, and wanted to quietly run away and go to jail. But I didn't have even a bad penny on me. One day she asked me, "Why are you always so sad and miserable?" I answered, "Do you see the demeanor and the atmosphere of this household? I want to run away and go to jail." My astonishment knew no bounds when, without a moment's hesitation, she said, "Then run away and go to jail." I said, "But I don't have a paisa. How do I run away anywhere?" With a smile on her face, she said, "Yesterday, *Abba* (my father) was here and gave me ten rupees. Take it and run away." She said this despite the fact that as per the customs and traditions of the times, that was her net savings. That money was no less than a benediction for me. I left home that night and reached Maulana Hasrat Mohani in Kanpur, and went from there to Bijnor and joined the *Madina* newspaper. After the Ahmedabad Congress, I took charge of the newspaper *Zamindar* in Lahore as its editor-in-chief, got arrested, and spent a year in Lahore Central Jail. In my lifetime, I was able to procure many means of sustenance, but those ten rupees that she gave me, and the way she encouraged me to jump into the movement and go to jail - although she was just an Urdu-literate young girl dwelling behind the purdah, and by that time, the mental picture of a jail was quite dreadful - has remained in my memory. She passed away on December 15, 1972. I consider it most fitting to dedicate this book to her memory.

Qazi Adeel Abbasi
1978

1

Background of the Concept of Khilafat

The concept of a centralized Islamic Caliphate or Khilafat is as old as Islam itself. In February of 1920, in his extensive presidential address to the Bengal Provincial Khilafat Conference, arguing for the Sharia or Islamic canonical law basis for Khilafat, Maulana Abul Kalam Azad had said[1]:

> *"Islam's canonical law, Sharia, calls for a Caliph and Imam, a community and spiritual leader, in every age. By Caliph is meant an autonomous Muslim sovereign, authority, and statesman who has the full power to protect Muslims and their populace and to enforce and execute their laws, and is strong enough to confront their enemies...*

> *"For centuries, the post of Islamic Caliphate has been in the hands of the Ottoman Empire, and at the present*

---

1   Maulana Azad's presidential address to the Bengal Provincial Khilafat Congress, in a revised form and with some additions, was first published in a book form under the title, *"Risala Masla-e-Khilafat aur Jaziratul-Arab"* (A Treatise on the Concept of Khilafat and the Arabian Peninsula) by Albalagh Press (Calcutta). Numerous editions of the book were published subsequently. The version from which this excerpt has been taken was published by Hali Publishing House (Delhi) in 1961 and appears on pp 265.

time, according to Sharia, they are the community and spiritual leaders of Muslims the world over. As such, it is the duty of every Muslim to extend them their allegiance and support. Those who deviate from their allegiance would be deemed to have removed the collar of Islam from around their necks. Those who fight against the Caliphate or support its enemies would be deemed to have fought God and his Prophet. It is the order of the Islamic canonical law that the Arabian Peninsula be kept secure from non-Muslim influence. This includes a part of Iraq, including Baghdad, and hence, if any non-Muslim government wants to occupy these lands or take them out from under the Islamic Caliphate and bring it under its influence, it would not be just a matter of losing an Islamic country, it would create a much larger and a particularly grave situation. And that is that infidelity would reign over the epicenter of the Islamic world. In such circumstances, it would be the prime duty of Muslims the world over to rise up and remove the occupier from this nation, and to dedicate all their energy to this task.

"Amongst the holy places of Islam, Jerusalem is revered in the same way as Mecca and Medina. To defend it, hundreds of thousands of Muslims have sacrificed their lives and countered eight campaigns of the European Crusades. It is the duty of all Muslims not to allow this place to fall in the hands of non-Muslims again, particularly to the occupation and control of Christian governments. And if such campaigns are under way, then to repulse these forces is not the duty of the Muslim

populace of this place alone, but every time and for every instance, that of every Muslim the world over."

The famous Muslim convert, English author, and translator of Quran, Mr. Muhammad Marmaduke Pickthall, past Editor of Bombay Chronicle, has written in his foreword to Dr. Syed Mahmud's book "Khilafat and England" published in 1921[2]:

"The religion of Islam is a complete set of rules governing a man's life and a repository of culture and genteelism, which has not yet reached the heights of its glory. The laws of God that universally apply to the human race and those laws, adherence to which are the basis for the advancement of human morality, cannot be found so explicitly stated in any book besides the Quran.

The Islamic culture is based on divine laws, and the Caliph is its worldly keeper, whether he is an Arab or a non-Arab, and whether his seat of power is in Baghdad, Medina, or Constantinople. The center of Islamic culture and advancement has changed with the change in the seat of the Caliphate."

Now, 50 years on, when the Caliphate has ceased to exist, if someone said that this was not a religious matter for the Muslims and all the Indians got it wrong, it would be quite an audacious thing to suggest. Islam's religious issues do not change with time. Being handicapped is another matter.

The leadership of the Khilafat Movement in India remained in the hands of Mahatma Gandhi from its inception till its end. In fact, it would be correct and appropriate to say that had

---

2   "Khilafat and England," Dr. Syed Mahmud, (Printed 1921), Foreword

Mahatma Gandhi not joined this movement with his full vigor and taken its complete load on his shoulders, the Khilafat Movement would not have been as forceful as it turned out to be. Mahatma Gandhi joined the Khilafat Movement with the announcement that this is a religious matter for the Muslims, and 'when our Muslim brothers are restless, how can we remain silent.' In his speeches and writings, Gandhiji had said over and over again that he joined the Khilafat Movement knowing full well that it was a sanctified issue for the Muslims. After the abolition of the Caliphate, Mahatma Gandhi said that even if he were an astrologer or a clairvoyant, and would have known that the Caliphate would collapse in Turkey, he would still have participated in the movement with the same zeal and determination. All the prominent leaders of India, such as Pandit Motilal Nehru, CR Das, Bipin Chandra Pal, Lala Lajpat Rai, Pandit Madan Mohan Malviya, etc. were supporters of this stand. Muslim scholars of every school of thought and every viewpoint and the leaders of Khilafat considered the "Caliphate" a purely religious matter and would argue for it accordingly. Any difference of opinion among the scholars and Sufis of India, in Firangi Mahal, Nadwatul Ulama, Bareilly, Budaun, and Amritsar, etc., belonging to all persuasions such as Hanafi, Deobandi, and Ahl-e-Hadees, and the *Sajjada-Nashin* of all the *Khanqah*, spiritual caretakers of the tombs of saints, was not of religious status in nature. Perhaps the religious scholars of India had never been in agreement on any issue in this manner before. Among the national leaders, Hakim Ajmal Khan, Dr. Mukhtar Ahmad Ansari, Maulana Abul Kalam Azad, Maulana Mohammad Ali, Maulana Shaukat Ali, Hasrat Mohani, the academics of Aligarh, and the leaders of Muslim League, anxious and restless, were ready to crawl over embers for the protection of the Islamic Caliphate and holy places.

Some people have compared the Islamic Caliph to the Roman Catholic Pope who maintains his religious authority and dignity despite being devoid of any sovereign rule. So, when a Khilafat delegation led by Maulana Mohammad Ali met with Lloyd George, and argued that the issue of the Caliphate was a religious matter of the Muslims and the British government should not intervene in it, Lloyd George said in his reply:

> "A second matter of the Caliphate's worldly power has been presented here. Mr. Mohammad Ali is very familiar with the fact that the question of a spiritual leader's worldly powers is not an issue unique to Islam. In the Christian world too, it has become a controversial issue. The frightful conflict with the head of the Roman Catholic Church regarding their worldly authority has raged for over a generation. Some Roman Catholics are in favor of worldly powers but there are some who are opposed to it. I do not wish to state my personal opinion, but when the Pope was stripped of worldly powers, his spiritual authority still remained strong as before, and even became stronger."

Mr. Lloyd George either feigned ignorance or was unfamiliar with the basic tenets of Islam. The Christian faith is based on just three years' worth of Jesus Christ's teachings. In the Christian religion, there are no laws or rules of governing; in fact, there is not even any mention of governing. Islam, on the other hand, has prescribed laws for every aspect of life, has laid down rules for governing, and gives instructions to take on the tumult of the world, which is impossible without the power to rule. Prophet Mohammad himself, in addition to his teachings of self-purification and high morals, was a soldier, the commander of an army, a thinker, and a governor as well, and it is the succession of those roles that is the Caliphate or the Khilafat. As mentioned earlier, in Islam there is no concept of a purely spiritual Caliphate that does not have politics, rule of law, governing, power and glory. In his final argument, Maulana Mohammad Ali said this and left it at that[3]:

> *"We were delegated with the responsibility to present diligently the matters of maintaining the worldly powers of the Caliph, restoration of the rights of Muslims to secure their holy places, and acceptance of their occupancy over them. We have presented these matters in front of the Viceroy and Mr. Fisher. We also wish to tell you that we will give priority to our religious matters at every opportunity."*

Maulana Abul Kalam Azad, in his article "Caliphate and the Republic of Turkey," has stated[4]:

> *"Here, it should remain clear that the arguments that were being presented in favor of the separation of civilian authority and the Caliphate, and were being presented in light of the division of duties and tasks, were mere displays on paper. Practically, no such division formally existed nor could it come into existence.*

> *"When the pope was deposed of all temporal powers, much of his affairs remained unfinished, such as*

---

3   Ma'arif Azamgarh, January 1973, *Mohammad Ali ki Yadein*, Salahuddin Abdul Rahman.
4   *Tabarrukaat Azad*, Editor: Ghulam Rasool Mehr, pp 266

forgiveness of sins, division of business licenses, amendments and abrogation of canonical laws and the monarchy of the Roman Catholic Church, supervision of the church's actions and congregation, etc. But when the last Caliph Abdul Majid Khan assumed his new position, there were no pending actions for him. Matters of forgiveness of sins or relating to heaven and hell were altogether nonexistent in the Caliphate's business."

The Caliphate of Turkey was spread over the three continents of Europe, Asia, and Africa, and although it was on the decline and Europeans had given it the nickname "Europe's Ailing Member," family members and dear ones always hold out hope for recovery and health till death finally strikes. Broken up parts of Turkey were being distributed, but along with that, measures of repair and revival were also under way, most significant among them being the appearance of Turkey's youth at the forefront in the form of the Young Turk Revolution. For that reason, hopes were rising. But when the situation turned and the pulse of hope became faint, anxiety soared.

Rt. Honorable Sir Ameer Ali, who held moderate views and a cautious attitude toward the British government, also felt constrained. He wrote an op-ed in The Times of India of London, the abstract of which was the same as stated above. His intent was to say that if the Turkish Caliphate did not survive, then Muslims the world over would be caught in a whirlpool of disappointment, that they had always thought of Turkey as the guardian of Islam, and they would be compelled to think of its decline as the decline of Islam.

The Khilafat Movement started at the time when the rise of the European nations was like the sun at its midday position, and Asia and Africa were sleeping as if they were dead. And soon after, the former started to decline and the latter started to awaken. That is, one era was passing and another epoch was taking birth. To quote Allama Iqbal, a new world and, to inhabit it, a new man was being created. Therefore, this book would not be complete till the past and the present, and the magnitude of both epochs, have been examined. At the same time, revolution came to Russia, and the people smashed the illustrious government of the Tzar to smithereens. The war between the Bolsheviks and Mensheviks also happened at the same time. Lenin and Stalin appeared with new philosophies for life, i.e. Marxism, and America started taking an interest in the affairs of Europe.

As far as Turkey and Islamic countries are concerned, all those things happened that had been feared for a long time. But, in addition to the question of an Islamic kingdom, the essence of self-awareness also started to take shape among the Muslims. The betrayals and treacheries of Sharif Hussein, Sultan Abdul Majid, Amir Habib, and Sultan Vehideddin reached their heights and then declined as well. India also stretched its limbs as it came out of slumber. Lokmanya Tilak's extremist party could not have dominated moderatism, and the English wanted to keep a firm grip on India by entangling the same moderates in its web of commonplace reforms. But one great human being, Gandhi, took the leadership of the entire nation in his hands, and in the storm of the moderate public's emotions of self-awareness, which was brewed by Gandhi, they all blew away like blades of grass.

Another aspect of the Khilafat Movement that is worth mentioning is that it laid the foundation for the independence for our country and sowed the seeds of Hindu-Muslim unity. For the first time, India got out from under the indignity of taking pride in being Britain's peasantry, and with newfound self-respect and self-reliance, its citizens learned not to be ashamed to call themselves Indians. The Khilafat Movement was a beacon of light that lit up India's conscience, and in that light saw and found itself.

It is true that the life and soul of the Khilafat Movement was Mahatma Gandhi, but in the same way it is also true that the Khilafat Movement gave Gandhiji the tools to unite India and set it on the path toward complete independence. That is why those who are interested in the history of the Indian Independence movement should also study the Khilafat Movement.

During the time of the Khilafat Movement itself, Jamiat Ulema-e-Hind came into existence, whose broadminded scholars acted on the messages of Congress and Gandhiji throughout the Independence movement. Many of its leaders were incarcerated for long periods of time for participating in the Salt March, Quit India Movement, and civil disobedience, and confronted the Muslim League till the very end in its opposition to the partition of the country.

Since the start of the Khilafat Movement, Muslim intellectuals of the finest hearts and minds were involved in it, such as Maulana Abul Kalam Azad, Shaykh al-Hind Maulana Mahmud Hasan, Mufti Kifayatullah, Maulana Abul Wafa Sanaullah Amritsari, Maulana Hussain Ahmed Madani, Maulana Muhammad Sajjad Bihari, Maulana Abdu Bari Firangi Mahali, Maulana Syed Sulaiman Nadvi, Maulana Inayatullah Firangi Mahali, Maulana Salamatullah Firangi Mahali, Maulana

Abdul Majid Badayuni, Maulana Saiyad Muhammad Fakhir Allahabadi, Maulana Ahmad Saeed, Maulana Syed Muhammad Dawood Ghaznavi, Maulana Azad Subhani, Maulana Habib-ur-Rehman Ludhianvi, Maulana Abul Qasim Sayf Banarsi, Mushir Husain Kidwai, Zafar-ul-Mulk Alvi, Hakim Ajmal Khan, Dr. Mukhtar Ahmad Ansari, Maulana Hasrat Mohani, Maulana Mohammad Ali, Maulana Shaukat Ali, Maulana Mazharul Haque, Dr. Syed Mahmud, Aga Safdar (Punjab), Zafar Ali Khan, etc.

These were the people who, besides being eloquent writers and orators, erudite scholars and thinkers, and researchers, were also practical crusaders. There were essayists among them, as well as poets and diligent and probing theologists. They also possessed a global understanding of western knowledge.

All these distinguished leaders of the community immersed themselves in this brave struggle with courage and boldness, the Khilafat Movement turned into the Independence movement of India, and all the political leaders of India fell behind Gandhiji single heartedly to march toward the goal of an independent India with determination and grit.

2

Basis for the Spiritual Unease Among Muslims

The Sanctity of the Issue of Khilafat

At the time the Khilafat Movement started gaining traction in India, there were many reasons for great anxiety among Muslims. First was the great affinity and heartfelt emotional attachment Muslims had for the central Islamic Caliphate. It was as if the Caliphate was the spirit of Islam and the foundation of the religion. The establishment of the Caliphate, its survival, and its stability were always considered matters of religious duty for the Muslims the world over. So, when the Mongol descendants of Hulago attacked Baghdad, Allama Ibn Taymiyyah emerged from his worship and study quarters with a sword in his hand and jumped onto the battlefield for its protection. The famous historian, Allama Ibn Kathir, during the long period shortly after the Mongol attacks when there was no Caliph, used to lament this fact in his writings annually at the start of the year. When Maulana Mohammad Ali took a delegation to London, and Lloyd George refused to support the continuity of the Islamic Caliphate, he was agonized much like a fish out of water, and publicly said that speaking out was the religious duty of Muslims. His final statement - 'we will raise these issues with priority at every opportunity' - was like a challenge that the valiant informal leader of the Muslim people threw at the head of a world's superpower to save the ship of Caliphate from drowning.

Turkey and the European Nations

The second major reason for the restlessness of Muslims was the rising power of European countries, particularly Britain, and its stubborn attitude toward Muslim countries in general and Turkey in particular. Muslims would remember with pride the time when Sultan Salahuddin Ayyubi defeated a braveheart like King Richard of Britain and other European Crusader countries to capture Jerusalem. Sultan Salahuddin, besides appearing in history books, appeared in stories, novels and various kinds of legends, arousing a passion of pride. They also used to take pride in how Sultan Mehmed Fatih conquered Constantinople, and then recited the following couplet of Saadi:

The spider is curtain-bearer in the palace of Chosroes
The owl sounds the relief in the castle of Afrasiyab

And their blood warmed with passion when they recalled the attack on Constantinople by the alliance of 52 princes of Christian Crusader countries under the command of the Duke of Burgundy, and how Bayezid I had charged at them on his horse like lightning, earning him the title 'Yildirim,' a Turkish word meaning 'thunderbolt.' And how Bayezid Yildirim, after his victory and the capture of the invading princes, released the commander of the Christian forces, Duke of Burgundy, taunting him to go and put together another alliance of Christian armies and come back; they will always find Bayezid ready for them on the battlefield. And then the numerous wars in which the Turks won glorious victories, prompting the late Akbar to croon:

Victorious are the Turks, triumphant the world over
Amazing are the Turks, may God protect from evil eye

They would also hold their heads high with pride when they thought about Turkey's naval prowess, which ruled the seas. Besides, with those Christian Crusades and Christian vs. Muslim slogans, the Europeans themselves, based on their own religious prejudice, had transformed the question of the Turks' very existence into that of protection of Islam.

Britain was at the forefront of the assiduous efforts to devastate Islam. Prior to 1914, it had made all necessary arrangements to disrupt the governance in Muslim countries. Their iron claws had gripped Egypt. Iran was already in control of Russia and Britain. France had occupied Morocco. Turkey was lost in the African province of Ottoman Tripolitania, or Tirablus-al-Gharb (Tripoli in the West). Turkey was like a seriously ill man taking his last breath. Allama Shibli has expressed this in the following way:

Morocco went, now Persia is gone, what is left to see
How long does the lifeless patient Turkey have to live

The following couplet also goes some way toward assessing the right emotions and feelings of the Muslims:

Someone ask these masters of human culture
How long these atrocities, how long this doom?

How long these reprisals for the victory of Ayyubi?
How long will you show us the scenes of the Crusades?

The war of nearly 500 years between Turkey and all of Europe was known to everyone, and the Muslims were justified in thinking that if the flickering flame of the Ottoman Caliphate were to die, there would be no dignity left for them in this world, and the Muslim world would take the shape of a caravan lost in a sandy desert. The ardor and passion and the sacrifice and selflessness that the Indian Muslims had demonstrated in the Battles of Balkan and Tripoli were fervently declaring that the collapse of the Caliphate was outside the tolerance of the Muslims.

The English, via colonialism, had started to pilfer and plunder from weak nations and to use the proceeds to treat their malady marked by an excessive desire for territory, and they had termed this greed and covetousness 'civilization.' They considered spreading this civilization their duty and, hiding their selfish intent under the cover of loud propaganda, they were colonizing the world. The following quote from Gladstone underscores this reality. Gladstone was a person who would shudder at the sight of anyone who had not gone through the Christian rite of baptism. He says:

> *"I am certain that we are all united in the love of this great nation of ours, which is our homeland. And that we are bound together with this kingdom which has entrusted our nation with such a God's trust that has never been the fortune of any people before."*

To earn the right to that trust, the English relied more on insidious deliberations and political trickery than the sword; their victims were generally Muslims with self-interest and Sultans and rulers who had sold their conscience. The English prepared logical albeit self-serving propaganda: they said their purpose was to bring civilization to the world. And with that Trojan horse, they made their way into backward cultures and, taking advantage of their poverty and illiteracy, looted their lands and resources and stuffed their coffers. The nature of this propaganda was such that people fell prey to it, since they were recipients of royal favors. The simple truth was that when the Renaissance period started in Italy and the progress in science turned all eyes toward Europe, it transformed into an industrial continent. And a market was needed for the products of the industrial continent. In the shadow of colonialism, using trade as the vehicle, they dumped their products in these markets, taking raw materials out of these colonies, and enriching themselves in the process. The famous English essayist Addison once remarked, "Indians are our plowmen and Chinese our potters." This colonialism was based on aggressive nationalism and there were some mutual competitions in play, but that was their internal matter. The colonized backward nations got nothing out of it. Since the ends were not pure, what were the chances that the means would have been pure? They handed out a lot of bribes and mostly got their way with them. Perhaps there is no corner of the world where they did not step through and make a country their slaves by paying out bribes. Regarding the French Revolution, historians of the world are in agreement that victory over it was achieved with the British Prime Minister Pitt's gold. Pitt was a mastermind, and was known as "The Captain who brought the ship to shore in a storm." He spent large amounts of money on bribes to stand up supporters of the revolution who went on a rampage of terrorism and barbarism till all of Europe trembled. The English were very adept at finding leaders in every movement who knew the ways to spoil, dismantle, and sideline the movement. Bribing these corrupt locals, they plundered and looted so many countries, decimated righteous movements, and led honest leaders working in their communities to fail. The reason for the servitude of Egypt was the same bribery. While drawing the borders of Afghanistan, they bribed the Afghan representative and included the frontier province in India. Durand had been appointed by the British government to demarcate the border. He was a very shrewd man and the frontier border is named after him. Only the Turkish soldiers and commanders did not fall for this greed. But while the Turkish soldiers and commanders were unique in that day and age, their sultans and ministers could not escape, and in the waning days of the Ottoman Empire, Sultan Abdul Hamid and a few of his ministers met the same fate of servitude.

Afghanistan's geographic position was considered very strategic at the time. It should be remembered that at the time of WWI, warfare was mainly carried out with horses and swords. Airplanes were just coming into military use. That is why it was critical to keep Afghanistan in a firm grip and for that purpose, Amir Habibullah, the ruler of Afghanistan, was made to be obedient and submissive. Sultan Abdul Hamid, the Islamic Caliph, and Amir Habibullah are considered key figures in the spheres of politics and war. Therefore, after making them their "servant" by generously endowing both of them with gold and bribing them with many promises, the English had to show them to be pious and God-fearing guardians of Islam, and passionate warriors who were fighting the heretics. The war chest had to be opened for these efforts too, and soon multiple efforts were underway to prove this falsehood to be the truth. This campaign was so successful that even today there is no dearth of sincere and impartial folks who consider Sultan Abdul Hamid and Amir Habibullah to be saviors of Islam, to the extent that they consider Turkish youths, or the Young Turks coalition, to have been bribed by the Jewish people.

The mind is blown with astonishment at this strange notion

An account of Amir Habibullah has been given by Dr. Abdul Ghani, who had been imprisoned by the Amir in a jail in Kabul. Dr. Ghani had written a book in English titled "A Review of the Political Situation in Central Asia." I met him in Lahore and he gave me a copy of the book. From that book I learned that Amir Habibullah had a French chef in his employ, who used to twist the neck of chicken and kill other birds and pigeons in a non-halal way and cook them for him. The Amir had established a women's department, which had army positions in it. Their job was to bring young girls from the mountains and employ them in everyday jobs. Amir Habibullah had a minister with the title *"mustaufi ul-mamalek"* (Chancellor of the Realm), whose name was Mirza Muhammad Hussain. He was officially a member of the British government's secret service. The Chancellor suspected Dr. Abdul Ghani of collusion with the party that, getting tired of the general situation, was getting organized and plotting to take control. Dr. Ghani's 14-year old son was hanged for the crime of rebellion and he was imprisoned. When Amir Amanullah Khan became the King of Afghanistan after the assassination of Amir Habibullah, he personally went to jail to release Dr. Ghani. At the Peace Conference in Rawalpindi after the end of the Third Anglo-Afghan War, Dr. Ghani was a member of the Afghan delegation.

After Amir Amanullah took over the reins of the government, he had the Chancellor arrested and made an announcement throughout the country asking people to assemble and watch the death of a traitor to the nation. Chancellor Mirza Muhammad Hussain was beheaded in public before a huge crowd. Before he was put to death, he was asked for three wishes. His first wish was that he be buried next to his wife. Amir Amanullah rejected that wish, saying that she was a chaste wife and someone as wicked and evil could not be allowed to lie beside her. His second wish was that his children be educated. Amir Amanullah said that although Sheikh Saadi had stated that "to kill a snake and look after its child is not a wise thing," this wish of his would be granted, since the children were innocent of any crime and were corrigible, even if it took some effort to rid them of the poison inside them. Amir Amanullah also expressed his great surprise that a vicious man like the Chancellor had delicate emotions of love toward his wife and children and that he would have thought that the Chancellor would be devoid of any human emotions. The third thing the Chancellor asked for was that his children not be deprived of his property. Amir Amanullah said that although the Chancellor acquired the property through deceit and selling his conscience, this wish would also be granted for the sake of the innocent children.

All these incidents were related to me in detail by Dr. Abdul Ghani, and I mention them here for two reasons: 1. To show how the wizardry of the Britain had enthralled the leaders of the Muslim world, and 2. To demonstrate how the English had succeeded in projecting Amir Habibullah as a warrior of Islam. I remember the time from my childhood when people truly looked up to Amir Habibullah with respect and admiration.

But a storm was brewing and those in the know were aware of it. Before Amir Habibullah's assassination, the students of Afghanistan had given him notice and demanded corrective action. I remember this statement in Dr. Abdul Ghani's book, which the youth of the Young Turks coalition went about saying:

"We can rule better than these guilty nincompoops"

But Amir Habibullah never paid heed to these notices and warnings, although rebellion had started within his own family and his estranged wife was most likely involved in his assassination. The people were seething with anger against him. The army was restless. The reason for this was that when the Islamic countries were facing attacks, and Enver Pasha was beseeching him to join in their defense, Amir Habibullah, as an envoy of the British, would find some excuse not to. The British Army had only 10,000 troops in India, and the British Indian Army troops were sent to Mesopotamia to fight the Turks. Had Afghanistan attacked India at the time, the British would have had to call those troops back. The result was that when General Allenby surrounded Jerusalem, the Turks were cut off from the west by the British Indian Army and from the east by the Arabs, and General Allenby was able to occupy Jerusalem.

This house was burned down by the lamp inside

The following statement in Maulana Hussain Ahmed Madani's autobiography *"Naqsh-e-Hayat"* Vol II, corroborates that[5]:

"Amir Habibullah, like most rulers, was not free of moral defects. Now this sickness had gotten advanced, and he

---

5   *Naqsh-e-Hayat* pp 173

had started reaching for the womenfolk of the nobles. Some virtuous ones among them committed suicide after being raped."

Maulana Mahmud Hasan raised the slogan of *"jihad"* the world over and pledged allegiance to "holy struggle" while living in Deoband. The Pashtun highlands, or Yaghistan as it has been referred to, 'land of the free and unruly,' was a hub of opposition to British rule. One of Mahmud Hasan's Pashtun associates at Deoband, Haji Turangzai (real name Fazal Wahid) had become a thorn in the side of the English, and now wanted to involve Afghanistan in the war. The English were successful in their propaganda with the help of the traitorous Amir Habibullah and the unconscientious Chancellor of the Realm.

Maulana Hussain Ahmed Madani writes[6]:

"In a few months of the war, the English had suffered massive loss of life and property, and the loud claims and determination had bit the dust. In the end, the old tactics that the English had used at difficult times in previous wars had to be utilized. Amir Habibullah Khan had to be put in the mix, tribal chiefs and freedom fighters had to be won over, and the path of bribery had to be assumed to bring back the few soldiers that were left, the details of which are as follows. The rural tribal chiefs of Yaghistan had to be enticed with loads of gold coins and currency, and a propaganda was put forth that Islamic canonical law does not allow for a "jihad" without the involvement of the ruler. That the ruler of Muslims in the region was the Amir of Kabul, Amir Habibullah Khan.

---

6   *Naqsh-e-Hayat* pp 185

That they should pledge allegiance to and merge with him in this holy struggle. That when the Amir Saheb rises and raises the ensign of "jihad", they should rise with him...The village heads and tribal chiefs were won over and could not think for themselves in the face of this propaganda. In the end, Haji Saheb faced defeat and there was confusion among the populace."

Maulana Ubaidullah Sindhi writes in his diary:

"The English gave a lot of money to the Amir to distribute in Yaghistan and get allegiance from the tribal Afghans for his kingdom. And the Afghans in Peshawar were told that if the Amir of Kabul launched a holy war, they should undoubtedly join the effort, but without the King this war was not permissible.

"Since a treaty had been reached earlier with Amir Habibullah Khan, the English were certain that he would never stand up against them in a holy war. That is why this game was played.

"After the general announcement, when pressure was exerted on Amir Habibullah Khan to leave the side of the English, initially by the Indian Muslims and the Turks and then by all Indians, Turks, and Germans, the Amir responded to the Indian, Turkish, and German delegation that until auxiliary forces reach Afghanistan, the war against Russia and Britain is a war of expediency.

"During that time, it was said that if the threat from Russia could be eliminated, frontier nations could attack India. To assess this risk, an Indo-Russian delegation (delegation of Dr. Mathura Singh and Mirza

Muhammad Ali) was proposed. When Russia's power weakened and this mission ascertained that Russia cannot attack Afghanistan, the Amir was reminded through his subordinates to keep his promise. When Amir Habibullah heard about it, he called the jirga, the traditional assembly which included army officers and national elders. When the Amir solicited opinions in this regard, other than Inayatullah Khan, who had been bought, everyone was in consensus that the fight must go on. The Amir was astonished and overturned it with a royal decree.

"After that, we (Maulana Ubaidullah Sindhi and his associates) were brought to a small house on the 1st of Ramzan, 1335 AH (1916 AD) and imprisoned. We were 25 men and that house was definitely not suitable for more than 10 people. We were under the strict watch of the Commander in Chief, General Nadir Khan. After some time, the Chancellor of the Realm took over our imprisonment and we were transferred to Jalalabad. And Amir Habibullah became the permanent king."

Sultan Abdul Hamid

The same was true of Sultan Abdul Hamid – the English had brought him into servitude. He had every inch of Turkey mortgaged. When a number of Christians joined the army, ignoring modern methods of war, he ended militancy. He had cannons and artillery removed from the forts at the Dardanelles Strait. He became the biggest landlord. He opposed reforms. Anyone who paid any attention to reforms was quietly assassinated by agents of the crafty Sultan.

The blood of the intellectual reformer Midhat Pasha is also on the hands of Sultan Abdul Hamid. And it wasn't just one Midhat Pasha; many innocent patriotic gentlemen became targets of the Sultan's oppression and tyranny at the behest of foreign interests. Not only his hands, but his entire garb is stained with the blood of innocent well-wishers of the nation and country. And why was all this happening? Just because the English did not want any reforms to come to Turkey and they wanted the rulers to slowly decline. Their main objective was to end the centralization of Islam, and Abdul Hamid was their most instrumental tool. But they promoted him as the "Guardian of Islam" and that title was accepted by a number of people, a sentiment that is echoed even today by many who look back at him with respect.

Maulana Zafar Ali Khan has accurately translated this propaganda of the English in his *"Ishaa'at-a-Baatil-o-Ikaaziyat"* (Publication of the Void and Invalid). But this used to be the kind of falsehood that would assume the matrix of fact and then there would be no dearth of people who would promote it. A number of educated writers and Sufi scholars had come under the influence of the English and people would take every word of theirs as though it was the gospel of the Quran and *Hadith*. Among these scholars, except for the blue-blooded Sufis who had inherited a place among the falcons of Islam, there were many glory-seeking foreigners. Who all are to be named? They devised such tales in praise of Sultan Abdul Hamid that they would make for a book if they were all compiled. Among the many traitorous acts of Sultan Abdul Hamid against his country and nation was the disarming of the Dardanelles Strait, which separates Asia from Europe. This 40 mile-long and four mile-wide strait connects the Aegean Sea with the Sea of Marmara. On both sides of the strait are mountains and this narrow waterway is the only way to get to Constantinople from the sea. Hence, on the mountains on both sides of the strait, many forts were built and were armed with cannons and heavy artillery. Anyone entering this strait would be met with heavy fire from these cannons and artillery, one after the other that an intruder could not escape. Following the orders of the English, Sultan Abdul Hamid had all the military fortifications demolished and the strait disarmed. Now the pathway for an attack was wide open. The naval powers of European countries had a free pass and Constantinople was in their grasp. It was only after the Young Turks deposed Sultan Abdul Hamid that they were able to immediately fortify the forts again, otherwise they would not have been able to defeat the Allied powers in WWI.

▌Reformers of the *Ummah*

Through these dark clouds, however, there was a glimmer of hope. Reformers of the *Ummah*, the supra-national community of Muslims, which mostly consisted of enlightened and broad-minded scholars, were constantly trying to improve the state of affairs.

> *A lifetime has passed since the fame of the triumphant who wandered*
> *We can adorn the rope and the gallows post all over again*

The first one to come to mind among them was Syed Jamaluddin Afghani. This astute scholar's relentless activism spread from Afghanistan to Egypt, through Iran, the Arab world and Turkey, and throughout the Muslim world, lighting the fire of rebellion everywhere. His message was of unity among the Muslims, which the English had given the demeaning term "Pan-Islamism". The English started the propaganda that Pan-Islamism aimed to subjugate and rule over the world, although this was far from the concept that reformism was promoting. The intention of Pan-Islamic unity that he promoted was simply to urge Muslim rulers to be reform-minded and to follow and implement the laws of the Quran. In countries that didn't have Islamic rule, the Muslims were urged to be patriotic, follow their faith in a broad-minded way, strive for freedom from colonial rule, and unite to create a central Islamic Caliphate so that they could be free of the handcuffs of Europe and the threat that Islamic countries and holy places faced.

The message of the great Indian crusader of Islam and the wise and intelligent scholar, Maulana Mahmud Hasan, was the same. He was foremost an Indian leader who campaigned vigorously for reform and independence in Islamic countries.

Holy Shrines

The third major cause for distress among the Muslims was the security of their holy shrines, which were coming under the control of non-Muslim powers, and due to conflict, being occupied by western countries.

The holy shrines of Mecca and Medina, the holy places of Jerusalem, and the monuments of Baghdad, Najaf, and Karbala were all under the guardianship of the Turkish Caliphs, who never called themselves the rulers of Hijaz, the Arabian province where Mecca and Medina are situated, and always considered their title to be "Sultans of Turkey" and "Servants of the Holy Shrines." They were the "Caliphs of Islam" and were called as such. The Sultans of Turkey had deep veneration for the holy shrines. They facilitated the expansion of the Great Mosque in Mecca and construction anew of the Prophet's Mosque in Medina, and secured all such historical monuments. They never collected any taxes from Hijaz. All expenses for the Ka'ba, or the Cube, the structure at the center of the Great Mosque in Mecca, and for the mosque, to the extent of the expense for the oil in the lamps that are lit there, were from Constantinople. Stipends for the scholars and academics there were fixed. The security of the holy shrines was particularly critical during WWI, the uprising of Mecca as a part of the Arab Revolt during the war, and, in particular, the settlement of Jews in Palestine. This was an issue that was very near the hearts of the Muslims. Allama Iqbal had penned an elegiac lament in such a pained tone on this topic:

The ruler of Mecca barters with the Prophet's faith
The endeavor of the Turks is found in the ashes and blood

Tyrants and flames once more on Abraham's race have glared:
For whom this new ordeal, or by whose hand prepared?

And how he calls out with such emotion:

May the Muslims unite in watching over the Shrine
From the banks of the Nile to the deserts of Kashgar

So that the foundation of the Caliphate may once again be firm
in the world
Search for and bring from somewhere the heart and spirit of
your ancestors

Ah you who cannot distinguish the hidden from the revealed,
become aware!
You, lovers of Abu Bakr and Ali, become aware!

It was inevitable that Muslims around the world would be anxious, and Indian Muslims were particularly perturbed.

Another Reason

Europe always fought wars with Turkey on a religious basis and labeled them the head and protector of Islam. In this way, it became threaded in the minds of the world's Muslims that the survival or fall of Turkey was the survival or fall of Islam. These wars have been briefly mentioned earlier and there is no capacity in this book to include more, although much more can be said about the fact that Europe and Russia always rose up in the interest and defense of the Christians' rights in the areas of Turkey where Christians lived, and incited them to rebel against Turkey. They equated Islam with ignorance. For instance, at the Brussels Geographic Conference, King Leopold II of Belgium said:

> *"To open up to civilization the only part of our globe which it has not yet penetrated, to pierce the darkness in which entire populations are enveloped, is, I venture to say, a crusade worthy of this age of progress, and I am happy to perceive how much the public feeling is in favor of its accomplishments; the tide is with us ..."*

The same was true for France and Germany, but England was the chief of the west at the time. Britain was the most powerful country. Its naval fleet was invincible, and that is why they sat on their island, safe and secure, while dreaming of world domination. And they named it "Spread of Civilization." Britain and Russia, in a competitive style, would raise the flag of Christianity to spread this so-called civilization, and would meddle in Turkey's affairs under the pretext of protection and guardianship of the rights of its Christian populace. There was bound to be a reaction to this in the Muslim world. The many wars that European nations fought with Turkey, they would regard them as Crusades against the Muslims. All this started at the time of Bayezid Yildirim and continued till the collapse of the central Islamic Caliphate. For instance, while paying tribute to General Allenby, who, after the failure of his command at the Western Front attacking German defenses, came from France and captured Basra, Baghdad, Jerusalem and other places, Lloyd George, the British Prime Minister, had said the following words:

> *"General Allenby's name will always be remembered for being an intelligent and worthy military commander who fought the last battle of the Crusades, bringing him a glorious victory. It is his good fortune that under his able command he was able to bring such a glorious end to a war that has seen the involvement of European armies for centuries. Now we must bury the thought that generations after generations, European military prowess was wasted on useless wars, because the British Army, under the command of General Allenby, has won the war to end all wars."*

This was a voice from deep down the hearts of Europe and Britain, and the reality of the situation manifests that. These campaigns had been going on for a long time and remained in full force till the very end. At the height of Turkey's ascent, the Ottoman Empire, besides including modern Turkey, extended into present day Hungary, Greece, Crimea, and Armenia in Europe, the Hijaz (Mecca and Medina), Jerusalem, Baghdad, Mosul, Basra, Syria, Arab countries along the Persian Gulf in Asia, and Algiers, Tunis, Tripoli, Alexandria, and Cairo along Africa's Mediterranean coast. How could Europe have tolerated this grand Islamic Sultanate? And the supreme kingdom of Britain, with an iron resolve to destroy it, rose up in the name of Christianity.

More than 50 years ago, I read a book by an Englishwoman. Unfortunately, despite looking for the book, I could not find it. If memory serves me right, its title was "The Arabian Peninsula." In it, she wrote in clear words that Britain and Islam cannot both survive in this world. According to her, two nations are crusading for superiority in the world, the English and the Muslims, and two languages want to dominate the world, English and Arabic. And one of those two will have to be annihilated. She was convinced that until the central authority of Islam was deposed and the Arab world was separated from this central authority and broken up into pieces, the power of Islam would not be crushed. She wrote about how English spies working toward this cause would chemically darken their skins to a tan color and go live among the madrasas (seminaries) and homes of the Arabs for long periods of time to understand their weaknesses and incite them against the Turks. It was the result of many years of discipline, hard work and sacrifice that Col. Lawrence could find enough material to be able to walk out in Arab garb like a commander during WWI and have the Arabs kill the Turks, putting a bounty on Turkish soldiers. Col. Lawrence himself was a part of the disciplined and hardworking intelligence team and also participated personally in several military engagements. The stories of his participation in the Arab Revolt in full regalia are fascinating.

Col. Lawrence was a short man, and because he did not measure up to the requirements, his application for military service was rejected. He worked for the intelligence and took on the work of inciting the Arabs to revolt. He had such a courageous will that he would ride on a camel for hundreds of miles, while running a fever, in the desert where there was nothing but gusts of hot wind blowing.

For a long time, the English had been working hard on two things, and their diligence is worth praising. 1. To break down the central authority of Islam. 2. To stand up the Arabian Peninsula against the rulers of Turkey.

Toward that end, the English with their bag of tricks had Turkey embroiled in internal and external strife. They would act as the Messianic guardians to Turkey's Christians and incite them to revolt, and the external strife would appear in the form of wars. The Turks could never find peace and were always involved in some war. Therefore, when the Young Turks deposed Sultan Abdul Hamid and started reform, as an English historian once said, instead of getting 20 years of peace they needed to bring these reforms, they got 20 years of war.

As far as India was concerned, its Muslims were in lockstep with the Islamic Caliphate and the Turkish rulers every step of the way. Hence, in 1897, when Greece started a war, the Indian Muslims collected money to help the Turks. In 1912, during the Balkan War, all the Muslims were uneasy and a lot of funds were raised. There were many people who left their homes for this purpose. Under the leadership of Maulana Mahmud Hasan, students of Deoband's Darul Uloom gave up their studies temporarily and left home to work for the war effort. I personally know a gentleman who left home for the entire length of the war and traveled from village to village collecting funds. He would have the accounting for all his collections published periodically in the famous newspaper of the time, *"Paisa Akhbar"* from Lahore. Suffice it to say, because of all these efforts, the Muslims of India developed a strong emotional affinity for Turkey and any perceived injury to Turkey weighed heavily on their hearts

During the Balkan War, as a daily routine, Maulana Mahmud Hasan would read a *Hadith* related to "jihad" or holy struggle. In this way, passion was incited among the students of Darul Uloom, and they petitioned for the institution to be shut down so they could devote their time to this struggle. That was exactly what Maulana's objective was. At that time, some people expressed their doubts that doing so would incur the displeasure of the government, which may be detrimental to the cause of Darul Uloom. Maulana stated that a similar event took place during the time of his teacher, and he had said that this institution was established to serve the faith. If the service to the faith itself was in trouble, then what use was the Darul Uloom?

The strong passion and a stirred up feeling among the Muslims during the Balkan War and the restlessness expressed by them for action is a long story. The Muslims of India were very anxious. The youth wanted to go there and enlist in the army and wage holy war. An advocate in

Faizabad by the name of Fayyaz Ali *Saheb*, who later went to Pakistan and lived there till his death, had written a novel called "Shameem," which was well received. The hero in that story finally left for Turkey to join the holy war. The poor and the rich alike donated money toward the cause, so that at least the Turks fighting for freedom would get some monetary help. Even those who were faithful to the government shelved their loyalty and openly jumped into the fray. Lucknow's distinguished barrister Mukhtar Husain delivered a heart-wrenching speech at a general rally in Lucknow's Aminabad Park, although he was included among the well-wishers of the government. The District Collector was also present there. When he expressed his surprise, Mr. Mukhtar Husain said that this was a religious issue for them. Allama Shibli, who held a prominent position for his understanding and insight of these matters, was constantly writing poems of heartache. Dr. Ansari took a medical delegation to Turkey which included some other prominent people. On their return, Allama Shibli welcomed them with a passionate poem, whose first couplet was:

> *We offer our thanks to Allah, the Singular: Al-Bari*
> *On the safe return of the delegation of Ansari*

The Turks had created the Red Crescent Committee in response to the Red Cross Committee. In imitation of that, Red Crescent Committees were formed in every city. When Maulana Mohammad Ali appealed for funds to support Dr. Ansari's delegation by advertising in "The Comrade" newspaper, the way the people responded as if with a *"Labbaik,"* or "I'm Ready" to God's calling, is best epitomized in Mir Mahfooz Ali's words. Mahfooz Ali was an associate of Maulana Mohammad Ali and manager of "The Comrade" newspaper, and this is what he had to say:

"The appeal caused it to rain money in the office of "The Comrade." The records kept in the newspaper's office are evidence that Rs. 10,000-15,000 are being received every day. And I am proof of that, as my hands are stiff from signing for all the money orders and parcels received."

The same was the situation at Maulana Zafar Ali Khan's famous daily newspaper *Zamindar*. It is legendary how Punjab gave heartily to the cause in response to Maulana Zafar Ali Khan's call.

And the same thing happened when Italy attacked Tirablus-al-Gharb (Tripoli in the West) and the English cut off the path of the Turks in Egypt. Enver Pasha went there in disguise and organized resistance. At that time too, the Muslims of India were agonized and restless, as can be sensed from this collection of couplets by Allama Iqbal:

Sick of this world and all this world's tumult
I left this earth and soared toward the sky

Angels led me to where The Prophet
Holds audience at the seat-of-mercy

Said The Prophet, O' Nightingale of the garden of Hijaz
Each bud is melting in your song's passion-flood

And like a scent comes here from the orchards of the earth—
What do you bring for us, what is your offering worth?'

'Master! there is no quiet in that land of time and space,
Where the existence that we crave hides and still hides its face;

Though all creation's flowerbeds teem with tulip and red rose,
The flower whose perfume is true love—that flower no garden
knows.

But I have brought this chalice here to make my sacrifice;
The thing it holds you will not find in all your Paradise.

See here, oh Lord, the honor of your people brimming up!
The martyred blood of Tripoli, oh Lord, is in this cup.'

It was understood that there was no path of action for the
Indian Muslims. India clung to the robes of the British under
its rule.

There is neither the permission to suffer, nor to complain

But the Muslims always considered the matter of Turkey
as that of protection of Islam and protection of the central
Caliphate of Islam, and by extension that of their faith, their
lives, and of their existence and survival.

3

Sphere of Action

The Muslims of India did not just speak words of empathy, lament and cry, or pray and shed tears of mourning to express their emotions. They presented actions as much as was possible. One example of these actions was the collection of valuable donations; the rich and the poor, the freedom fighters and the pro-British government, all gave freely and with gratification. The second example is that of those associations and conferences that were established despite the difficulties and hardships of the prevailing restrictions. At that time, for more than a century, Firangi Mahal (Lucknow) was the guide of Indian Muslims for religious and cultural values and the center of rational instruction. The same Firangi Mahal which had produced such great minds as Mulla Nizamuddin and Bahrul Uloom Maulana Abdul Ali, whose fame spread throughout the Muslim world. This was where such an erudite scholar as Maulana Abdul Hai arose, who, despite his death at the age of only 39, left a legacy of thousand great scholars who were his students. There wasn't a book that he hadn't annotated with explanatory notes. And then there was that exalted personality that shone in this same Firangi Mahal, who was not only a very learned scholar and a man of high morals and virtues full of foresight and insight, but was also restless due to a shared agony with the Muslim community and was diligently at work in the Islamic world with his broadminded deliberations and strategies: Maulana Abdul Bari. What a stature he had at the time, evidenced by the following passage from Salahuddin Abdul Rahman's *"Mohammad Ali ki Yadein"* (Memories of Mohammad Ali), in which he has described the Khilafat Delegation's meeting with Mr. Fisher:

> *"Maulana Syed Sulaiman Nadvi made a short speech on this occasion in which he said that he just wanted to add that he was perhaps the first Indian Maulvi to have come there and that he was not a political person at all. He said that Maulana Abdul Bari Saheb, who belongs to the famous family of Firangi Mahal in Lucknow, has sent him expressly to represent Maulana Bari, so that he could make it clear to the Government of His Royal Highness that this is no political matter for them, but purely a religious matter."*

Maulana Abdul Bari's attractive personality was generous and liberal and he met every person with grace and courtesy. His name was taken with respect in all corners of India. It is a matter of much happiness for me that I had the honor and privilege of receiving his blessing. The way it happened was that I was traveling in a train. I had already heard his name. Word came that he was on the same train in a 2nd Class carriage. I presented myself and within a few minutes, I felt as if I had played in his lap when I was a child and there was no one as close to him as I was. I found out that every person who met him would be under this presumption that Maulana's hospitality was the most generous toward them. After that, I went often to meet him and stayed there. My God! The crowd that would be there dining with him. Once I was there and I had an upset stomach. How he would come to me again and again with offerings – have some rice-lentil medley, some tapioca pudding, or rice and yogurt, and banana. As if I were a child in the home and he was coaxing me to eat something. On one side of the courtyard was an open hall. During the month of Rabi' Al-Awwal of the Islamic calendar, which is the month of the birth of Prophet Muhammad, a lamp would be lit in one corner of the hall, and people would gather there. Hazrat Maulana would also be in attendance. A gentleman would read from the book of *Hadith* and translate, and the gathering would appreciate it. Every spring has its fall. Sometime after my last visit, I went to see Maulana Mohammad Mian Firangi Mahali. Maulana Nasir Mian Firangi Mahali sent someone along to guide me. When I reached the house, I was startled and involuntarily cried out, "Oh my! This is Hazrat Maulana Abdul Bari's home!" The guide nodded his head in affirmation. My heart sank when I saw how desolate the place was. Then I started looking for that small room where I used to stay, which was a few steps down. People there pointed to the open hall in front and said that it was in its basement and had now been shut, but my memory couldn't confirm that. Perhaps it was my memory that was failing me, but it suggested that the room was in between the two open chambers.

The Legal Struggle

In the matter of the Caliphate of Turkey, Firangi Mahal was the center of the legal struggle. Maulana's instincts had surmised that it would rain even before the clouds gathered, and had laid the foundation of *Anjuman Khuddam-i-Ka'ba* (Society of the Servants of Ka'ba), in which Maulana himself was a servant of the Servants of Ka'ba. This society created a fervor in every member of the Muslim community of India and a passion of great affinity with the Islamic Caliphate and the holy shrines. It was as if it was the first step toward an action and a movement.

Afterwards, during the Khilafat Movement too, Firangi Mahal remained a center of activity. Maulana Mohammad Ali was a disciple of Maulana Abdul Bari, and Firangi Mahal was where he and Shaukat Ali were conferred the honorary title of "Maulana." And they truly did become Maulanas. They wore an '*abaa*, a long gown, at all times and in every public gathering. Dense beards and faces that had a splendor. Once, at a rally, it was prayer time. I heard Maulana Abdul Majid Badayuni say to Maulana Mohammad Ali, "Please lead the prayers. It will be a pleasure and joy for me to pray behind you."

Till the time that Maulana Mohammad Ali, with his exemplary compassion for the community, and ignoring his own health, took on the load of the Khilafat Movement, it was Maulana Abdul Bari whose name had come to be the essence of the movement. "Mahatma's Gandhi's order is Maulana Abdul Bari's decree" was the sentiment carried in many newspaper advertisements. In the Khilafat Movement, the direct action that took place was on the grounds laid by Maulana Abdul Bari, who also had a big hand in taking the Khilafat Movement forward from there, establishing the Jamiat Ulema-e-Hind, and uniting the Islamic world and the Muslims of India against the British.

Establishment of the Khilafat Committee

When and where the Khilafat Committee was established, I tried very hard to ascertain, but I have to admit that I did not succeed. Some people suggested that the All-India Muslim Conference that convened on December 18, 1919 is what turned into the Khilafat Committee. That does not seem right since the conference passed a resolution to give thanks to the Khilafat Committee. On the basis of this and some other events, a few said that the Khilafat Committee was established in 1920. Those narratives don't appear to be true either. Circumstantial evidence suggests that Maulana Abdul Bari established the Khilafat Committee in Lucknow, which later shifted to Bombay as other people there took the responsibility to carry it forward. This has been confirmed in Shah Moinuddin Nadvi's book "Hayat-e-Sulaiman" in which he writes:

"I spent a lot of time searching for any documented evidence as to when, where, and on whose efforts the Khilafat Committee was established but unfortunately I was unsuccessful. I went to the home of Maulana Abdul Bari and met many people there. I exchanged letters with Mufti Muhammad Raza Ansari, who is compiling material on the life of Hazrat Maulana. I also established contact with various publishing houses. An associate went to Bombay and looked for the archives in the Khilafat offices there, only to find out that the office had been out of commission for some time. He could not even find any archived copies of the "Khilafat" newspaper. The scholars in Bombay expressed their inability to be of any help. I wrote to Maulana Imtiaz Ali Arshi Saheb, who wrote back with a lot of information which confirmed my understanding of a lot of issues, which was very comforting, but he too didn't have anything to say about

the matter of when, where, and how Khilafat Movement was established.

"As has been written, Firangi Mahal was the center of all Islamic movements. An example of that, as informed in a letter from Mufti Muhammad Raza, the Anjuman Khuddam-i-Ka'ba (Society of the Servants of Ka'ba) was established at the home of Hazrat Maulana Abdul Bari in December 1912. The office bearers of this society, besides Maulana Abdul Bari, included Mr. Shaukat Ali, who had a BA from Aligarh and later became known as Maulana Shaukat Ali, and Mr. Mushir Husain Kidwai, Barrister. There were many other founding members of the society. The formation of this society indicates that Maulana Abdul Bari, with his enlightened conscience, had assessed what was to come, and hence started this movement. It would be no surprise that this society is what turned into the Khilafat Committee or came about under its influence. In any case, what is for certain is that the Khilafat Committee had been established in Bombay before the All-India Muslim Conference took place. The rest are guesses, estimates, and conjectures."

Jamiat Ulema-e-Hind

It is very likely that the pain that the mutual differences between the scholars of Islam was causing the Muslim community and the precarious situation of the world's Muslims was what motivated peers with understanding and insight to bring scholars of all schools of thought together. But before anything else, Maulana Abdul Bari convened a gathering of a few scholars in Delhi's famous Syed Hasan Rasool-Numa's

Khanqah, and impressing on them how delicate the situation was and what was needed to be done, urged them to agree and unite and led them in taking the following pledge:

"Assembled at the shrine of Delhi's famous holy saint and with the Omnipresent and Omniscient God as our witness, we pledge that in our common national and communal issues we will remain united and unanimous, and we shall not let issues of divisions and differences create disagreements among us. Also, in matters related to the struggle of the nation and the country, we will bear with patience and fortitude the hardship and violence meted out by the government and will remain resolute and determined. In matters of the congregation, we will take actions with confidentiality and trust."

The intent here is not to write the history of Jamiat Ulema but to show, as is evident in the words above, that the hearts of the Muslims were heavy and that they were searching for that path of action which doesn't just appear like a divine revelation but is achieved after much stumbling.

In November 1919, on the occasion of the Khilafat Conference, a powerful congregation with representatives from all regions of the country had assembled in Delhi. After the conference, there was a session of all the leading scholars presided by Maulana Abdul Bari, and that was when Jamiat Ulema was established. Putting mutual differences aside, the way in which these leading scholars got together on the same platform for a particular cause, i.e. the survival of the Caliphate, can be best gauged by the fact that the famous leader of Ahl-e-Hadees and a crusader of the community in the true sense, Maulana Abul Wafa Sanaullah Amritsari delivered the keynote address.

The following Maulanas were in attendance at this gathering in Delhi:

> Abdul Bari, Salamatullah Firangi Mahali, Sanaullah Amritsari, Muhammad Sindhi, Asadullah Sindhi, Saiyad Muhammad Fakhir Allahabadi, Muhammad Anis, Khwaja Nizamuddin, Kifayatullah, Muhammad Ibrahim Darbhanga, Khuda Bakhsh Muzaffarpuri, Abdul Hakim Gayawi, Muhammad Akram, Munir-uz-Zaman, Muhammad Sadiq, Syed Muhammad Dawood, Syed Ismail, Muhammad Abdullah, and Azad Subhani.

It was perhaps the first time that these scholars came together in this way for the cause of the Islamic Caliphate, scholars who had grown so distant from each other due to their differences that some had even resorted to calling each other infidels. Squabbles related to groupism and ideological disputes had become an everyday affair, to the extent that violence and even killings had started happening in mosques. Those who would not even greet each other in the past were now standing on the same platform as one, ready to act together with all their might. This was the omnipotence of the Khilafat Movement, which had awakened the conscience of every Muslim, whether a learned or a common person.

Scholars of Divinity and Jihad by the Sword – Fantasies of a United Democratic Government in India

There was another group of men, self-aware and God-fearing, that was unconcerned with worldly causes and was embellishing the field of holy struggle. As Nushoor Wahidi said in the following couplet:

The history of passion is that in every era of wisdom
We made arrangements for rope and the gallows post

This arrangement started with the education and indoctrination from Shah Waliullah Dehlawi and continued through his son, Shah Abdul Aziz (died 1824), who issued a decree declaring India to be Darul Harb (land of war) under British dominion and pronounced that it was obligatory upon Hindus and Muslims to wage war against the British government for freedom, liberty and justice. Hazrat Syed Ahmed Shaheed was a disciple of Shah Waliullah who embarked on jihad and clashed with the Sikhs. But his campaign was not against the Sikhs as much as it was indirectly against the British. The Sikhs were loyal to the British government and occupied a strategic position, like a strong fortress between India and Afghanistan. The objective of Syed *Saheb* has been stated in Maulana Hussain Ahmed Madani's "*Naqsh-e-Hayat*" as follows:

"Since Syed Saheb's real objective was to exterminate the dominance and power of the English over India, under which both the Hindus and Muslims were distressed, he invited the Hindus to join him in this endeavor, and made it clear to them that their sole purpose would be to end the rule of foreigners in the country. Their purpose would not be to decide who rules over the country after that. Those who will be eligible to rule, be they Hindus, Muslims, or both, will rule. Subsequently, the letter he wrote in this regard to Raja Hindu Rao, minister and brother-in-law of Daulat Rao Sindhia, Maharaja of Gwalior state, is worth a careful study. It sheds a light on his real intentions and his viewpoints on the governing of the country."

Maulana Madani goes on to reproduce this letter, which is long, and then draws the following conclusions about Syed Ahmed Shaheed:

1. *He considered the English strangers, foreigners, and alien to India, and exasperated by their hegemony and domineering attitude, was determined to fight them.*
2. *He considered India his homeland*
3. *He never considered the purpose of jihad to establish their rule*
4. *He considered Hindus and Muslims to be equal partners in the fight against oppression and the trampling of rights, and considered the purpose of jihad to be the winning of freedom from the alien oppressors for both the communities.*

Further, as a summary, Maulana Madani writes that the Independence movement that these scholars started to join in the early 19th century, which included Shah Abdul Aziz Dehlawi, his family members and his disciples among those who laid its foundation stone, did not have even a hint of sectarianism or narrowmindedness, nor was their purpose to have worldly gains, territorial conquest, selfish interests, obtaining positions, or taking others in servitude. Nor was this movement started to bring any person or section of society to power, but had only a true democracy as its desired objective.

This has been mentioned here to present a practical example of the spirit of the unity of Islam. As has been mentioned before, the intent of the unity in Islam was not to establish an Islamic autocracy, but to bring a revolution in every Islamic country for reform. And in countries where there were non-Muslims as well, the intent was to join them in vanquishing tyranny and establish a clean democracy. Just as in Muslim countries, where a transparent government based on Islamic principles was sought to replace the interference and meddling from foreign powers, great revolutions needed to be started all over the world to establish a government that cared for the welfare of its people.

This movement was still limited to India as if it was the first iteration. For the second iteration, a guide and a leader for the 20th century was needed. This came in the form of Maulana Mahmud Hasan who set off earthquakes with their epicenter in Deoband.

Maulana Mahmud Hasan made schemes for revolutions in all of the Muslim world. On the surface, Maulana was an Indian academic, scholar, commentator, and a specialist of Prophet Muhammad's traditions, whose occupation was discharging the duties of the principal of Deoband's Darul Uloom along with teaching religion and indoctrination of knowledge. But in addition to those things, he was also a tireless activist and a refined thinker and politician. He was actually a complete realization of this dream of Allama Iqbal:

> *More difficult than the conquest of the world is the task of seeing the world;*
> *When the heart is reduced to blood, only then does the eye of the heart receive its sight.*

> *For a thousand years the narcissus has been lamenting its blindness;*
> *With great difficulty the one with true vision is born in the garden.*

Ostensibly, Maulana had no time left from his duties of principal of Darul Uloom, his work translating the Quran, the compilation and arrangement of annotations in texts, the teaching of Prophet Muhammad's traditions, authoring textbooks, and guidance and counseling to be able to pay any practical attention to political thought, which is very tedious work and whose results show after much hard work, a lot of time, and in the final stages of the mission. But how does one account for the fact that Maulana had distributed the action plan for revolution and reform throughout the Islamic world? His sharp foresight was focused hundreds of years in the future. His view was of lasting peace and prosperity for the nation and the community. He was observing how the English had spread their net throughout the world, which had resulted on the one hand in India's servitude to them, and on the other, the devastation and destruction of the central Caliphate and Islamic countries. To counter this, he launched movements in India to establish a united independent democracy as well as making schemes for the security and survival of the Islamic countries. And both of these fronts required clashing with the English. At the time, England was the world's most powerful colonial power, and there was no way to survive without going to war with her.

It is a pity that history has draped a curtain over Maulana's narrative and if anything is known about his revolutionary movements, it is only that he started a struggle in Yaghistan, which has been mentioned earlier. And in India, a roadmap for a proposed democracy was presented, for which Raja Mahendra Pratap, a well-known revolutionary, was made the president. These events provide guidance toward Maulana's life principles, but there are no known details. The historical accuracy of the proposed democracy was preserved by the former Home Minister of the Government of British India, Sir William Vincent, by making fun of it. In a speech at the Central Council, he said about the proposed democracy that the answer is a proposal too. It is a pity that Sir William Vincent wasn't around to see that the proposed democracy became a reality. This is an indication of Maulana's political position within India, which has been documented by his young student, Maulana Hussain Ahmed Madani, as detailed in his booklet titled *"Muttahida Qaumiyat"* (United Nationality). And Allama Iqbal, under misapprehension from this text, criticized the Maulana, debates ensued, and ultimately Allama Iqbal had to admit that he had misunderstood. In this context, the poet and scholar Iqbal Ahmad Khan 'Suhail' wrote a number of couplets and poems in Persian in response. While, unfortunately, there is no room to discuss them here, suffice it to say that although the Maulana was of that breed of men who not only dreamed early on of a joint democratic government in India but even invited martyrdom to see it to fruition, no legacy of his remains in the Islamic world. It is true, however, that sitting in Deoband he breathed life into revolutions in Kabul, Constantinople, Cairo and the Hijaz. The lack of any material on this topic is largely due to the fact that Maulana did not share his deepest thoughts even with his close associates. This was the perfection of a combination of leadership and intellect. Maulana Abdullah Sindhi was perhaps one of the closest persons to him. He writes that Maulana said to him, "Abdullah, go to Afghanistan." He asked, "Hazrat, why?" Maulana didn't say anything. Then one day again Maulana said, "Abdullah, go to Afghanistan." He again asked, "Hazrat, why?" Maulana was again quiet, but his face had a disagreeable expression on it. Maulana Abdullah writes that now he was worried that if the Maualana asked him again to go to Afghanistan, he would have to comply. And that is what happened. After a few days, Maulana again asked him to go to Afghanistan. Now the assertion was clear. Maulana Abdullah went to Afghanistan and states that when he reached there, it was clear why he had been sent. But beyond that, Maulana Abdullah is silent about the details, leaving observers to the speculation of their minds and understanding. Another incident was narrated to me by Maulana Muhammad Manzoor Nomani. He said Maulana Abdullah Sindhi had told him that Maulana Hussain Ahmed Madani never revealed any secrets. He once told Maulana Abdullah that someone would come to meet him at such and such a place at such and such time and asked him to note down whatever he said and not to ask him anything. And that man came at the indicated time and place and stated quantities of guns, ammunition, and other items, which were duly noted and the man left. Questions were neither permitted nor asked. Later people found out that Maulana probably had an armaments warehouse in Rajasthan, which the English never found out about. Another incident is from when Maulana Abdullah Sindhi had to depart and he needed money. He wrote to Seth Abdullah Haroon asking for Rs. 2000 to be sent to him by a certain time. When the money didn't arrive by the requested time, Maulana was surprised. The next day in the afternoon there was a knock on his door. When Maulana Abdullah stepped out, he found Seth Abdullah Haroon standing there. He handed him the Rs. 2000, said the message to him was delayed and that was why he was late in getting the money to him, and left immediately. Maulana Sindhi went straight and stayed with Sir Abdul Qayyum and then slipped out and took a path through the jungles, but had to spend all the money giving bribes at checkpoints. Now he was empty handed, and sent a coded message to some person, who sold off everything he had and came and gave him Rs. 1500. The foregoing story points to an affair that is confirmed by the following narrative:

> *"The details of the incident are described as follows. Maulana Abdullah Sindhi knew that the police and CID were on guard. His escaping to Afghanistan was very difficult if not impossible. Therefore, he decided to come across as a simpleton, and went directly to Peshawar to stay with Sir Abdul Qayyum, whose son-in-law was an army officer responsible for the security of the frontier. Maulana repeatedly said to the army officer in a pleading tone that he needed to go to Afghanistan for a goodwill deed. God's reward would be his if he made a place for him in the many trucks of his that cross the border. The officer would laugh to himself thinking how naïve this man was to ask him something like that, and he would just ignore the request with cursory responses. Maulana's plot was to lull the officer into ignoring his whereabouts. That is how it transpired, and when Maulana was convinced that the officer was no longer cautious about his whereabouts, he slipped out one night and took another route. From Peshawar he went to Quetta, a mountainous route through the jungles. The money that Seth Abdullah Haroon had given him was in the form of guineas. There were checkpoints along the way where he had to give bribes to get past and ultimately the money ran out while Maulana was still on his way. Hence, Maulana sent a coded letter to Sheikh*

Abdul Rahim, who was Hazrat Maulana Mahmud Hasan's trustworthy associate. Sheikh Abdul Rahim was Acharya Kriplani's brother who had converted to Islam and had joined Shaykh-al-Hind Maulana Mahmud Hasan's struggle and movement. Maulana asked him to send money and indicated a place where he would be to receive it. Sheikh Abdul Rahim sold some household possessions and jewelry to raise the money and sent it to the indicated location. Maulana received the money and moved on to Afghanistan."

In 1921, when I was on the editorial staff of Bijnor's *Madina* newspaper, I had also joined the non-cooperation movement. Abdul Latif Kiratpuri was the president of Bijnor district's Congress and we had grown close to each other on account of working together. He was a serious minded man. One time, after the verdict in the Karachi case, there was a grand rally in Kiratpur which I attended. In this way I was able to see his hometown as well. In my opinion he was a very observant and intelligent man.

Abdul Latif Kiratpuri had narrated to me how he had served Hazrat Maulana for a long time, and one of his duties was to read to him the translations and summaries of news articles in the *Pioneer* newspaper. Abdul Latif *Saheb* once told me that Maulana had formed a secret society by the name of *"Mukhlisiin"* (The Sincere Ones), which had very selected members. If he wrote a recommendation letter for anyone, he would say everything in it but never end with "Sincerely." That word was reserved for the members of the society. And if he wrote to anyone saying that so-and-so was a 'sincere man,' and should be given Rs. 10,000, the recipient of the letter would sell all his possessions if he had to and give the person the money. Abdul Latif told me that Hazrat Maulana's scheme appeared to be to incite the spirit of rebellion among the frontier tribes and start a grand army of holy warriors. For this purpose, a few scholars were sent there who used to teach Quran, and particularly elucidate those portions of it that talk about jihad, which previously these scholars would just gloss over. The result was that a passion of struggle was ignited among the tribals and they became strongly opposed to the English. It came to the point that the tribals would give their young sons firearms, and after coming home from work, would ask them how many Englishmen they killed that day. An armament factory was also established there, where they made their own rifles and pistols and some tribals still do. They were such good marksmen that they would say, "As God is our witness, our bullets never hit the ground." When things reached that state, Maulana Abdullah Sindhi was asked to establish an Islamic university in Fatehpuri. Consequently, in 1333 AH, or 1912-13 AD, Maulana Sindhi established an institution by the name of *"Nazaair Al-Ma'arif"* in Delhi's Fatehpuri Masjid. Maulana Ahmad Ali of Sheranwala Darwaza in Lahore was a student and close relative of Maulana Sindhi who had migrated to Kabul and was later called back. He used to live in a chamber of the Sheranwala Darwaza mosque. All he did was teach the Quran. I too studied the interpretation and commentary on the verses of ten chapters under him. He had interpreted the entire Quran in the light of a holy struggle to the extent that he had a Quranic interpretation for why the rulers should not interfere with the religious issues of the subjects. Maulana Ubaidullah Sindhi had a student by the name of Abdul Hai Farooqui who had documented Maulana

Sindhi's Quranic interpretations and published them in the form of a book under the title *"Tafseer Quran."* The title he gave to the chapter on the verse *Surah Al-Baqarah* was *"Khilafat-e-Kibriya"* (Magnificence of the Caliphate).

The historian Najibabadi told me that Maulana Sindhi had once asked him to say in one word the objective of the teaching of Quran, then answered the question himself as "governance." Maulana Ahmad Ali would ask the scholars who came to study the interpretation and commentary of Quranic verses under him if they knew how to ride a bicycle. If they said no, he would give them his bicycle and they would be allowed to attend his lectures only after they had learned how to ride it. He used to say that if they didn't know how to ride a bicycle, how could they drive bigger things and conduct a jihad. In this way, the education of the Quran was being made common and the passion for holy struggle was being aroused for a particular and a pure purpose.

Of foreign lands, Maulana Ahmad Ali said that Afghanistan's Shaikh-al-Islam, Turkey's Grand Mufti, Al-Azhar University's vice-chancellor, and the scholars and muftis of Egypt were his cohorts in that they had the same point of view. This much we know from books that Afghanistan's religious leader, Shaikh-al-Islam, was a graduate of Deoband. Iran's *Mujtahid al-'Asr* (lit. Leading Jurist of the Age), during the time when the Shah of Iran had given the exclusive contract for importation of tobacco to the English, was unconcerned with matters of jihad. Members of *"Mukhlisiin"* (The Sincere Ones), posing as laborers, started unloading the crates of tobacco from the ships, and when the English supervisors were drunk from alcohol plied by them, they would open the crates and inspect them. They took these crates to the *Mujtahid al-'Asr* to show him how armaments were being smuggled into the country. *Mujtahid al-'Asr* issued a decree saying, "*Tambaaku naushiidan dariin zaman haram ast*" (Smoking tobacco is forbidden at this time). In the evening, when the Shah went into his quarters, unlike the usual routine, his hookah had not been prepared. When he called out for it, no one answered. The Shah got very upset and he shouted angrily, "Did no one hear what I said?" That's when his wife came in, told him he would not get his hookah that day, and informed him of the *Mujtahid al-'Asr*'s decree. The Shah immediately held court, summoned the *Mujtahid al-'Asr*, and asked him what kind of a decree that was, given that Islam is a universal religion till the end of time. How could smoking tobacco be forbidden at this time but not others, and forbidden in Iran but not in Turkey. *Mujtahid al-'Asr* asked for a private audience, then narrated the entire story to the Shah. The result was that the English monopoly over tobacco import ended.

It is a pity that Maulana's program did not succeed, which he narrated as follows. Anis Ahmad joined the *Nazaair Al-Ma'arif*, and talking about his asceticism and piety, and his love for the Turks, he recalled when, on hearing about the defeat of the Turks in the Balkan War, he got very agitated, staggered and fell on the first floor of the Fatehpuri Masjid, which had an open roof and no parapet and he was at risk of falling off and meeting his death. As a result, Maulana Ubaidullah Sindhi had complete confidence in him. I had met Anis Ahmad as well as his father Idris Ahmad, who was the principal of Bijnor Government High School and had such a stature in the British Secret Service that he had direct contact with the Governor-General. Anis Ahmad betrayed Maulana to the British and the government decided to arrest him. At the intercession of Dr. Mukhtar Ahmad Ansari, Maulana came to know about it and he escaped to Hijaz to continue his work. His feeling was that from there he would be able to better implement his scheme for the Islamic world, but WWI broke out in 1914, Maulana did not get an opportunity to seek the help of the Turks to come to Afghanistan, and he was imprisoned in Malta. With him were Maulana Hussain Ahmed Madani, Maulana Aziz Gul and others.

Whether my stated narrative of Abdul Latif Kiratpuri is borne by history or not, it needs to be included for completeness when we take full account of the state of affairs. I note the following particulars:

1. It is evident that Maulana had created a system of jihad and rebellion in the entire Islamic world. His objective was to end the colonial policies of the English and establish a united democracy in India. Every movement before Gandhi was based on violence. It is entirely unlikely that such a big movement could be started in all of India without an organization behind it. Therefore, the existence of "The Sincere Ones" seems appropriate.

2. Maulana kept everything related to the movement close to his chest. He never took anyone into confidence. Others knew only as much as he deemed necessary. There are two strong pieces of evidence in support of that. First, Maulana Ubaidullah told Maulana Muhammad Manzoor Nomani that when he got to Kabul, Amir Habibullah personally gave him an envelope containing instructions for the work he had

to do there. This also suggests how all-encompassing, strategic and compiled with consciousness the movement was. It is another matter that Amir Habibullah was in it for selfish interests. Second, Maulana Ubaidullah also told Maulana Muhammad Manzoor Nomani that he was in Karachi when he received a note from Shaykh al-Hind saying that a person would meet him and that he should note down confidentially what he had to say and not ask him any questions. Sure enough, a man approached him at the Karachi Masjid and gave him some information about a magazine as well as details about guns, ammunitions, bombs, etc. Maulana Ubaidullah noted down the details and when he went to Deoband, he delivered them to Shaykh al-Hind. He never knew what it was all about. Now we learn through traditions that Maulana had set up a magazine press where armaments were stored, which the CID never found out about. People also say that the press was in Rajasthan.

3. There appears to be evidence for the development of code words and coded messages, which is the hallmark of large revolutionary organizations. It was these code words that were used by Maulana Ubaidullah to ask Sheikh Abdul Rahim for money. And the way in which Sheikh Abdul Rahim arranged for the money and brought it to Maulana Ubaidullah also lends credence to Abdul Latif Kiratpuri's suggestion that if the society's members wrote "sincere" to describe someone, they would go to any lengths to help that member out.

4. The envelope that Amir Habibullah gave Maulana Ubaidullah in Kabul had a specific list of tasks that needed to be carried out.

5. Constantinople's Grand Mufti not issuing a decree against Mustafa Kemal Pasha and accepting exile and captivity in Malta is also a significant event. It was due to the influence of Maulana. Kiratpuri's contention that Maulana Mahmud Hasan had spread his net against the English in the entire Islamic world also appears credible.

6. Raja Mahendra Pratap's activities in Afghanistan, which were toward the independence of India, and his working together closely with Maulana Ubaidullah are also significant events in these series.

Maulana Madani has written:

"Hazrat Shaykh al-Hind was not just brimming with knowledge of Quranic interpretation, Prophet Muhammad's traditions, jurisprudence, principles of logic and philosophy, mathematics and geometry, and contemplative sciences, but his understanding of Arabic, Persian, Urdu prose and poetry, teaching aptitude, composition of articles, poems, lyrics, and rhyming couplets, etc. were so memorable that the listener would be awed. In addition, Hazrat had a broad and deep understanding of history and political events. His understanding of India's economic, political, trade, industrial, educational, administrative, war, health issues etc. also was so deep that he would impress even the academics of these disciplines. He was a voracious newspaper reader and was an enthusiastic follower

of contemporary global affairs. However, the British government and events in India forced him to put his life on the line to oppose the English tyranny and oppression and never gave any threat a chance to intimidate or affect him."

Once I said to Maulana Hasrat Mohani that Maulana Mahmud Hassan had been impressed by Maulana Azad's writings. Maulana Hasrat appeared agitated and asked if he had heard me right. Maulana Mahmud Hasan being impressed with someone's writings? He was something else! That was the status of Maulana Mahmud Hasan, may God have mercy on him.

Abdullah Haroon Jafar, Dr. Ansari, Maulana Mohammad Ali and all other Muslim leaders being obedient and submissive toward Maulana, besides being a commentary on his status, also goes to show how much work he had done inside India toward its independence. There were even plenty of revolutionary organizations, and the objective was that when, according to plan, Afghanistan or the independent frontier tribes were to attack India, all the armaments would come out. The idea was to violently overthrow the British government and gain independence for India.

The second conclusion that can be deduced is that the society of "The Sincere Ones" played an important role in this. The one moving part of a code word would mobilize the delivery of thousands of rupees across the land. Hazrat Shaykh al-Hind's scheme was like a brick-kiln: cool from the outside but blazing inside.

Maulana had assembled a group of people who devoted their lives and would sacrifice it for the nation. They were teeming with a revolutionary spirit, deeply in love with Islam, willing to sacrifice their lives for freedom, and filled with commitment and determination. Maulana Sindhi was like a thorn in the eye of the government. Hence, when he started for Afghanistan, CID was eager and active to arrest him. A person who resembled Maulana Sindhi was arrested and a telegram was sent to the Viceroy that Ubaidullah had been arrested. The person who had been arrested was a member of "The Sincere Ones." He went silently to jail, and when he was certain that Maulana would have reached Afghanistan, he protested why he had been arrested and that he wasn't Ubaidullah Sindhi.

Abdul Latif Kiratpuri also used to say that Maulana's activists were spread throughout the world. These people were very pious and abstemious, devout and godly, but they were permitted to even ply alcohol if it helped them get something out of it. It was by getting the English supervisors drunk that the activists had discovered arms in tobacco crates in Iran. It is well known that the English get drunk very quickly and easily.

Suffice it to say that this was an armed struggle in a vast battleground where wannabe martyrs were hard at work to hollow out the roots of the British government, just as the English were working hard to eradicate Islam from the world. Along with their all-out effort to protect and preserve the Islamic Caliphate, freedom for India, just as the freedom of other nations of the East, was a paramount objective of these leaders. Another benefit they wished to derive from this was that by expelling the English from such an auriferous country as India would cause the colonial British empire to collapse, and its evil eye and sharp teeth would not remain in existence.

Looking back today, who can say that these people were not successful or the Khilafat Movement did not succeed? Those who say that lack in understanding of and need to study more the politics and history of the Independence movement and the process of cause and effect.

4

The Great Wars and Indian Politics

World War I 1914-18

Serbia, Montenegro, Greece and Bulgaria started a war with Turkey to break it up into pieces. After deposing Sultan Abdul Hamid, the Young Turks took the reins of the government. It hadn't been very long when, in October 1912, this war broke out. When the war started, everyone surmised that Turkey would win, and that is why the British and French Prime Ministers issued a joint statement declaring that geographic boundaries would be preserved whoever won. But the result was different and Turkey was defeated. After that, the two Prime Ministers changed directions and blatantly declared that they saw no reason why the victors shouldn't get the spoils of war. This war ended in May 1913, and on May 30, 1913 a treaty was signed in London which ceded many provinces of the Ottoman territory to the Balkan League. After that, Serbia, Greece, and Romania attacked Bulgaria and this Second Balkan War ended in August 1913 with the last peace treaty being signed in the Romanian capital Bucharest, under which Serbia gained a lot of territory.

On June 28, 1914 the heir presumptive to the Austro-Hungarian throne, Archduke Ferdinand was assassinated in Sarajevo. Sarajevo was the capital of the Austro-Hungarian province of Bosnia, which was once a part of the 10ᵗʰ century Serbian state. Austria declared Serbia responsible for this assassination, and on July 28, 1914 declared war on Serbia. Russia had been a supporter and guardian of Serbia for some time and put its armed forces on alert. Germany tried to dissuade Russia, but when they did not agree, Germany declared war on Russia on July 30, 1924, the day that Belgrade was being bombarded. France was allied with Russia and so, on August 3, 1914 Germany declared war on France as well and asked Belgium for the right of way to attack France.

In 1839, Britain, the German Confederation, France, Austria and Russia recognized and guaranteed the independence and neutrality of Belgium. Invoking that treaty, Britain gave an ultimatum to Germany not to ask Belgium for the right of way and, on not getting a commitment back, declared war on Germany on August 4, 1914. On August 23, 1914 Japan declared war on Germany and gradually the conflict became a World War, which America, whose policy heretofore was to keep away from the politics of Europe, also joined in 1917, i.e. toward the end of the war. Britain and its allies came to be known as "Allied," which included the following countries: Britain, France, Italy, America, Japan, Belgium, China, Greece, Portugal, Romania, and other small countries and principalities totaling 17.

Turkey Joins the War

Britain's actions against the Turks were out in the open. Britain had explicitly helped and supported the capture of Turkish territory and ceding it to the control of others. For example, in the 1877-78 Russo-Turkish war, two Turkish provinces, Bosnia and Herzegovina, were ceded to Austrian control with British support. Later, in 1908, the two provinces were included in the Austro-Hungarian empire. Britain had occupied Egypt and cut off the path of the Turks there during the Tirablus war. There was a pattern to this intent. Young Turks had brought about reforms and tried to win the support of the British but were eventually disheartened by the stance taken by Britain and France in the Balkans. Come what may, Turkey joined the war on the side of Germany.

The German army was considered very strong at the time. Germany had used their knowledge of science and technology to develop such armaments that the world had no concept of. A fort in Belgium that was considered indestructible was blown up by Howitzer cannons as if it was made of cotton wool. Serbia was blown to smithereens. France started to recede. Those who faced Germany in the beginning suffered heavy losses.

As soon as Turkey entered the war under the leadership of Enver Pasha, it forcefully attacked the Caucasus Mountains area. But soon it had to retreat and Russia captured Turkish territory. On February 2, 1915 the Turks invaded the Suez Canal in Egypt but they were unsuccessful there too. Now the Allied forces set their targets on Constantinople in an effort to oust Turkey from the war. On February 19, 1915 the joint naval forces of Britain and France invaded Dardanelles Strait. The Allied forces were under the impression that since the forts on both sides of the narrow strait were not armed with cannons, which had been removed by Sultan Abdul Hamid under orders from his English masters, their navies could easily navigate it to reach Constantinople. But the Allies suffered heavy defeats since the cannons and artillery had been reinstalled in these forts as soon as the Young Turks came to power, and all kinds of armaments had fortified the strait. Protected by hundreds of cannons, and given there were no warplanes at the time, it was not possible for naval ships to breach the strait. But now it became an issue of honor for the Allied forces. After having to retreat on February 19, 1915 they attacked again and again with intense planning on February 23, March 6, and March 18, 1915, for the supervision of which Lord Kitchener himself was present there, but to no avail. The Allied forces were unsuccessful in these attacks and so, on April 25, 1915 joint land-sea attacks started. The idea was to land Allied troops on the Gallipoli peninsula, proceed over land to Constantinople and capture it. But just as they had thwarted the naval attacks, maintaining their traditional courage and bravery, Turks under the able guidance of their commander Mustafa Kemal Pasha handed the Allied a resounding defeat and in the end they retreated after suffering losses of 31,389 dead, 78,740 injured and 9,708 missing, according to the count of the Allied themselves. The bravery and chivalry of the Turks in that battle was an unprecedented demonstration of their courage. But in Mesopotamia, due to the Indian forces composed of both Hindus and Muslims and the treachery of the Arabs, the Turks suffered defeat after defeat. In the beginning, the Turks established themselves as valiant, but later they suffered losses in Mosul and in the region of the Euphrates river, even losing Tikrit to British occupation on September 28, 1916. Then General Townshend, commanding British and Indian forces, advanced toward Gaza. Such was the fate of Palestine that on March 26, 1917 British and Indian forces attacked the heavily fortified city of Gaza. But after two days of intense battle, the

British had to retreat. Then General Allenby was sent from France to take charge, and on October 31, 1917 his forces captured Beersheba, and on November 7, 1917 Gaza also fell. After that, by November 16, 1917 General Allenby's forces had pushed the Turks as far back as Jaffa, and on December 9, 1917 they declared victory over Jerusalem and the Turks retreated from there.

By spring of 1918, General Allenby had crossed the Jordan River and his forces had blocked the Turks from retreating toward the west. On the eastern front, the joint forces of Amir Faisal and General Lawrence had cut off their way. Toward the end of October, 1918, General Allenby entered Aleppo and the victory over Palestine was complete. Finally, on October 30, 1918, in Moudros harbor on the Greek island of Lemnos, peace talks started and Turkish military actions ended that day.

In the journal *Mashriq* dated March 13, 1919 on page 18 under the title "Notes and News," the following text appears:

"His Excellency the Commander-in-Chief delivered a statement to the Viceroy's Legislative Council in which he briefed that to date India has sent 579,252 men to various battlefields as follows: Iraq Arab 302,199, Egypt 140,419, France 86,382, East Africa 34,511, Persian Gulf 24,401, Dardanelles Strait and Salonica 9,717, and Aden 17,57. The losses suffered by these forces are as follows: 19,010 dead, 61,916 injured, 3,341 missing, 6,146 prisoners, and 1,223 believed to be prisoners. Non-military personnel sent to these theaters are in excess of 500,000."

On November 9, 1918 Germany called for truce. The German Chancellor Kaiser Wilhelm II had earlier abdicated his throne and fled into exile. Conditions for an armistice were laid down and later, the Allied countries reached separate peace treaties with the vanquished countries.

State of Affairs in India During the War

Till that time, Congress was a moderate party whose objective was to promote friendship between Britain and India, and to slowly establish self-governance in the shadow of the British government. Congress stood with Britain and Mahatma Gandhi supported the English, including the recruitment of Indian soldiers. Non-violence had not permeated his conscience yet. Revolutionary political parties that wanted to establish their government through violent means had no interest in this war. This was a European matter and the world had not shrunk to the small size it is today. In fact, as I have mentioned earlier, even America remained away from European politics. In 1917, by declaring war on Germany, America showed interest in Europe's politics for the first time.

As far as Muslims were concerned, they were in a strange predicament. On one hand, every Muslim had a deep reverence for Turks of the Ottoman Empire. On the other, the Aligarh Movement started by Sir Syed had taught them the lesson of unwavering fealty to the British government, making them its strong supporters, even slaves. They were convinced that their survival in India implicitly depended on preserving British rule. That is why some Muslims were caught in a strange dilemma. They were either those who relied on government jobs and assistance or were feudal lords, nawabs, or *taluqdars* (estate owners, barons, or land tax collectors) or those who were under their influence. The predominant reason for this dilemma was the Aligarh Movement that Sir Syed had started. After the failure of the Indian Rebellion of 1857, a great personality that arose from among the Muslims was Sir Syed. He was a very learned, broadminded, and intelligent man and had a great mind. He was extremely affected by the Muslims' backwardness and poverty. He observed that the Muslims did not have access to schools or colleges, and contemporary modern knowledge and learning was not reaching them and their children. All in all, there were a few Arabic madrasas where outdated curriculum and Dars-i Nizami syllabus (the system of Islamic education developed by Mulla Nizamuddin Sihalivi of Firangi Mahal, which is used in many Asian madrasas and Darul Ulooms). After considering these factors, he decided that it was essential to take advantage of the good attributes of western culture. Conservatism had seeped into every fiber of the Muslims' being so much that they found it difficult to accept any modern thought, particularly despite the fact that they were caught in a vortex of despair and hopelessness. Sir Syed traveled to England. He visited Cambridge and Oxford Universities. He observed their clubs, their debating, their sportsgrounds, and thought how necessary all these things were in addition to religious education. He wished there were universities like Cambridge and Oxford in his own country. There too, students would have debating clubs and excel in all kinds of sports. He decided to create a new framework for the Muslim society.

Sir Syed was such an enlightened and wise man for having foreseen a scenario that no one could have dreamt of at the time and gave his all to achieve it, down to the residential characteristic of the university, the need and benefits of which are modern concepts, and was also a dream of Sir Syed. He took many features of Oxford and Cambridge Universities, and he kept an eye on the practice of religion as well, saying that just as the students of these English universities went to church, praying in mosques and teaching of religion should be made a requirement. Like in the English universities, he implemented an attire but did not choose western clothing. The attire required was a Turkish hat, white cotton trousers and a Turkish coat, with shoes and socks. Anyone not in that attire could not enter the dining hall, where meals were served and eaten together. In short, Sir Syed took religion and worldly affairs and combined it with modern learning and culture to construct a new society and there is no bigger proof of his greatness than to see that this construct is attractive and desirable to everyone today. Sir Syed was an extremely sincere man and even-tempered, patient, serious, forbearing and single minded. He broke the fetters of customs and traditions and devised new rules for culture and the way of living which are relevant even today. Sir Syed was a great man, the kind that is born once in centuries. He gave the Muslim community the capability to think, a wisdom that captured the minds of the community, and a number of intellectuals gathered around him. Historians such as Allama Shibli, poets and thinkers such as Hali, writers such as Dr. Nazir Ahmad, and generous, resourceful and sincere folks such as Nawab Mohsin-ul-Mulk, Maulvi Zakaullah, and Nawab Viqar-ul-Mulk, all became concordant with Sir Syed and his determined helpers. They came together to create a college that today is known by the name Aligarh Muslim University, which gave the Islamic community of India some true activists and all that it needed. Sir Syed never allowed sectarianism to enter Aligarh. If he had kept Aligarh only for Muslim students according to the law of the times, there would have been no obstacle to such an arrangement, but in a large-hearted move, he opened up the school to every class and thought, every religion and community, keeping the atmosphere broadminded. The first student to graduate from Aligarh was not a Muslim, he was a Hindu. One can gauge Sir Syed's thinking and disposition from this.

From 1883 till 1894, Sir Syed maintained this modality. His writings and speeches from the time indicate that Sir Syed considered the nation to be composed of both Hindus and Muslims and was in favor of not just a shared government but a shared culture, and he laid the foundation of what is called secularism today. The Mohammedan Anglo-Oriental College was a congenial confluence of Hindu and Muslim students and teachers. The first graduate of the college was Ishwari Prasad and, along with Allama Shibli and Dr. Ziauddin Ahmed, Jadav Chandra Chakravarti and Bhavani Chandra Chakravarti were among the teachers there. Out of 47 faculty, 17 were Hindus occupying key positions. The first 'vote of thanks' of the MAO College was given to the Maharaja of Patiala. That is why Allama Iqbal gave the following message to 'The Tombstone of Sayyid,' which is absolutely true and based on facts.

If your aim in the world is religious education
Never teach your nation world's abdication

Do not use your tongue for sectarianism
Resurrection Day's tumult is hiding here

Your writings should pave the way for unity
Beware! No heart should be hurt by your speech

Sir Syed filled every nook and cranny of the college in Aligarh with Hindu-Muslim solidarity, national unity, and secularism. Sir Syed dreamt that the young generation of the time would receive a modern education and training while staying true to Islam and that dream came true. Students of Aligarh proved to be examples of this Persian maxim:

Get acquainted with present-day Aristotle
Make time with instruments and be new

But keep traveling, going to places beyond
Don't get lost till you reach your destination

The college thrived. Once a professor of mine, an Englishman, told me that he met a friend of his in Calcutta who asked him where he was going. When the professor replied Aligarh, the friend said, "Ah, Aligarh, where the students wear red hats made in Fez and play such good cricket!"

Sir Syed gave courage to the community, motivated them to work hard, and brought hope to where there was only despair. He told them to realize their shortcomings and overcome them, because God doesn't bring change to a nation that doesn't bring about a revolution within itself. He taught them self-awareness and self-confidence, and righteousness of words and deeds, and with his patience and perseverance, breathed new life in a lifeless body of the Muslims.

Aligarh Muslim University is still the same today, its character is the same, its conscience is the same and its way of thinking is the same.

In this way, the great personality of Sir Syed was a revolutionary one. He had said that philosophy would be in our right hand, natural sciences in our left hand, and we would wear the crown of the "Oneness of God" on our heads, and he accomplished that. The seed of secularism that he sowed in the college has blossomed into a robust tree today, and no storm of ill winds has been able to bend it.

Sir Syed and India's Politics

But Sir Syed appeared on the political scene of India when, after the failure of the Indian Rebellion of 1857, the Muslims were very demoralized. There was an endless sequence of murders, hangings, and sequestering of property, which continued for a while, and soon after regaining complete control, the British government had started excluding Muslims from junior level employment. Indians never got senior level positions anyway. Sir Syed was extremely affected by this situation, and after some time he came up with this solution for it:

1. Muslims have to be brought out of poverty.
2. Independence of the country should be delayed as much as possible, and a complete charter of support for the government has to be created to take the Muslims out of poverty and allow them to lead respectable lives. Otherwise, in an independent India with ¾ Hindus, the ¼ Muslims will be crushed. Along these lines, a speech of Sir Syed was published in the January 11 or 12, 1888 newspaper that he had delivered on December 28, 1887 in front of a crowd of civil and military officers of the Taluqdar government of Awadh, lawyers, newspaper reporters, academics

and intellectuals, Shia and Sunni scholars of all sects and schools of thought, and student youths from India and England. In his speech, he emphasized that Muslims should absolutely not join Congress because if a representative government was formed, the future of the Muslims would be dark and they would not get anything but devastation and achieve nothing but perpetual slavery. Sir Syed had stated three reasons for that:

i. Hindus and Muslims are two separate nations. Suppose that the British left with their armies etc. Who would rule the country then? It is obvious that both Hindus and Muslims cannot sit on the throne together. One would have to overpower the other. To expect that both will have equal rights is to hope for the impossible and the impractical.

ii. An elected government in India is irrelevant for the reason that in the event of an election, Muslims shall vote for Muslims and Hindus for Hindus. In such a case, the ratio of representatives would be 75:25.

iii. Muslims should fully trust the British government. They can protect their rights and give them effective representation in the administration.

The esteemed audience of the speech and the environment and the times in which it was delivered caused it to be widely publicized. In Indian newspapers, there was anger and uproar over it, but the London newspaper The Times published it on June 16, 1888, declaring it one of the best political discourses in an Indian voice.

Sir Syed advised Muslims to stay completely away from politics and devote themselves to getting an education. Sir Syed's objective in declaring politics as the forbidden fruit was to dissuade Muslims from contributing to driving the English out of the country as he considered them most protective of the Muslims. But Sir Syed could not stop the Muslims for long, and gradually semi-political societies were being established, and finally, in 1906, Muslim League came into being. Muslim League was under the control of Nawabs and Taluqdars and its appearance was very elitist. Later on, forced by general opinion, when it did take the name of a starter government, it used the term "suitable" to qualify it. This was the Muslim League about which Maulana Zafar Ali Khan had stated:

The League that turns on its side once a year

Muslim League held only annual meetings. Other than during the short duration of the Khilafat Movement, it stuck to its convictions that resulted in the partition of the country. Because of this, the Muslims had to face dreadful misery and are still facing hardships that are evident to everyone.

More than 90 years later, when we read Sir Syed's speech, we find it lacking as political thought, although as far as his educational services are concerned, he does appear to touch the sky with greatness. Some people take sections of Sir Syed's speeches from here and there and use them to try and prove that he was a nationalist, but that would be a distortion of history. For example, Maulana Saeed Ahmad Akbarabadi has discussed Sir Syed's political beliefs and, on the basis of two speeches of Sir Syed from 1884 that were prior to the 1888 declaration, has tried to demonstrate that he was not only a nationalist but a revolutionary[7]. There is no doubt that the resources that he needed to rid the Muslims of their poverty and its bases hadn't materialized yet and as stated earlier, there was not even a trace of sectarianism in him. Sir Syed was a large-hearted and clear-minded person, but later, as a means to an end, there was a storm of a revolution in his thinking as far as the freedom of the country was concerned. Hence in 1887, three years after he delivered those speeches, he declared in front of a large gathering, that Hindus and Muslims were separate nations and India was not ready for a representative government.

Sir Syed's absence from Syed Ameer Ali's proposed National Muhammadan Conference can absolutely not be used to arrive at the conclusion that he was not opposed to sectarianism in politics; in fact the real reason was exactly that for the sake of the protection of the Muslims, he wanted to keep India under British rule and was against Muslims taking part in political activity. It was for that reason that he opposed the Indian National Congress and created "The United Patriotic Association" to stand against it and promote the continued yoke of slavery around India's neck. He actively opposed Syed Jamaluddin Afghani's movement and deemed it wrong to have Indian representatives in the Viceroy's Council. No student of history can ignore these facts. Maulana Akbarabadi has also acknowledged that whether it was a joint platform of Muslims and other Indians or an exclusive Muslim organization, Sir Syed was convinced that it would be harmful for Muslims to participate in any political movement.

But why was he thus convinced? What were the reasons and the bases? It was nothing more than his desire to not see even

---

7   *"Burhaan,"* Delhi, Month of September, 1972 pp 158-166

the slightest change in the ruling regime of the country, and that's where Sir Syed differed from the moderate Congress leaders.

Maulana Akbarabadi has also reproduced that speech of Maulana Hali in which he has declared the participation of Muslims in politics as their incompetence. Maulana Hali had stated that "the truth is when we look at the lofty ideals of Congress and then look at ourselves, we are reminded that we should abstain from having too many sweets."

But the English also said the same thing, that the Indians are unfit to rule and that they were giving them training. Then, presenting the sayings of Hali in support of the thoughts of Sir Syed would be futile. Hali was a great poet, a righteous man, and a sincere person, but it is from his *Musaddas-e-Hali* that we learn that he is prone to composing elegies and sees wounds everywhere he looks. Besides, he was always a supporter and companion of Sir Syed. As the late poet Akbar said:

Story of Sir Syed's life from Hali you should hear
The conqueror's condition ask of the balladeer

Sir Syed was awestruck by the British government but was equally impressed with the English culture. Anyone who has studied the journal *Tehzeeb-ul-Akhlaq*, later known as the Aligarh Institute Gazette, and has looked at Sir Syed's speeches would know what a big fan he was of the habits and manners of the English, and of their lifestyles and their ways. In fact he considered Eastern style to be uncivilized and backward.

His thoughts regarding religion were similar. As a result, the commentary he wrote on the Quran denied the concepts of angels, jinns, miracles, and bodily ascension. On the question of whether the *Mi'raj*, the heavenly ascension of Prophet Muhammad, was spiritual or corporeal, he writes, "All that the Mohammedans must believe respecting the *Mi'raj* is that the Prophet saw himself, in a vision, transported from Mecca to Jerusalem, and that in such vision he really beheld some of the greatest signs of his Lord."

It would be audacious to say about Sir Syed that he could neither gauge that the country would gain independence nor could he predict what would happen to the Muslims after that, or to say that he had no solution for the problems of the various communities of India, particularly the Hindus and the Muslims, and therefore assumed a path of escapism. The man who brought about such an intellectual revolution, who did not pay heed to the norms of the time, and who crushed all outdated superstitions, could not have been so short sighted. Albeit it is possible that Sir Syed, with his foresightedness, could have understood that as things stood it would be very difficult for him to change the status quo, and adopted this policy for a transitional period. We should also not forget that Sir Syed started his political work in the last stages of his life, and he was eager to succeed in his mission.

Muslim League, which was purely a Muslim organization that opposed an independent India except for a short duration during the Khilafat Movement when the passions of the Muslims were at its peak, was a necessary byproduct of Sir Syed's policies. Allama Shibli composed the following couplets on the political policies of the Muslim League[8]. In his

---

8   Islam, Arshad, "Allama Shibli and the early Muslim League: A dissenting voice," *Intellectual Discourse*; Kuala Lumpur Vol. 21 Iss. 2, (2013): 197-219

poem *Ingratitude*, Shibli outlines the objectives of the Simla Deputation of 1906 for securing separate representations for the Muslims, which led to the founding of the All India Muslim League.

> *When Hindus secure some rights through great struggle,*
> *We should also get some share in it in the name of Panjtan.**
> *When the lion hunts some prey and brings it home,*
> *The fox rushes there and says "Me too, my master."*

(*Panjtan: the five holy persons of Islam, viz. Muhammad, Ali, Fatimah, Hasan, and Husain)

After mocking the League in its early days, Shibli remarked ironically that if anyone asked about the virtues of the League, in brief it could be said that it was simultaneously a benefactor of the community and a slave of the rulers.

> *I do not deny the greatness and power of the League,*
> *The country rings with sensation, with noise*
> *Government also casts on it a benign look*
> *The rich and famous as well give it a sweet smile*
> *It's the training ground of the new leaders*
> *Stepping stone of pride and public exhibition too;*
> *In brief, its merits, if someone asks, are that*
> *It is at once patron of the community and servant of the rulers*

These couplets had no effect on Sir Syed, although it cannot be denied that he did not accept even a minimal change in the ruling government either. He wanted the British to continue ruling over the country and for Muslims to take no part in politics. And that is what came to be known as the Aligarh Movement.

▍Aligarh Movement and the MAO College

Some people did not distinguish between the Aligarh Movement and Aligarh's MAO College. There were also some who considered the college and the movement to be in the same camp and as such expressed hatred and enmity toward them although such an equivalence is patently wrong. MAO College was an educational institution and like other educational institutions, people with varied thinking graduated from there. This college produced stalwarts such as Dr. Zakir Husain, Maulana Hasrat Mohani, Rafi Ahmad Kidwai, Maulana Mohammad Ali, Maulana Shaukat Ali, Khwaja Abdul Majid, Tassaduq Ahmad Khan Sherwani, and Dr. Syed Mahmud.

The English, with the demonstration of their artful propaganda, did not exercise much tolerance for this either and, through their mouthpieces, spread the notion that the religious decree that the Islamic scholars had issued against Sir Syed was due to the fact that Muslims were disgusted with western education. This was a blatant lie. No Islamic scholar ever opposed the learning of English language, modern thought and sciences, etc. Syed Jamaluddin Afghani, who had issued the decree against Sir Syed for flagrant violation of the religion, was himself a strong proponent of this education. The truth is that Sir Syed's violation in the minds of the Islamic scholars was in the way he wrote Quranic commentary and how he was encouraging the Muslims to march in the steps of the English who were then engaged in spreading the net for the destruction of Islam the world over. The scholars had expressed their weariness with him over these issues. Syed Jamaluddin was harshly critical of Sir Syed in his article "The Status Quo of Aghorian."

(It should be noted that the Aghori are a group of ascetic sadhus whose practices are considered contradictory to orthodox Hinduism. Here, Aghorian implies naturalism). The implication is that the accusation of infidelity against Sir Syed was because he was deemed a naturalist, not because he was imparting western education.

On this topic, the opinion of one of the greatest scholars and researchers, and a wise man, is stated below, after which there will be no need for additional proof. On October 20th, 1920, in his presidential address to the gathering convened in Aligarh to lay the foundation of Jamia Millia Islamia, Shaykh al-Hind Maulana Mahmud Hasan stated:

> *"Those among you gentlemen who are knowledgeable and aware know that our elders never issued a decree of infidelity for learning a foreign language or for acquiring the knowledge and art of other nations."*

In his book *Asbab-e-Baghawat-e-Hind* ("Causes of the Indian Rebellion"), Sir Syed himself has written:

> *"When big colleges were established in the cities, right from the get-go, some people were terrified of them. In those days, Shah Abdul Aziz, who was a widely known Maulvi of India, was alive. The Muslims asked him for his opinion. He gave a clear answer that enrolling in these English colleges and learning the English language is alright according to Islam. After that, hundreds of Muslims joined these colleges."*

All this background is being stated here to underscore that, starting in 1888, the shackles of servitude to the English and the training that had been given to have trust in the

English had worked well on one section of the community. That is why, when the British government promised them protection of the Islamic Caliphate and holy places, this section of the community believed it and had no emotional distress in not only supporting English forces in their war against the Turks, but even opposed the Turks in Jerusalem. In this way, Muslims in large numbers were ready to take down the citadel of Islam. This indicates, as evidenced by later upheaval in India, that all these feelings were on the surface, while deep in the hearts of Muslims was a different sentiment. Just as Sir Syed could not keep the Muslims away from politics despite his all-out effort and the Muslim League slowly came into existence, the voices that religious scholars had raised for the freedom of India in the shadow of the Islamic faith also could not be contained, and made room in the hearts of the Muslims of India.

Modus Operandi of the British During WWI and Failed Opposition

When Turkey joined WWI in 1914, the Islamic Caliph declared "jihad" or holy war and ordered Muslims all over the world to join the struggle. In an English journal "Graphic," a photo appeared of the Sultan of Turkey declaring holy war in a public rally, with a caption underneath it that read:

THE SULTAN PROCLAIMING JEHAD (HOLY WAR)
TURKEY PRONOUNCING HER OWN DEATH

In Afghanistan, Maulana Ubaidullah Sindhi tried to convince Amir Habibullah to fight against the British, but Habibullah was a friend of the English and beholden to them for the stipends they gave him. It was next to impossible to convince such a person to join a fight against the British. But motivated by this unrealistic hope, many intelligent and talented students from wealthy families, despite facing hardships, reached Afghanistan. Among them was Maulvi Mohammad Ali Qasuri, who had an MA from Cambridge University and was a scion of a respectable and educated family of status from the Qasur district of Lahore. He later came to India. I had personal relationships with the members of the Qasuri family. Conforming to the Islamic code of style and dress, he was involved in commercial business and missionary work. He was religious and knowledgeable, and a man of wealth as well. God had blessed him with both faith and acuity in worldly affairs.

The Turco-German alliance wanted India to be attacked somehow. Shaykh al-Hind suspected that this objective could not be achieved only through the efforts of Amir Habibullah, and hence made Yaghistan a center for tribal rebellion as well. The Islamic Caliph had sent the order for jihad to Amir Habibullah, and a Turco-German mission came to Afghanistan as well for that purpose. Aibak has written:

"But the Afghanistan Government, which was influenced by pro-British sentiments, was not persuaded by this mission. Amir Habibullah was empathetic to this mission, but maintained a good relationship with the English as well. On the one hand, he assured the mission that if Turco-German forces were to reach the Afghan border, he would immediately declare war against the English, but on the other he would report all his talks with this mission to the British government."

After the assassination of Amir Habibullah, the statement given by Lord Curzon, the British Foreign Secretary, puts a seal of confirmation on Habibullah's betrayal of Islam[9]:

"Lord Curzon, in his conversation with a gentleman, expressed the government's deep sorrow and regret on learning of the death of Amir Habibullah Khan. He said that Amir Habibullah was a true friend and well-wisher of the government. During the war, during difficult times, he always proved to be a sincere friend."

The efforts to turn Turkey and Germany toward India remained rather unsuccessful. For this purpose, a Turkish military contingent left for Afghanistan by way of Iran. The commander of this campaign was Rauf Orbay of the Balkan War fame, when at great risk and with exemplary bravery, he commanded the *Hamidiye* cruiser in renowned attacks against Greek naval fleets. But sadly this campaign of the Turkish military contingent was a failure when the presence of British and Russian forces in Iran did not allow it to advance toward the Afghan border and had to return to Turkey. A Turco-German mission in 1916 also returned unsuccessfully from Afghanistan. Maulana Mahmud Hasan too maintained his ongoing struggle in Mecca, defying the Indian Government by secretly going to Hijaz, an extraordinary feat given capabilities of the British secret service. As soon as the Indian Government found out about Maulana's departure, a telegram was sent to Bombay for his arrest. But Maulana left before he could be arrested. Then a telegram was sent to the captain of the ship in which he was traveling, but the telegram was received after he had disembarked at the Sa'ad ad-Din Islands for the purpose

---

9   Weekly *Mashriq*, Gorakhpur, March 13, 1919, pp 3

of quarantine. In Hijaz, among other people, Maulana met Enver Pasha and Jamal Pasha, who were visiting Medina at the time, and they entered some collateral agreements including support for the tribal populations. With the insight of Maulana Hadi Hasan, these collaterals were delivered to the tribal leaders, once again defying the secret services. Enver Pasha was of the opinion that Maulana himself should go to the tribal lands, and he himself wished to do that, but the passage was blocked. The decision was made to go via Istanbul, and Maulana met Ghalib Pasha in Taif to prepare for the journey. But during that time, the Sharif of Mecca attacked Taif and the Arab Revolt against Turkey commenced. Maulana returned to Mecca facing many difficulties. There he was asked to sign off on a decree that leveled charges of infidelity against the Turkish nation, rejected the authority of the Ottoman Sultan, and declared the revolt of the Sharif of Mecca righteous and laudable. The decree had resulted from an inquisition at the behest of the Government of India and was brought to Hijaz by Khan Bahadur Mubarak Ali Aurangabadi for the signatures of the honorable religious scholars. Its title was "From the scholars of Mecca *Mukarrama* who teach at *Haram Sharif*, the Noble Sanctuary." Maulana refused to put his signature on this decree.

The gunpowder that the religious scholars had packed in India needed just one spark to explode into a fireball, but regretfully the time never came because of the treachery of some of their own. However, the scholars fulfilled their duties regarding the central Islamic Caliphate and the struggle for the country's freedom, and added another accomplishment to the list of their enlightened deeds as detailed in Maulana Muhammad Miyan's books *Ulama-e-Hind Ka Shandaar Maazi* ("The

Glorious Past of the Islamic Scholars of India") and *Ulama-e-Haqq Aur Unke Mujahidana Karname* ("Struggles and Deeds of the True Scholars of Islam").

A Wooden Trunk

Shaykh al-Hind Maulana Mahmud Hasan kept the writings and documents of Ghalib Pasha and Jamal Pasha locked in a trunk that he had specially constructed with hidden compartments so that these papers would not be visible on the inspection of its contents. Maulana Hadi Hasan, Rais Khan *Saheb* of Jahanpur in district Muzaffarnagar, and Haji Shah Bakhsh Sindhi left for Bombay with this trunk but when they arrived at the port, there was a huge police presence there expecting Maulana Mahmud Hasan to alight from the ship. A trusted associate of Maulana took this trunk, slipped out of there with the trunk among his other baggage, and as per the plan, sent it ahead by parcel post. Maulana Muhammad Nabi Khan of Jahanpur received this trunk, took out the documents, and was in the process of copying them when the police raided his place. British intelligence agencies were in a heightened state of security and aware that certain documents had been shipped in a wooden trunk. Maulana Muhammad Nabi stuffed the papers in the pocket of a waistcoat and hung it on a coat hook. In the six hours the police spent searching for them, they never looked at the waistcoat hanging on the hook. The police also had information that Haji Ahmed Mirza *Saheb* was going to take the documents to a photographer to make photocopies of them. The police raided the photographer's shop but did not find anything there either as the documents had not yet arrived. The documents were delivered to the photographer after the raid, photocopies made, and distributed where they needed to go.

Maulana Hussain Ahmed Madani has written in his book that what Maulana Sindhi wrote in his diary, that these photocopies were burnt, is not true. Maulana Madani writes:

"These documents and collateral would have proven very useful and would have been very helpful for Turkey and its Caliphs, but when America's large troops and stockpile of arms came to the aid of the Allied, the fortunes changed."

On disembarking from the ship, Maulanas Khalil Ahmad and Hadi Hasan were arrested and were repeatedly interrogated, but they were trusted men of Maulana Mahmud Hasan who were ready to lay down their lives for him. The police could not learn anything and they were soon released.

Maulana Mahmud Hasan was arrested in Mecca and sent to Malta. Before that, Dr. Ansari, his brother, and Hakim Abdul Razzaq had sent Rs.1000 for Maulana to Mecca through a relative of his. These incidents convey the omnipotence of this movement that Maulana had started.

Silk Handkerchiefs

There are many famous stories about silk handkerchiefs. Some say that Maulana Mahmud Hasan had given the silk handkerchiefs to the sincere activists of his revolutionary party. The handkerchiefs were made in such a way that if a few of the silk wires were pulled out, Maulana Mahmud Hasan's name would appear. This was a symbolic act within the party to garner trust among its members, and these kinds of handkerchiefs were given specifically to those operatives who had been commissioned to murder English officers and the secret had to be revealed on a particular day at a selected time, etc. etc. As stated earlier, history has draped a curtain over many a Maulana's narratives, but the historical status of the silk handkerchiefs appears to be that under Maulana Mahmud Hasan's scheme, Maulana Ubaidullah Sindhi was living in Kabul and was inciting the tribal Afghans to attack India. These Afghans were also in communication with the revolutionary organizations of India. When the documents of Enver Pasha and Ghalib Pasha were delivered safely in the wooden trunk and distributed successfully among the tribals, to arouse passion and excitement among revolutionary parties and the Muslims of India, the details of those proceedings had to be conveyed to Maulana Mahmud Hasan immediately so that he would know that the grounds had been furrowed. Besides that, there was a provisional government installed in Kabul whose President was Raja Mahendra Pratap, the Prime Minister was Barkatullah, the Minister of the Interior was Maulana Ubaidullah Sindhi, and there were other customary appointed officials. Their claim was that they were the true representatives of India, that India had rebelled from Great Britain, and that if India was attacked, the chances were bright that the attack would succeed. Their objective was to establish friendly relations with various governments to form an alliance against the English. Hence, with much pomp and show, Raja Mahendra Pratap took a delegation to the Tzar of Russia with Dr. Mathura Singh and others. Similar missions were sent to China, Burma, Japan, France, and America, a difficult task given that this government in exile was empty-handed. This information had to be briefly delivered to Maulana Mahmud Hasan as well.

The passage from Afghanistan to Hijaz was totally blocked. The only means of sending a message was through India.

For this purpose, two letters containing the proceedings of Kabul were embroidered on silk handkerchiefs using *khat-e-gulzar*, a style of calligraphy in which letters are shaped to resemble flowers with flourishes. These handkerchiefs were given by Maulana Ubaidullah Sindhi to a recent convert to Islam by the name of Sheikh Abdul Haq, who had been raised by Khan Bahadur Rab Nawaz Khan, father of Allah Nawaz Khan. The handkerchiefs were to be delivered to Sheikh Abdul Rahim in Sindh. In a third such letter, Sheikh Abdul Rahim was advised to send the previous two handkerchiefs to Shaykh al-Hind Maulana Mahmud Hasan through a trustworthy courier, and if no such person was available, then to go there himself under the pretext of performing Hajj. This is the story of the silk handkerchiefs.

Allah Nawaz Khan was considered a reliable man, but Sheikh Abdul Haq delivered these handkerchiefs, or the letters, to his father Rab Nawaz Khan, who turned them in to Sir Michael O'Dwyer, Governor of Punjab, in exchange for some rewards, and the scheme failed. Further discussion of this matter is irrelevant to the topic.

I have taken a complex topic, which has entangled many a mind, and written about it in a plain manner without giving much detail. Suffice it to say that Shaykh al-Hind used silk handkerchiefs in a manner which appears to have inspired Maulana Ubaidullah.

Promises of the British Government

On November 2, 1914 the British government issued an official proclamation which was delivered in every town and village along with the declaration of war.

> *"The Muslims of India are assured that in this war, we or our allies shall do nothing which hurts their religious beliefs and sentiments. Islam's holy places shall be protected from blasphemy and all practicable care shall be exercised to maintain their respect and sanctity. There shall be no proceedings against the holy center of the Caliphate. We are fighting only the Turkish Government which is under the influence of the Germans, not the Islamic Caliphate. The British government, not just on its own behalf but also on behalf of the Allied governments, takes responsibility for these undertakings."*

This was an answer to the call for jihad by the Islamic Caliphate. Many a naïve Muslim, particularly army soldiers and officers, fell for it and accepted it as a national war.

On January 12, 1915 Lord Harding, the Indian Viceroy, made this pledge in the Legislative Council:

> *"The Allied governments have made an announcement regarding protection of Islam's holy places in the Arabian Peninsula and Iraq. The British government has also announced that if there is a need, we are ready to attack external forces to carry out this protection and we will not allow any harm to come to these places. No matter what direction events may take us, let there be no doubt that in the matter of the protection of holy places, there shall be no encroachment or meddling and Islam shall remain among the supreme powers of the world."*

In the same manner, Lord Cromer delivered the following speech in the House of Lords on April 20, 1915:

"There is no need for me to affirm that I am in agreement with the opinion of the noble Marquess that the matter of the Caliphate should be settled by the Muslims themselves, but I cannot remain without saying that it is not sufficient for the Caliph to be just a Muslim, but it is also imperative that he should be a Muslim who is not under the influence of any European power."

Mr. Lloyd George, the Prime Minister of United Kingdom, stated in a speech on January 5, 1916:

"We are not fighting this war with the objective of depriving Turkey of its seat of government or of the fertile lands of Asia Minor, where people of Turkish ethnicity live."

These magical words were not only casting a spell, but the passion and excitement that had been stirred by the call for jihad by the Islamic Caliphate started to subside. Muslim soldiers and army officers, whose numbers had reached hundreds of thousands, marched to war. Only 10,000 troops remained in India. If the Afghans and tribals had attacked India at the time, the Indian troops would have to be called from Mesopotamia and history would then have changed course. These announcements also helped to generally bring down the angst among the people. But there was a section of those with fundamental wisdom who were not going to be consoled like a child by such rhetoric. Islamic revolutionary parties were hard at work and so was the government's intelligence division, which was composed of mostly Muslims. The orders of the government regarding the youth that was escaping and running away to Afghanistan was that when caught they should be hanged from the nearest tree. But the sacrificers of the nation would walk all night and hide during the day, would go without food, swim across rivers, and keep on going. These frenzied efforts give an indication of the passion that had been aroused in their hearts.

Maulana Mohammad Ali's Confinement

The intellectuals of India could not control their passions either, and so, right after Turkey's declaration of war, Maulana Mohammad Ali wrote an article in his universally famous English newspaper "The Comrade" whose title was "Choice of the Turks." In the article, it was posited that Turkey had no choice but to take the side of Germany against the Allied. Maulana Mohammad Ali was still Mr. Mohammad Ali at the time and his past position was one of support for the government. But a love of Islam was in every fiber of his body, and in this delicate time, his emotions and his beliefs were dominant over his past.

Maulana Abdul Majid Daryabadi, in his compilation "Mohammad Ali: A Few Pages From His Personal Diary," has written:

"'The Comrade' had caused a sensation and now that Hamdard was released, it too was causing a sensation. The young and old gravitated toward them but Mohammad Ali's steps were now day by day hurrying rather quickly toward Islam. In May 1913, in the city of Kanpur, in connection with making a new road, the municipality and the collector knocked down the bathroom of a mosque and when the Muslims strongly protested, they were even shot at by the police at a rally. There was a lot of turmoil, and among the protest

leaders was Mohammad Ali. 'The Comrade,' in its protest and critical articles, raged at even the Governor of the province, Sir James Muston, let alone the District Collector. In any case, the rulers at the time were not tolerant of strong criticism from Muslim voices, but Sir James Muston also considered Mohammad Ali to be his old "loyal friend." Naturally he was upset. On the other side, in the matter of the Balkan War too, Mohammad Ali was front and center in expressing empathy for the Turks, and now he had a beard on his face as well.

"All this was going on when, in November 1914, Turkey allied with Germany entered Europe's Great War in opposition to Great Britain, and 'The Comrade' wrote a lengthy explosive article entitled 'Choice of the Turks' in response to an article in The Times (London). How and for how long could the English ignore this matter. 'The Comrade' was immediately shut down and Mohammad Ali arrested. That Mohammad Ali who until as recently as a year or two ago was the apple of the eye and a favorite of prominent officials."

The above excerpt from the pen of Maulana Mohammad Ali's biggest admirer and India's great writer and intellectual has freed me of any doubt that Mohammad Ali's position was one of loyalty to the British government, so that it can be demonstrated how many revolutions were born from the passion associated with the matter of the Caliphate.

Maulana Mohammad Ali was first incarcerated in Rampur, followed by Mehrauli, Delhi, and Lansdowne, and then transferred to Chhindwara. And when that didn't satisfy the authorities either, he was sent to the Betul jailhouse.

The authorities perhaps surmised that Maulana Mohammad Ali would go down in one strike, would be apologetic, and would follow up with petitions of regret and remorse. But the manner in which he received the orders for his incarceration is best narrated by Qazi Abdul Ghaffar *Saheb*, who was one of the many influential people of the time who had gathered around Mohammad Ali, and was on the editorial board of *Hamdard*:

> *"It was the time of such ease that when the orders for the arrest came, I was not in the office but was called in, and when I came close to the door of Mohammad Ali's room, I heard a roar of jubilation and thought there must be some really good news. But entering the room, I see officers serving the arrest warrant and hearty congratulations being exchanged, and in this excitement, the voices of the two brothers were the loudest, as they laughed and congratulated each other."*

Ghalib's apropos couplet perfectly defines the situation:

> *Ask not the delight of those for martyrdom who wait*
> *Unsheathing of the sword for them is cause to celebrate*

The arrest of Maulana Mohammad Ali had created an uproar in the country and nearly 150,000 telegrams were sent to the Viceroy and the Home Minister of the Government of British India demanding that the arrest warrant be rescinded. If anything came out of this effort, it was only that an officer came with a document, and Maulana Mohammad Ali and Maulana Shaukat Ali, who were incarcerated together, were told that if they signed it they would be released. This document only contained a declaration of fealty to Great

Britain. The Ali brothers said that they would be willing to sign the document if only the following statement were to be added to it: "provided that the practice of this fealty would not be an impediment to the restrictions placed by the practice of the Islamic faith." They essentially declared that their primary fealty was to the religion of Islam. The debate was ongoing when the mother of Ali Brothers, who would later become famous by the name '*Bi Amma*,' entered the fray and declared that her sons were never disloyal to the government but that religious duties trumped everything. If they were to sign this contract unconditionally, she said, may the Lord give her wrinkled hands enough strength to choke both their necks. Mohammad Ali had already become a hero of the Indian Muslims for writing the article "Choice of the Turks," and for the hardships he had faced by happily accepting his incarceration. This refusal to bow to the English enhanced his fame and popularity.

Maulana Abul Kalam Azad

At the same time, another star had arisen in the political sky whose light had started to match that of other luminaries. Maulana Abul Kalam Azad had joined the ranks of distinguished scholars at a young age owing to his wisdom and knowledge. In 1912, his Urdu weekly newspaper *Al-Hilal* proclaimed its prominence in all of India. *Al-Hilal* was a liberal Islamic publication. In his autobiography "India Wins Freedom," Maulana Azad has written:

> "*The first edition of Al-Hilal was published in June 1912. Al-Hilal brought about a revolution in Urdu journalism and very soon gained unparalleled popularity. The public*

was attracted to its beautiful script and printing, but more than anything to its imparting a strong patriotic message, and it aroused a revolutionary passion among its readers. There was so much demand for Al-Hilal that within three months, the old editions had to be republished because every new subscriber wanted all the editions since the beginning.

"The leadership of Indian politics was in the hands of the Aligarh Party at the time. Its members considered themselves trustees of Sir Syed's policies. Their foundational principle was that Muslims were loyal to the British Crown and should keep themselves away from the Independence movement. When Al-Hilal raised a voice contrary to that principle, and its popularity and its publication increased day by day, they feared that their leadership was in danger. That is why opposition toward Al-Hilal started to the extent that its editor-in-chief (Maulana Azad himself) received death threats. But as much as the leadership would oppose Al-Hilal, its popularity would rise that much. Within two years, Al-Hilal's subscriptions reached 26,000. Such numbers had not been seen earlier for an Urdu journal."

In this context, an interesting incident comes to mind. Maulana Azad received many letters saying that if he went to Lucknow, he would be killed. Maulana went to Lucknow and wrote about it: "I got down at the Charbagh station by myself and awaited the attackers but none came. It is sad that our people don't even have someone that would honor anyone."

It should be remembered that *Al-Hilal* started in 1912. This was an era when the Muslims had dreamt of the central

Islamic Caliphate being safe in the hands of the determined, the courageous, and the brave Young Turks, had been disillusioned by the Balkan War, and were suffering from severe anxiety. Allama Shibli has filled the voice of worry in the hearts of Muslims in the following couplet:

The flood of misfortune sweeping in from the Balkans
How long can it be stemmed by the smoke of their cries

Al-Hilal's passionate expression of its claim and its new attractive style of writing gave courageous and fearless interpretation to those passions that were layered deep in the hearts, asserting its right to moral leadership. Its popularity was inevitable since it was the voice from the hearts of the readers themselves. The leaders of the Aligarh Movement had no strategy to save the sinking ship of Islam. Besides, *Al-Hilal*'s tone and style were especially catchy.

Where do I get that portrait from?
That awakens from the dreary dream of neglect

Al-Hilal was indeed that seraph that had awakened even those in eternal sleep. The English considered *Al-Hilal* a rebellious newspaper and in that they were right. The government demanded a surety bond of Rs. 10,000 from *Al-Hilal* for it to refrain from publishing rebellious material. This caused an uproar throughout the country and people started wiring money to Maulana Azad in droves. If he had kept all that money, it would have amounted to hundreds of thousands of rupees. But Maulana Azad replied to all the donors saying that *Al-Hilal* was his newspaper, he reaped the profits from it and he would bear the expense associated with it. The bond money was deposited and immediately forfeited. A second time, Rs. 20,000 was demanded, that too was deposited and later forfeited. All these payments were made by Maulana himself.

Maulana Azad was earlier a member of a revolutionary party. He writes in "India Wins Freedom":

"In those days there were only middle class Hindus in revolutionary groups. In fact, all of the revolutionary parties were against the Muslims. They believed that the British government was using Muslims against the Indian Independence movement and the Muslims were a pawn in the hands of the government. East Bengal had become a separate province and its Lt. Governor, Sir Bampfylde Fuller had openly stated that the government considered Muslims their beloved spouse. Revolutionaries were of the thinking that the Muslims were a roadblock toward freedom and, like other roadblocks, they too needed to be removed."

Maulana Azad was becoming a fly in the face of the government. He was always trailed by a CID officer. It was a fact that when Maulana Azad met someone, no matter how much later he met them again, he would immediately recognize them. Abdur Razzaq Malihabadi in his book *Zikr-e-Azad* writes that Maulana Azad saw him eight years after their first meeting and immediately recognized him. I experienced something similar. I first met Maulana at Bradlaugh Hall in Lahore, and when I met him four or five years later at Delhi railway station with Mohammad Ali Qasuri, he immediately said, "Say, Adeel *Saheb*, I hope you are well." It was a result of that remarkable memory that he could reproduce text verbatim from books with reference to page and paragraph.

The legend is that it would happen quite often that Maulana would be going on a train and a decrepit fakir would come and say, "In the name of *Allah*, give this poor man a few paisa," and Maulana would say, "Khan Bahadur So-and-so, Deputy Superintendent of CID, why are you getting worried. Come sit and have tea." Or it would be a sadhu saying, "In the name of Bhagwan,....," and Maulana would say "Rai Bahadur So-and-so, Deputy Superintendent of CID,..."

The articles in *Al-Hilal* and Maulana Azad's revolutionary behavior had created such a sensation that an Englishman in Basti, Collector RP Dewhurst, who was a student of Maulana Muhammad Farooq Chiryakoti and a scholar of Arabic and Persian, used to translate *Al-Hilal* into English and send it to the British India Government. People tell stories of strange incidents from the time of Dewhurst. He would not let any lawyer present their arguments in English and would insist that they do that in Urdu. He once asked a person his name, who replied, "Nasrat Ali." He immediately corrected him, "*Nusrat* Ali." The person said he was sorry, using the accepted pronunciation, "*Ghalti hui.*" Dewhurst corrected him with the strict pronunciation, "*Ghalati hui.*"

A year after the war broke out in 1914, the government used the Press Act to seize the *Al-Hilal* Press. This made no difference to Maulana Azad's daring acts nor did his footsteps miss a beat. Five months later, he established the *Al-Balagh* Press and started printing *Al-Hilal* there. *Al-Hilal* Press was in Calcutta as was *Al-Balagh* Press. In any case, the government could not have allowed *Al-Hilal* to be published during wartime. And Maulana's perseverance and fortitude had made it clear that the Press Act alone would not suffice to stop him. And so, the Defence of India Regulation was used to banish Maulana Azad from Calcutta. The governments of Punjab, Delhi, UP, and Bombay had already used this regulation to preemptively ban Maulana Azad's entry into those provinces. Only Bihar remained among the convenient provinces and so Maulana Azad went to Ranchi, but six months later he was arrested and remained incarcerated there till December 31, 1919. On January 1, 1920 Maulana Azad was released along with other detainees through a royal decree. This is a brief sub-chapter about the brave struggles of an intellectual crusader and a scholar, and subject matter expert of Islamic thought.

Maulana Azad also founded a party called *Hezbollah* with the objective of bringing Muslims into politics via religion. He made another similar effort which will be mentioned later. The *Hezbollah* party was in its initial phase when a tumultuous era prevented the party from putting any acts on the record. The fact is that Maulana Azad considered politics to be an integral part of religion and his creed from the beginning was to get out from under the servitude of Britain and establish a joint democratic government of united nationality in India. That is why he used to oppose the Aligarh Movement with utmost courage and in his customary charming and passionate manner of speaking. Maulana could not come to terms with the Aligarh Movement and always impressed upon the Muslims its defects and ill effects.

Temporary Peace or Protracted War

We have examined the proclamations of statesmen and the Government of Britain; now let us see which of these conditions they imposed and enforced after winning the war.

On October 30, 1918 Rauf Orbay, Ottoman Minister of Marine Affairs, and Admiral Somerset Gough-Calthorpe, Commander-in-Chief of the Royal Navy's Mediterranean Fleet, put down their signatures agreeing to the following conditions:

1. *The Straits of Dardanelles and Bosphorus and all the forts on their banks shall be vacated by the Ottoman forces and surrendered to the Allied forces.*
2. *All Ottoman forces shall be disarmed.*
3. *The Ottoman Naval fleet shall be handed over to the Allied.*
4. *The Allied shall have the right to occupy any Ottoman territory "in case of disorder" threatening their security.*
5. *All ports and railways shall be made available for use by the Allies.*
6. *All telegraph lines shall come under the control of the Allies.*
7. *Turkish soldiers that have been arrested shall remain imprisoned.*
8. *Turkish soldiers stationed in Hijaz and Tirablus shall lay down their arms.*
9. *Soldiers of the Allied armies that have been arrested shall be immediately released.*

These conditions were perhaps unprecedented in their humiliation of any vanquished by the victor. The draft of the armistice with Germany was very different. With full authority in their hands, the English occupied Constantinople and started a search for Turkish leaders with the intent of prosecuting them. The Prime Minister Talaat Pasha, the War Minister Enver Pasha, the Minister of the Navy Jamal Pasha, and others escaped to Europe and when they returned, they went underground. There are strange stories about how they would change disguises and take various measures to hide themselves. The Islamic Caliph Sultan Abdul Hamid hung the yoke of slavery around his neck and hoped that he would get a pension and retire in the shadow of wealth and a life of comfort and leisure. The Grand Mufti and other scholars of Islam also fell prey to an inferiority complex.

The conditions of the temporary peace accord disappointed and demoralized the Indian Muslims. They now felt that lasting peace would only come when there was no Turkey left, nor the Islamic Caliphate, the holy places, Palestine or Jerusalem. In a state of confusion and helplessness, the Muslims held prominent meetings and consultations. The objective was to prevent the British government from bowing down and doing what the Muslims feared.

Search for a Path Forward

On October 30, 1918 Turkey signed an armistice and subsequently, in May 1920, the Treaty of Sevres was signed imposing the conditions of this truce on Turkey. This was a very tumultuous period with much frenzy in people's minds and a search for a plan of action. On the one hand, the British government had promised the world's Muslims protection for the central Islamic Caliphate and Islam's holy places. On the other hand, Zionist groups had been promised a nation in Palestine. It was not an easy task to meet these two contradictory promises. A Royal Commission was established for this purpose. The commission, in its report, mentioned both these promises saying that the government had made two contradictory promises, that it would have to renege on one of them, and that it had no choice but to stand guilty of breaking one of the promises. The British government had promised to bring reform in India in exchange for its support in the war; a high ranking committee was making explorations for this reform in London. The promise of self-rule was made to India by Mr. Montagu through a royal announcement dated August 18, 1917. A few months later, Mr. Montagu came to India and toured the country with the Viceroy to gauge the sentiment of the people. Moderate Indians had taken a delegation to England to present their point of view. Some of the questions being asked were: What were the rights of the Muslims? Should Sindh be made a separate province? Should reforms be brought to the Frontier provinces as well?

In 1916, there was a pact between Congress and Muslim League and a mutual agreement known as *Miisaaq-e-Millii* ('The National Covenant') was created. The following points were decided:

1. *Regarding the Provincial Councils, it was decided that the larger provinces have up to 125 members and the smaller provinces up to 50-75 members.*
2. *4/5th of the members should be elected. The right to vote should be expanded and proper representation of all minorities should be assured. The Governor should have the right to appoint 1/5th of the members.*
3. *Muslim representation should be assured through reservations of seats as per the following details:*

Name of Province	% of Muslims in Population	% of Muslims Members in Council
Punjab	55	50
Bengal	53	40
UP	14	30
Bombay (Sindh)	20	33
Bihar and Orissa	10	25
Central Province	4	15
Madras	7	15

At the time this 'National Covenant' was drafted, Maulanas Mohammad Ali, Shaukat Ali, and Abul Kalam Azad were incarcerated. Mr. Jinnah was the President of the Muslim League. Neither the Muslims nor the Hindus were satisfied with the covenant. Muslims objected to the fact that they were in the minority in the councils of provinces where they were in the majority, and the Hindus did not like the fact that there were reserved seats for Muslims in the councils of provinces where Muslims were in the minority. Historians and political experts are of the decisive opinion that Congress made an egregious blunder in accepting this covenant since it accepted separate elections for Hindus and Muslims. The castle of Pakistan was later constructed on this foundation. The covenant was also a major roadblock for both Hindus and Muslims on the path to attaining independence as it would distract from that movement, create conflict between them, and divide them.

The issues concerning the Muslims of India went beyond the Arabian Peninsula, Palestine, and Jerusalem: the establishment of the central Islamic Caliphate in Turkey was paramount to them from a religious perspective and they were not willing to consider Medina and Jerusalem outside of the domain of the Caliph. The promise by the English to bring reforms to India was being studied in London but in the meantime, on January 18, 1919, the Rowlatt Bill was passed by the Imperial Legislative Council in Delhi. The Rowlatt Committee had been working on the bill since 1917 but its drafts had everyone dissenting. Its passing caused a fireball to erupt in India, and everyone despaired that dissent was useless and the Rowlatt Bill would become an act no matter what. With the exception of a few lickspittles for the government, the voice of the entire nation rose up against the Act. All political parties and their leaders were in consensus. The goal of the Bill was to deprive Indians of all kinds of freedom and to bind them in servitude. People wondered how this Bill could follow the royal announcement of 1917 promising self-rule to India.

Muslims found that this was a golden opportunity to raise their voice against the English and joined their Hindu compatriots. A heartwarming sight of Hindu-Muslim unity appeared on the scene. The result was that all of India became a volcano which was spewing lava. There was a great uproar against the Bill all around, but the Muslims set out with the proverbial 'burial shroud tied around their heads,' i.e. ready to fight till death in a decisive final battle. Islamic scholars were holding rallies in various places. There were conferences of scholars in every province and these scholars started joining political parties as well, which was a new trend. For instance, in 1919 the second annual conference of the Islamic scholars of Bengal was presided by Maulana Azad Subhani, Principal of the Madrasa Al-Hayat in Kanpur, and was attended by Maulana Abdul Bari, who at the time was considered the principal Islamic scholar of India. The same year, many scholars attended the Muslim

League conference as well, for which a vote of thanks was given to them in one of the conference's resolutions. Muslims were ready to put their lives on the line. There was no town or village where rallies were not held and Muslims had not expressed their anxiety.

Mrs. Besant and Home Rule

On September 1, 1916 the Home Rule League started its campaign for democracy in India under the leadership of Mrs. Annie Besant, an Englishwoman who was a proponent of Indian political and social causes. Its purpose was to orchestrate an agitation against the constitution to obtain a self-rule government in India, not in return for the support of Indians in the war, but because it was their right and justice demanded it. But now it appears that Mrs. Besant's objective was merely to take the focus away from complete independence for India. She was also a proponent of the Hindu religion. But when India truly stirred and took a step toward freedom for the country, she started to oppose it. When Mahatma Gandhi's non-cooperation picked up steam and students started to leave colleges to join the movement, in a speech in front of students and the general public at a rally in Allahabad, Mrs. Besant, who was a powerful orator, asked with the full force of her oratory, "When did the Hindu religion make it permissible for a son to disobey an order from his father? Is there an instance of a son going against his father's wishes?" The speech was in English, and a student of the Muir Central College of Allahabad stood up and said angrily in English, "Prahlad violated his father's wishes!" Mrs. Besant was nonplussed and sat down.

Before that, Lokmanya Tilak had raised the slogan '*Swaraj* (self-rule) is my birthright and I shall have it.' He even advocated for *Swaraj* by 'all means necessary.' At that time, Tilak's trial was going on in London which was incurring extensive expenses. Maulana Hasrat Mohani was a disciple and a big supporter of Tilak, and had said this about him:

O' Tilak, O' pride of patriotism
The knower, follower, believer, and articulator of righteousness

You were the first to bear O' son of India
Hard work, imprisonment and pain in the service of India

These myriad anxieties all indicate how much unrest there was in the heart and lack of peace of mind. Although there was a search for the solution no matter how many sacrifices it would take, there did not seem a path forward.

The Arrival of a Leader

To sum it up, Mother India was having the pangs of labor, the child of complete independence was to be born, a midwife was needed, and the nobles and common people all were waiting. A leader was needed who would enter everyone's hearts, whose hands would be on everyone's pulse to recognize their conditions, guide them along the right path with a serious minded strategy, whose mind was enlightened and his heart in the right place, and who could be depended upon by the entire populace. And it was then that Mohandas Karamchand Gandhi appeared on the horizon of India rising as both its sun and its moon, and soon after, all the leading stars of Indian politics faded away, bowing their heads toward him. This was the same Mahatma Gandhi about whom a Deputy Collector of Basti, who later became Commissioner, Mr. Yadav told me a joke. He said he had once gone to London and was a paying guest in a house. One evening, everyone was sitting around the fireplace when a boy of six or seven years asked, "Mother, can I ask you a question?" The mother said no and that first he had to whisper the question in her ear. Yadav *Saheb* earnestly insisted that the boy be allowed to ask the question. After making some formal conversation, the question that the boy asked was, "What kind of a plague is Gandhi?" Yadav replied that Gandhi was not a plague but the name of a person. The boy jumped up with surprise and with an astonished expression on his face, said, "What? Gandhi is the name of a person? I thought it was a plague!"

Mahatma Gandhi was truly a plague for servitude. A plague for England's pride, arrogance, conspiracies, and breach of promises.

Mahatma Gandhi not only took a keen interest in the matter of the Caliphate but also promised to support the Khilafat Movement. And he not only promised to support the Khilafat Movement, but he jumped onto it, and very soon the Muslims and all of the Muslim leaders took him as their own leader.

Maulana Mohammad Ali and Maulana Shaukat Ali called him *Bapu*. After being sentenced at the Karachi trial, when they were on their way back to jail, people asked them about the status of the movement. They replied that they were in jail, but all they knew was that after the Prophet of Islam, only the rule of Gandhiji applied. Maulana Azad Subhani had entered Gandhiji's ashram and wore clothes that covered up to his elbows and knees. Maulana Abul Kalam Azad was speaking and acting in unison with Gandhiji. Shaykh al-Hind passed away early and there was no one to take charge of the Muslim leadership. At the Ahmedabad Congress, a friend of the Shaykh al-Hind, Maulana Aziz Gul said in a speech:

"We have accepted Gandhi as our leader. If he asks us to go forward, we shall go forward. If he asks us to go back, we shall go back. But Gandhi should know, we Muslims don't even follow our Caliph when he deviates from the path of truth. As long as Gandhi is on the path of truth, he is our leader."

But this is all that came later. October 30, 1918 to May, 1920 was a period of sentimental and spiritual anxiety, boundless passion, readiness for all kinds of sacrifices, and an active quest for a path forward.

It would be an injustice not to mention Hasrat Mohani here. Maulana Hasrat Mohani always skirted Mahatma Gandhi. Since he was a disciple of Tilak, his point of view was very different. Maulana Hasrat Mohani was a completely political being and believed in full independence from the British government. And he believed that Gandhiji, being a disciple of Gokhale and hence of moderate thinking, would make peace with the government on 'dominion status,' i.e. under the shadow of the British Empire. But detailed discussion on Hasrat will come later. How can any mention of Hasrat not be made when discussing the history of that period? For now, suffice it to say here that even in disagreement, he stood by Gandhiji in every movement. What other way was there?

In the same way, there was a great man in that age whose selfless service, clear vision and worldview, whose disregard for any redemption, praise or reward, whose high-mindedness and silent sacrifices are strewn all over the pages of history. This was Dr. Mukhtar Ahmed Ansari, whose feats can be found all around, but to put them all together and compile them would be very laborious. Nonetheless, a casual study reveals the depths of the sense of righteousness in his heart, the courage and thoughtfulness with which he took over the reins of the community at a delicate time and served the freedom movements.

Rowlatt Bill

At the same time, under the pride of victory and intoxicated with power, the English decided to pass the Rowlatt Bill. The moderate political parties in India had taken a delegation to London to ask for reforms. They were working there as well as at home in India. They were anticipating a royal edict. Mrs. Annie Besant was publicizing the demand for Home Rule. There were some notable leaders working with her, Gorakhpur's Munshi Ishwar Saran among them. There was a forceful agitation under way against the Rowlatt Bill to prevent it from becoming law. Muslims were burning with rage and the only effect it had until then was that they were fully united on the matter of the Caliphate and were raising their voices for it. The English, unconcerned with all these affairs under the influence of their pride and power, were oblivious to the opposition and did not stop working toward the Rowlatt Bill's passage. In fact, the Lieutenant Governor of Punjab expressed such a defense of this bill that it became clear it would become an act. It was possible that if trouble had not come looking for the English, they could have worked moderately and quietly, but instead they published the bill in the face of strong opposition to it. As a result, Gandhiji entered the fray in opposition to it. He convened the Satyagraha Sabha and started taking membership signatures for it. All the prominent leaders signed up for it and the common people also lined up to put down their signatures. Thus began Mahatma Gandhi's non-violence based *satyagraha,* or 'truth force.' This was the first revolutionary step that Gandhiji took and showed the path for attaining freedom. This was a new turn that history took, a new politics, a new determination and perseverance; a unique and novel approach for success and achievement was taking birth. The nation was emerging from the old imaginations and entering the era of a new style of thinking and a renewed appreciation for revolution, where they could recognize themselves and become free.

The Rowlatt Bill's oppressive laws are briefly summarized below:

1. *The government was given the powers to demand bail bonds or surety bonds from any individual.*
2. *The government could detain any person anywhere.*
3. *Stay orders or restraining orders were deemed authorized to be issued in some ordinary cases as well such as on news publications, pamphlet distribution, participation in processions and rallies, etc.*
4. *The government could order any person to report their presence to the police at given times.*
5. *The government could arrest anyone without a warrant and without telling them their crime.*
6. *The government could keep anyone in prison without a trial or a sentence from the court*
7. *The government could ban the entry of any Indian who was outside the country.*

8. *If any banned material was found in anyone's possession, even if there was no intent to sell of publish such material, the mere possession of it was enough to be worthy of a punishment*

The bill was published in February of 1919. Mahatma Gandhi had just recovered from an illness and was convalescing at his home in Ahmedabad. He became very restless, and said to Vallabhbhai Patel that if a few people could be convinced to draft a written protest, a *satyagraha* could be started. Subsequently, a small conference was held at Satyagraha Ashram on February 24, 1919; Vallabhbhai Patel, Mrs. Naidu, BG Horniman, Shankarlal Banker and others attended. It was decided there that a written declaration would be drafted and people's signatures taken on it. It was also decided that a 'Satyagraha Committee' would be established which would draft a strategy by which everyone would abide. The effect of this oppressive bill on Gandhi, a man of action with the disposition of a fakir, was similar to that of gasoline on a fire. Hence Gandhi gathered the determination to start the *satyagraha*, and the Satyagraha Committee, on March 23, 1919, decided upon the strategy to print literature that was banned and would be confiscated, and distribute it. It was also decided to do things that would violate the laws governing the registration of newspapers. The government, instead of softening its approach, presented a bill in March 1919 amending the criminal code and passed it to become an act on March 18, 1919. Under this act, the government had assumed several powers to squash civil liberties. The Satyagraha Committee decided upon the day of April 6, 1919 to act on its decided strategy. The plan was for people to abstain from eating all day and then gather in the evening at a certain place and pray to God. They would gather barefoot and without any head coverings, and all shops and businesses should remain shut. Gandhiji advised that during this *satyagraha* it was imperative to remain hungry and to keep shops and businesses shut. He believed that this would increase the people's spiritual strength, which in turn would make their hearts speak the truth and therefore be well-received in the court of God. Gandhi was inspired by the fasting requirements in both Hindu and Muslim religions as his justification for abstaining from food and the idea was preached in all parts of the country. Just as the thirsty find water, the entire nation, Hindus and Muslims, joined this plan of action and were ready to sacrifice their all for it.

On April 6, 1919 Gandhiji himself initiated *satyagraha* in Bombay by launching the newspaper *Satyagraha* without obtaining the requisite approvals for it. In addition, he started selling literature, books, and magazines which were not allowed to be published. Mrs. Sarojini Naidu was with him, but the government did not intervene. In Bombay, Gandhiji asked the public to assemble in the Chowpatty maidan. There, after taking a dip in the ocean, a procession was carried out and a rally was held. Gandhiji was there and then left for Delhi by way of Agra and Mathura. On April 9, 1919 when the train reached Kosi, an officer of the Punjab Government advised him that he was not allowed to enter Punjab. Gandhiji ignored that advice. When the train reached the next station Palwal, the governments of Punjab and Delhi declared that he was not allowed entry into Punjab and the Indian Government ordered him to return and remain in Bombay. Gandhiji refused to obey the order. An English police officer ordered him to get off the train but he refused, saying that he would get off only if he was arrested.

The police officer placed his hand on Gandhiji's shoulder and that's when he got off the train. From there he was returned to Mathura and then back to Bombay on a special train.

At Palwal station, Gandhiji wrote a message to the people of the country, gave it to Mahadev Desai, telling him that he was going to act in Gandhiji's place. The gist of the message was:

1. *My arrest gives me freedom. I got what I wished for, i.e. that the Rowlatt Act should be repealed or I should be sent to jail.*

2. *Now it remains for you to fulfill your duty, which according to the pledge of satyagraha is now your responsibility. Fulfill this duty; there is success in that.*

3. *The satyagrahis who have embarked on this great struggle, if they deviate by a hair from the path of truth and righteousness or they bring harm to any English people or Indians, there will be a lot of harm to this cause.*

4. *I am confident that Hindu-Muslim unity, which I believe in my heart has descended into all of the nation's hearts, will now show its true colors.*

5. *In the end, my faith is that the secret of our success and freedom lies in our strength to bear hardships and difficulties and not in the reforms meted out by England, no matter how extensive and far reaching those reforms may be.*

6. *It is my hope that all Hindus, Muslims, Sikhs, Christians, Parsees, Jews, and all those who were born in India or have assumed residence here will participate fully in this national struggle. It is also my hope that women and children will be as much a part of this as they want to.*

(Mohandas Karamchand Gandhi)

Swami Shraddhanand's Speech at Jama Masjid

Due to a miscommunication, Satyagraha Day was celebrated early in Delhi on March 30. The government was now preparing with all its might to crush this movement and the army was called in for this purpose. The grand rally in Delhi was ordered to disperse. The police and the army were armed with machine guns among other armaments. There were firings on two occasions. A few people died and many were injured.

It was that March 30 when Hindu-Muslim unity reached its zenith: the Arya Samaj leader, Swami Shraddhanand, gave a speech from the pulpit of the Jama Masjid and the Muslims, with much pleasure and delight, allowed him to. After that, when a procession was taken out and it reached Chandni Chowk, Swamiji opened up his chest to the bayonets on the rifles of Gurkha soldiers. This incident received a lot of publicity and all of India went wild with passion.

Those loyal to the government were on the lookout and erupted in a furor over allowing a Hindu into a mosque. Maulana Abul Kalam Azad, who was incarcerated in Ranchi at the time, picked up his pen, and prepared a detailed defense with references to authentic *Hadith*. He gave such a befitting response that it silenced all the critics. Then taking a defensive tone, they started saying that the pulpit was the place of sanctity of Hazrat Bilal; why did they have to let Swamiji stand there? But as the proverb goes, the snake had slipped away, there was no use now beating that line on the ground that looked like it.

It wasn't just Delhi and Bombay; there was no city in India large or small where huge rallies attended by anywhere between 15,000 and 100,000 people did not take place. People abstained from food all day long, came to the rallies barefoot and without any head covering, and prayed to God with emotion and urgency for justice. All of India had boiled over. Some prominent people started speaking in unison with Gandhiji. Maulana Hasrat Mohani, who had never been a proponent of Gandhiji's *satyagraha*, was front and center in this battle. All that Hasrat *Saheb* needed was a front to fight, and die fighting, for the freedom of the country. Dr. Ansari, Swami Shraddhanand, etc. all joined the fray. Someone named this unique thing *Silent Opposition* in Urdu, which has been stated in English as 'Passive Resistance.' Gandhiji distributed a note among the people in which he pointed out the faults of the Rowlatt Bill, saying that reforms were possible, whether they were enacted or not. He continued that the need of the time was to reach a reasonable and just agreement on this matter. He declared that the Imperial Civil Service officers could remain in India only as the servants of the Indian people, and not just on paper but in practice. He also cautioned the British Chambers of Commerce that its presence in India was viable only if it strove to fulfill the needs of the Indians, and not if they were bent upon the destruction and devastation of Indian industries. He stated that, "On the basis of the mentioned drafts, we should become more vocal in our dissatisfaction with and criticism of the government, whose authoritarian activities are giving testimony against it." This note was sent as a *satyagrahi* to the Viceroy. The Viceroy invited Gandhiji to discuss the matter. And Gandhiji went to meet the Viceroy.

The summary of the discussion between Gandhiji and the Viceroy, which the newspapers published in a very concise form, is as follows:

Gandhiji: We shall strictly abide by our 'Passive Resistance,' i.e. *Silent Opposition.*

Viceroy: There was haste in initiating this 'Passive Resistance.'

Gandhiji: I thought that the foundation of the British government was spiritual power.

Viceroy: My opinion regarding that is on the contrary, and I doubt your statement.

Gandhiji: If the foundation of the British government is absolute power, then all of India should be considered disloyal. In such a situation, I shall be the first person deserving to be called disloyal.

That day, clear sentiments were put in words: *satyagraha* was a philosophy. But the public got an opportunity to express their sentiments and they took it. The Muslims were already extremely anxious due to the matter of the Caliphate. Now the Rowlatt Bill was a challenge for both the Hindus and the Muslims. A leader had been found and a strange scenario of Hindu-Muslim unity unfolded.

The Massacre of Jallianwala Bagh

After the proposal for the *satyagraha* opposition was approved on March 1, 1919, in Amritsar and other districts of Punjab, just like in the districts and towns of other provinces, a *hartal* or a strike with passionate demonstrations took place on April 6.

The government turned up in full force to crush those demonstrations. Their pride of victory and power was at its height, and the British government made the same mistake that Gen. Yahya Khan made recently in East Pakistan, which resulted in the creation of Bangladesh. The government forgot that the public's emotions cannot be crushed. It is said that when a storm hits a calm ocean, there is no power other than the Almighty's that can ask it to stop. The army was on the move at all times. Machine guns were prominently displayed. But Gandhi, the dervish, had conjured such an image of the future that there was no going back to sleep.

Adamantly committed to crushing any sign of unrest, the government arrested Dr. Saifuddin Kitchlew and Dr. Satyapal on April 10, 1919 and expelled them from Amritsar. On April 15, 1919 martial law was imposed in Amritsar and Lahore, where the movement had picked up steam.

On April 10, 1919, enraged by the news that Gandhi had been arrested, there was a mass gathering in Amritsar. Since it was the early days of the movement and people had not fully understood the principles of *satyagraha* and the concept of non-violence, they attacked a bank and killed some British officers and a British woman. A building was burned down. Police quickly brought the situation under control but Gen. Dyer reached Amritsar in command of 2000 troops. On the morning of April 13, Gen. Dyer proceeded through the city with several city officials, announcing a ban on all processions and public meetings of four or more persons. The announcement included a warning that, if necessary, weapons would be used to quell crowds that violated the curfew to gather for demonstrations. But the public ignored these orders and announced a public rally for 4:30 that evening in Jallianwala Bagh. When Gen. Dyer heard about this, he was mad with rage and arrived in Jallianwala Bagh with troops armed with machine guns. He had all the exits blocked and ordered the troops to fire on the crowd and keep on firing until all the ammunition was exhausted. The outcome was 379 dead and 1200 injured. No aid was given to the injured nor were they taken to the hospital. They just lay there in agony. The Martial Law remained in effect for a month and a half after that, under which a curfew was imposed in the city from 8 p.m. till 5 a.m. Curfew violators were to be shot on sight. All the cars and other means of transport had been impounded without compensation. Electric lights and fans had been confiscated. Harsh punishments were meted out on merely the slightest suspicions. When someone tore down a banner announcing the Martial Law order from the walls of Sanatan Dharam College, many students, professors, and all male residents living in the compound of the college were arrested and forced to march for three miles before they were released on bail. 1000 students of the college were asked to report to the authorities every day, for which they had to walk 16 miles every day. People were whipped at the slightest suspicion. There was an alley in Amritsar where some people had attacked an English person. Residents of that alley were made to crawl on their stomachs for a long time. It was a long alley, and if anyone faltered, they were whipped. Orders were given in Lyallpur that if an English person passed by, Indians should get down from their vehicles and if holding an umbrella over their heads should fold their umbrellas and stand respectfully on the side with their heads bowed. Army was sent out into the rural areas, where they would round up anyone they wished and whip them. Places were bombed by aircraft and crowds were fired upon to spread terror among the residents. When some railway tracks were uprooted, residents of a village nearby were fired upon indiscriminately without any inquiry.

All of India was shaken up on hearing of these incidents. It should be remembered that this India was now Gandhiji's India. There was sincere and emotional condemnation of these incidents from all quarters. When this news reached England, the general opinion was very much affected by it. An old Englishman, whose son had recently come to India as an Indian Civil Service officer, clenched his teeth on reading the news of the Jallianwala Bagh massacre one morning and said angrily, "I did not send my son to India to commit such ghastly crimes. I shall call him back." An investigative tribunal was set up for Martial Law. English officers acknowledged these atrocities, saying:

> *"The purpose of our actions was to annihilate any thought of rebellion in the minds of the Indians."*

During WWI, India had given Britain hundreds of thousands of soldiers, two billion rupees, and blood and sweat. This is what they got in return.

The affairs of the Caliphate were arousing boundless passion, and now there were these insane procedures and conspiracies to strengthen the British government's position of terror and barbarism and the shackles of slavery. The government was not only breaking their promise to the Muslims, they were breaking their promises to India. The country was now ready for a complete struggle for freedom, and Gandhiji's forward-looking leadership, courage, and boldness were coming to life in their full color.

Rabindranath Tagore's Response

The Jallianwala Bagh incident shocked the renowned philosopher, intellectual, and Nobel laureate Rabindranath Tagore to such an extent that on April 30, 1919 he renounced his knighthood and stated that "such mass murderers aren't worthy of giving any title to anyone."

Laborers had gone on strike in Ahmedabad and the city had become an erupting volcano. On the request of the people, Gandhiji went there on April 13, 1919. The next day, April 14, the laborers called off their strike and peace returned to the city. This made it clear that Gandhiji's intent was not anarchy, but a conscientious awakening of the people and to prove its effectiveness.

There was a session of the Congress Committee on April 20, 1919, but Gandhiji did not go to Punjab simply because he was bound to get arrested and that would have caused agitation among the people. And the experience up until then had been that the public had not adhered to non-violence.

After that, to investigate Jallianwala Bagh and other dreadful incidents, the government set up the Hunter Commission. Then, Gandhiji suspended the civil disobedience movement. The real reason was that the people were not yet ready for *ahimsa* or 'nonviolence,' and the success of *satyagraha* depended on two principles: truth and nonviolence. On taking the step to suspend *satyagraha*, Gandhiji's dignity rose to touch the sky.

During that time, the government shut down The Bombay Chronicle and deported its editor, BG Horniman to the United Kingdom. Soon after that, in association with 'Young India', Gandhiji started a newspaper *Naujivan*, with himself as the editor, Mahadev Desai as the publisher, and Shankarlal Banker as the printer.

The Afghanistan War of Independence

Days of misfortune had arrived for the English. Afghanistan too stretched itself awake. The area of Afghanistan is around 245,000 square miles and its population is less than 10 million. This is a mountainous country. Many areas of the country are uninhabited. The Hindu Kush and Himalayan mountain ranges have peaks reaching 20,000 feet in many places. Peaks are often covered with snow. There are three passes that provide a route to India. Khyber and Gomal Passes lead to Punjab and Bolan Pass into Sindh. To the east of Afghanistan is the Frontier Province, to the west the Iranian province of Khorasan, to the north Bukhara and Russian Turkestan, and to the south Balochistan. Its geographical location is such that it was always a battleground for geopolitical contentions. Sometimes it was under the influence of Russia and sometimes that of Britain. After going through different eras, Abdur Rahman Khan, who had friendly relations with Britain, became Amir of Afghanistan in 1880. On his death in 1901, his son Amir Habibullah became the ruler. He came fully under the control of Britain. He was also a man of poor habits and manners. The English had promised him a large sum of money after the war as compensation and had also promised that he would be made the Islamic Caliph. In his greed, Amir Habibullah kept Maulana Ubaidullah Sindhi and his associates captive for a long time. Although he always called them his guests, he opposed all revolutionary movements. Maulana Ubaidullah Sindhi had founded a provisional Indian Government in Afghanistan, with Raja Mahendra Pratap appointed as its president. But Amir Habibullah never allowed this government to function. How could they function when they were confined to small and dark rooms and monitored every minute, all under the pretext of being 'guests' of the Amir.

But the Afghanistan Independence Party, which had come into existence through the efforts of Syed Jamaluddin Afghani, was active in the country. It had influence over the entire Afghan army. Begum Alia Hazrat and Amir Amanullah from the royal family were also active in it or supportive of it.

One time, Amir Habibullah went to Jalalabad on a hunting trip. On February 20, 1919 he was fishing when a fish jumped out of the lake and started fluttering. Amir Habibullah said that someday every man's soul would flutter like that and depart the mortal body. The same evening, an assassin entered his room, shot him dead, and disappeared.

Zafar Ahmad Aibak[10] has written:

"A week before his death, Amir Habibullah Khan in his Friday sermon had declared himself 'Amir of the Believers' and 'The Islamic Caliph.' It appears that Amir Habibullah was awaiting the fall of the Ottoman Caliphate so that he could declare himself Caliph. The

---

10 *Aap Biiti*, Vol I, pp130

same week, the Amir demanded from the English the price for his neutrality. He sent mules to Peshawar to transport the payment back to him for helping the English in the war by remaining neutral, i.e. for the harm he had brought to the Islamic world by ignoring the benefits of the Islamic Caliphate and the struggle for it, and now he wanted his reward and compensation for it. But look at the glory of the Almighty, neither did he have in his destiny to become the Islamic Caliphate nor did he have in his fortune the money he could spend on comfort and luxury."

After Amir Habibullah's death, the army erupted. They arrested Sardar Inayat Ullah Khan and Sardar Nasrallah Khan and brought them to Kabul, and announced that Amanullah Khan had become the Amir of Afghanistan. As soon as he took the reins of the government in his hands, Amanullah Khan started preparing for war and piled his forces on the border. Maulana Ubaidullah Sindhi sent messages to India on behalf of the provisional government saying that in case of war, everyone should be ready to rebel and to support the attacking forces.

After the declaration of war, Mr. Chelmsford, the Viceroy and Governor General of India, issued a statement on May 10, 1919 to inform "the loyal subjects of the great emperor," parts of which provide confirmation of our point of view. For instance:

"His Excellency suggested that one reason for this 'astonishing foolishness of Afghanistan' was the unrest in the country after those responsible for the assassination of Amir Habibullah were punished.

By declaring war, Amir Amanullah is trying to divert the people's attention. To break off the close relations with the Government of British India is, to some extent, the late fruit of those efforts in Kabul of their German friends who gave the late Amir the motivation to stay on the path of righteousness and loyalty.

"The evidence that His Excellency has in his hands makes it obvious that the excuse the Amir has made for his treachery is that India is in a state of rebellion, which in his country would be a basis for covert action. Amir has told his subjects that in India there is neither safety for people's assets and possessions nor for their religion...Amir has made arrangements to distribute such documents and announcements, and has also made arrangements to bribe such newspapers that he hopes can be bought...this suicidal mistake of the Amir to test his strength against such a power that was victorious and triumphant in the biggest war the world has seen. The government has the omnipotent power to exercise with priority what it wishes to, and it will positively exercise it to punish this criminal activity."

Sardar Muhammad Saleh Khan was sent as the Commander. On May 2, 1919 he started a battle before the war was declared from Kabul. The English bombardment from airplanes injured Saleh Khan's leg and he retreated screaming, "My foot has been martyred, my foot has been martyred." Amir Amanullah immediately removed him from his command and asked for opinions as to how he should be punished. Everybody's opinion was that he should be hanged, but Amir Amanullah decided that he should be dressed as a woman and kept inside the home. He also declared that if Saleh Khan were to be found outside in male's clothing, his murder would be considered lawful. Everyone had the right to kill him. Taking advantage of Sardar Muhammad Saleh Khan's removal, the English forces captured Dakka. Now Gen. Nadir Khan arrived at the battlefront and after a series of offensives, lay siege to the garrison of Thal. Gen. Dyer was dispatched to face Nadir Khan. Gen. Dyer had a statement issued at the time in the official English newspaper "Civil and Military Gazette,' in which he stated that Nadir Khan attacked his troops as one strikes a single star in the vast sky. Gen. Nadir Khan had decided to surround and capture Peshawar. Gen. Nadir Khan's brother, Gen. Mahmud Khan, had defeated the English forces on another front but on May 27, 1919 Amir Amanullah decided to end the war and issued an order for the Afghan forces to leave the Indian soil and retreat to 20 miles inside the frontier.

Amir Amanullah's state of mind was such that when Muhammad Saleh Khan was removed from the battlefront and the English bombarded Kabul from airplanes, he would set out with a rifle and fire at the planes despite Hazrat Alia Sultan telling him it was futile. These absurd acts reveal what courage and valor he had. The only objective of that war was to have the English lose their influence over Afghanistan and the God-given country of Afghanistan truly become a God-given country. The predicament for the English was that their Indian troops had not yet returned to India and in Russia, the Bolshevik regime under Lenin and Trotsky had been established in 1917. Despite its internal problems, Russia was fully supportive of the independence movements of India, Afghanistan, and all other subjugated countries.

In this altercation, it was impossible for the English to teach Afghanistan a lesson of the kind it had in the past. And hence a mutual declaration to end the war came quickly.

Rawalpindi Conference

To reach a permanent truce, representatives of both parties met in Rawalpindi and on August 18, 1919 an accord was reached between the two countries. Under this accord, the English recognized Afghanistan's complete independence and Afghanistan accepted the borders as they existed at the time.

At the Rawalpindi Conference, the English representative Hamilton Grant gave a speech first, in which he severely reproached Afghanistan for starting the war. He then said, "What status did Afghanistan have to stand up against us, but we took pity on Afghanistan and considered it inappropriate to continue waging war against it." After that, the Afghan representative Sardar Ali Ahmad Khan spoke forcefully. His speech was deemed amazing by the Anglo-Indian newspapers. The Afghan delegate said, "You are the one who started the war and you are the one who is asking for peace. You have an absolute undue arrogance concerning your power. You were very weak in comparison to Germany, but it was the Allied who won. You were with the Allied, that is why you won. How do you know what would have happened if we had found our own alliance..." At that point the conference was temporarily suspended. The full statement is as follows:

"Regarding the statement that the British government is so much more powerful than the Afghan government that if the war had continued, the result would have been in favor of the British, Sardar Ali Ahmad acknowledged

> *that the British at this time certainly have more men, cannons and warplane, but wasn't that the case with Germany too in the European War, and didn't Germany drop bombs on London the same way that the English did on Kabul? But who won in the end? Britain was on the winning side because it was with the Allied. It had found an alliance. The same possibilities of being a part of an alliance are available to Afghanistan as well. In such a situation, one party to a peace conference should not be permitted to say to the other that they would have won the war had it continued. The Government of British India should not be under the misconception that the Afghans are an inattentive and ignorant nation."*

Maulana Ubaidullah Sindhi was very restless for the freedom of his homeland India, but by staying abroad and depending on foreign nations, he did not create a good impression on the Hindus of India. There was suspicion about his intention and the English through their propaganda had created the impression that the Muslims were plotting an attack by Afghanistan and helping them to establish not a unified national democracy but an Afghan Islamic government. There were many accusations and clarifications exchanged on this topic for many years. Every nationalist Muslim had to answer to the charge of being "Afghan people," to the extent that Maulana Mohammad Ali was asked once and he replied that if Afghanistan came to get India its freedom, we would help them and if they came to conquer India, we would resolutely oppose them. In 1920, Maulana Hasrat Mohani, who had just returned from Allahabad, told me that there was a meeting at the home of Sir Tej Bahadur Sapru to ponder over the question of what our position should be if Afghanistan was to attack India. Maulana Hasrat stated that he said at the meeting, what is to be gained from hiding the real question behind that question? Everyone knows that Afghanistan does not have the strength to attack India. The real question to be pondered is what our position should be if Russia attacked India. Sir Tej Bahadur asked him to state what he thought our position should be. Maulana Hasrat said, "We shall write odes to welcome them." Sapru *Saheb* said, "But wouldn't they make us slaves?" Hasrat *Saheb* replied, past experience tells us that their policies are not colonialist, they just bring freedom to slave countries. Sapru *Saheb* said, "Maulana, they will loot your home." Maulana said, "Let them as much as they want, at least we will get our freedom." These incidents speak of how much anxiety there was among the Muslims in 1919. The English had won the war but the fire of the freedom struggle had spread everywhere.

Amir Amanullah Khan

O' Amir, the fortunate one, the illustrious one
Young and with a solid foot, the mature one

From the beginning, Amir Amanullah Khan spoke the slogans of jihad and reforms. He used to give passionate and forceful speeches. He used to ask his subjects to sleep with a gun under their pillow, because they could never know when he would call them up for jihad. With a pretense of strength, he would call upon himself, "In the path of Amanullah Khan, always be prepared to give your life." He released all those who had been imprisoned for their libertarian thinking, which included India's Dr. Abdul Ghani (who has been mentioned earlier), and he respected them all very much. That is why he included Dr. Abdul Ghani in the Afghan delegation to the Rawalpindi Peace Conference. He ordered his subjects to store six months' worth of food in their basements (Afghanistan is a very cold place and even cooked food doesn't go bad for six months). He introduced the custom of using indigenous items. He asked the people to wear their indigenous clothes. If he saw an officer of the government in non-Afghan clothes, he would get close and praise the attire and then take out scissors and cut a piece from it, saying "as a sample," ruining the clothes in the process. He would wander around alone at night, and since it was his order that no one wander around alone at night, a policeman once arrested him. He rewarded the policeman. Amanullah introduced education in current affairs and sciences in the country and even sent some boys to London for schooling, but a religious scholar went with them. His instructions were that when the Christian students went to church, these boys should study the Quran.

He believed in Islamic unity and the central Islamic Caliphate with his heart and soul. Hence, when a representative of the British Crown came to get Amir Amanullah Khan's signature on the conditions for a peace agreement and told him there will be complete peace between Afghanistan and England, he replied they were only establishing neighborly relations. He said that the English's treatment of the Ottomans, the atrocities they were committing in Smyrna, and their treatment of the Islamic scholars in India made peace with them impossible.

Afghanistan had become free. It was standing on its own two feet, having taken off and thrown the shackles of British slavery, and was talking about self-reliance and self-awareness. There was a time when the English proposed Afghanistan as a summer retreat. The Afghans massacred the English residents of Afghanistan. In retribution, British forces trampled Ghazni and Kabul. That era had passed as the revolution that had come to pass in Russia, and the foreign policy that Lenin espoused made the English wary of starting a second World War, and nor could they. In this way, the seed of independence that Maulana Mahmud Hasan had planted was bearing flowers everywhere. The independence of Afghanistan imparted a timely and exemplary strength to the Khilafat Movement and through it to the Independence movement of India, and mention of its implication is indispensable, although the deceitful political tricks of the English had not ceased and were saying:

Do not think that the work of the taverns is done yet
There are thousands of goblets of wine on the grapevines

All-India Muslim Conference

As mentioned earlier, there were protest rallies being held throughout India related to the Khilafat Movement, and demands were being made that the central Islamic Caliphate be preserved in Turkey and that the holy places, the Arab Peninsula, Jerusalem, Palestine, Baghdad, Najaf al-Ashraf etc. remain under the authority of the Caliph, as per the promises and the pledges. But Turkey's fate had not yet been decided, and the general public as well as the close observers were of the decisive opinion that the leadership of British and Indian governments be apprised of the emotions of the Muslims so that the Peace Conference Committee that was working under the three superpowers, America, Britain, and France, be influenced to make decisions consistent with these emotions. For that purpose, rallies were being held throughout the country, where resolutions were being passed. In this connection, a grand rally was held under the name of "All-India Muslim Conference" in Lucknow on September 18, 1919[11]. Scholars and religious leaders of all schools of thought and from all over India attended this conference. It is said that the conference attracted a very large crowd and there was no section of the Muslim community that was not represented there. The representatives to the conference were as follows:

1.	Honorable Nawab Zufiqar Khan	Lahore
2.	Mr. Agha Muhammad Safdar	Sialkot
3.	Maulvi Ghulam Mohiuddin	Qasur
4.	Maulana Abul Wafa Sanaullah	Amritsar
5.	Honorable Nawab Sarfaraz Husain Khan	Patna
6.	Honorable Khwaja Muhammad Noor	Gaya
7.	Honorable Syed Nurul Hasan	Bankipur
8.	Honorable Sir Fazal Bhai Karim Bhai	Bombay
9.	Haji Jan Mohammad Chotani	Bombay
10.	Honorable Seth Ibrahim Haroon Jafar	Poona
11.	Seth Abdullah Haroon	Karachi
12.	Honorable Sir Asad Ali Khan	Madras
13.	Honorable Muhammad Abdul Quddus	Madras
14.	Honorable Maulvi Fazlul Haq	Calcutta
15.	Honorable Maulvi Abul Qasim	Burdwan

---

11 Chaudhari Khaliquzzaman, in his book "Pathway to Pakistan," has claimed that the conference was his brainchild. However, his claim has not been verified by any other source. This percept also does not add up since Khaliquzzaman was just a student of LLB at the time and to organize such a large conference was beyond the capacities of a student. In addition, the list of the representatives in the conference does not include his name.

16.	Maulvi Mujibur Rehman	Calcutta
17.	Dr. Mukhtar Ahmad Ansari	Delhi
18.	Honorable Syed Raza Ali	Allahabad
19.	Hakim Muhammad Ajmal Khan	Delhi
20.	Sheikh Zahoor Ahmad, Barrister	Allahabad
21.	Maulvi Mohammad Faiq	Faizabad
22.	Maulvi Mohammad Yaqub	Moradabad
23.	Honorable Syed Ale Nabi	Agra
24.	Tassaduq Ahmad Khan Sherwani	Aligarh
25.	Sheikh Abdullah, Lawyer	Aligarh
26.	Hafiz Mohammad Halim	Kanpur
27.	Hafiz Hidayat Husain	Kanpur
28.	Maulvi Fazlur Rehman, Lawyer	Kanpur
29.	Sheikh Shahid Husain Taluqdar	Barabanki
30.	Munshi Nawab Ali, Lawyer	Barabanki
31.	Maulvi Syed Nabiullah, Barrister	Lucknow
32.	Munshi Muhammad Nasim, Advocate	Lucknow
33.	Munshi Ahtisham Ali, Raees-Kakori	Lucknow
34.	Chaudhry Nematullah, Lawyer	Lucknow
35.	Dr. Mohammad Naeem Ansari	Lucknow
36.	Sheikh Mohammad Ali Haider Khan	Lucknow
37.	Syed Zahoor Ahmad, Lawyer	Lucknow

It was also decided that Syed Zahoor Ahmed, Honorary Secretary of All-India Muslim League should be in charge of recording the proceedings of the conference. These names in and of themselves reveal the nature of the All-India Muslim Conference. The headline of its advertisement was "A Matter of Life and Death for the Muslims," and it went on to say:

> *"It is not a baseless statement that the future of the Turkish Sultanate, and Turkey and Constantinople themselves,*

are in some degree of apprehension, as suggested by the occupation of lands in the aftermath of the war and the deposing of our Caliphs and Sultans not only from Turkey to Shiraz, but also in many other provinces and European parts of Turkey and Constantinople itself. It is also under consideration that lands acquired this way be given under the control of the Christian powers of Europe. As for those territories which were determined to be left under the control of the Sultans, it appears that the thought is to curtail their royal powers. These proposals have not been finally approved by the Peace Conference that is meeting in London but these reports have been received and it is anticipated that Great Britain supports many if not all of these proposals. Detailed submissions and strong objections have been submitted to the Peace Conference through the British government and the British delegation, but so far it has produced no desired result. The latest newspaper reports are heartbreaking for the Islamic world.

"Most of the people who are in favor of these proposals seem to ignore how deeply they will hurt the emotions of the Muslims.

"All-India Muslim League and some other parties are fulfilling their duty. Donations have been solicited and rallies have been held at different places or are going to be held soon so that the Muslims of India can express their sentiments. Therefore, for this purpose, we are taking the courageous step of inviting everyone to an All-India conference to be held on December 2, 1919. We are requesting that all members of the Muslim

*League and other political parties as well as all Muslims,
whether they are disposed to politics or not, to make the
effort to attend this special conference and to participate
in the discussion there and express their true emotions
regarding the Sultan and the Sultanate of Turkey."*

Mr. Ibrahim Jafar had been elected president of this conference
but he could not reach on time, so the name of Maulana
Abdul Bari was proposed for president and it was approved
unanimously. In the post-afternoon prayer session, Mr. Jafar
assumed the presidency and read a part of his presidential
address. The complete printed address was distributed among
the attendees.

The proceedings of the conference are reflected in the
following resolutions that were enacted.[12]

The conference's first resolution was regarding the
preservation of the supreme authority of the Caliphate and was
presented by Maulana Saiyad Muhammad Fakhir Allahabadi
and seconded by Maulana Syed Hasan Arzoo. The second
resolution expressed disapproval for taking large territories
of the Ottoman Empire such as Iraq, Arabia, Palestine, Syria,
Armenia etc. away from the Turkish Sultanate and putting
them under the rule of non-Muslim powers and emphasized
the need for the Arabian peninsula to remain under Muslim
control. It was presented by Maulana Abul Wafa Sanaullah
Amritsari, editor of *Ahl-e-Hadees*, and seconded by Sheikh
Abdullah, a lawyer from Aligarh.

The third resolution was to maintain the small geographical
region of Thrace under the control of the Turkish empire

---

12 *Mashriq* (Gorakhpur): Vol 11, September 25, 1919

according to the definitive promise of the British government and to maintain Constantinople as the seat of the Caliphate. This resolution was presented by Mr. Abbas Tyabji, Barrister and Chief Justice of the princely state of Baroda, in a passionate speech in English, and was seconded by Syed Jalib, editor of *Hamdam*, in a speech in Urdu in which he presented its synopsis.

The fourth resolution about the expulsion of Greeks from Smyrna was presented by Maulana Syed Sulaiman Nadvi in a painful and emotional speech which reminded the attendees of the past glory of the Muslims and, for a short while, turned the conference into a gathering of mourning.

In the fifth resolution it was stated that all of the four resolutions above be sent to His Excellency, the Viceroy, and to appeal to him that he recommend and forward them to the Imperial Government.

The sixth resolution declared October 17 to be a day of prayer for Turkey and for holding rallies in its support.

The seventh resolution expressed appreciation for the work done by Bombay's Khilafat Committee and expressed the need to establish its branches in cities in other states. In conclusion, Maulana Abdul Bari gave a vote of thanks to the president and all the attending delegates for their time, and the president in his concluding remarks thanked the Lucknow native, expressed his pleasure at the conference's success and prayed for the continued success of their efforts[13].

The objective of presenting the proceedings of this All-India Muslim Conference in detail is to note the following points:

---

13 *Mashriq* (Gorakhpur): Vol 11, September 25, 1919

1. Muslims from all over India, whether they were members of His Excellency's Council or His Honor's Council, or had titles of Khan Bahadur and were chiefs of nobles and lords of lords or were poor or were scholars or college educated or belonged to any one group or class of thinking were equally anxious and had raised their voices in a united and organized manner, which was the voice of all of India's Muslims.

2. There was no formal plan of action and that is why there was a reliance on pleading with and submitting petitions to the British government, sending delegations, making speeches, and holding rallies. The result of the Peace Conference was also anticipated, but the main issue was the lack of a plan and hence the movement was getting by on entreaties and complaints. But these entreaties and complaints were about to give birth to a strategy for the future.

A summary is presented here of the reports published in the weekly *Mashriq* about the passion and excitement expressed by the Muslims of India within a few months of October 30, 1918, when hostilities ended between the Ottoman Empire and the Allied. *Mashriq* was published from Gorakhpur under the editorship of Hakim Ibrahim and was an established stooge of the British government. But it reported all the news and kept its opposition at a high level. Maulvi Farooq of *Hamdard* newspaper had given *Mashriq* two alternate names. First, he called it "*Mashrik,*" since the newspaper's name was written as such in English on its cover page. The second name he had given it was "Opposite Direction," which was very interesting as a play on *Mashriq* vs. *Maghreb,* or East vs. West. In any case, its reporting on the Muslims' passion and excitement is extremely reliable. There is no testimonial better than the one given by those in opposition.

Selected sections from articles in *Mashriq* are presented below[14].

▍Day of Prayer

Gorakhpur:

Conforming to its movement, the All-India Muslim Conference Anjuman Islamia, in planning for a day of prayer at the Jama Masjid on October 17, 1919 and Khilafat Day to express their pain and grief, organized a meeting of Hindus and Muslims on October 16, 1919 at 5 p.m. at the bungalow of and presided by Munshi Abdullah Khan Shakir Ali *Saheb* Barrister which was attended by a number of the Hindu brothers. It was decided by consensus that on Friday, October 17, 1919 Hindus and Muslims shall close their businesses and pray for the continuity and survival of the Turkish Sultanate and the Islamic Caliphate. Consequently, on October 17 the Hindus and Muslims closed their businesses and the shopkeepers in Alinagar, Urdu Bazaar, Jafra Bazar, Sahabganj and elsewhere throughout the city kept their shops closed the entire day. In every mosque, after the Friday prayers, passionate prayers were held for Turkey and the Caliphate. Many Muslims assembled in the Jama Masjid on leaving their mosques. The crowd was so dense that people were packed all the way up to the gate. After these prayers, the Muslims of old Gorakhpur recited *Durood Sharif* and *Istighfar* supplications. Everyone was very emotional. Many Hindu brothers were in attendance. The Friday prayer at the Gorakhpur Jama Masjid was led by Maulana

---

14 *Mashriq* (Gorakhpur): Vol 23, October, 1919

Fakhir *Saheb*, who coincidentally had arrived there that day. After- prayer supplications were recited with such ardor and depth of feeling that the attendees' hearts were restless and they involuntarily exclaimed their impassioned feelings. It is impossible to describe its atmosphere in words. After that, Maulana Mamduh gave a pithy and impressive speech with a concluding prayer for the Caliphate. And right then, the common Muslims gathered there established the local chapter of the Khilafat Committee, electing Qazi Firasat Husain its President, and Hakim Maulvi Muhammad Mohsin and Maulvi Zahoor Uddin (Member, Municipal Board) as its secretaries. Telegrams were sent to the Viceroy of India and to the Khilafat Committee, and the resolutions of the All-India Muslim Conference were ratified. Lawyers and members of the Municipal Board, Babu Abhay Charan, Babu Jagdamba Prasad, and Babu Nawal Kishore, and many other Hindu dignitaries and common people heartily participated in the proceedings.

Azamgarh:

Here, Khilafat Day and the plaints and urgency expressed regarding the cause were successfully observed with much passion and expression of outrage. All the Muslims fasted, prayed for the survival of the Caliphate at the Jama Masjid, and ratified the resolutions passed at the All-India Muslim Conference held in Lucknow. All the businesses of the Hindus and Muslims were closed. The local administrative secretariat was also shut for two and a half hours.

Lucknow:

A day of plaints and prayers was observed on October 17, 1919 with much activity. At 1:00 p.m., a Friday prayer was held at Shah Pir Muhammad *Saheb*'s *Teele Wali Masjid* which was attended by more than 10,000 Muslims who prayed for the continuity of the Turkish Caliphate. There were post-prayer supplication recitals in many other mosques of the city. Right after the Friday prayer, people gathered under canopies and outside at the Rifa-e-Aam and the large grounds behind it. The place was packed and many Hindus were in attendance. Mr. Mukhtar Husain, presiding over the rally, gave an impassioned speech. The resolutions were ratified and it was decided that its copies shall be sent to England's Prime Minister, the Secretary of State for India, the Viceroy of India, and the Lieutenant-Governor of the United Provinces.

Banaras:

Khilafat Day was observed in Banaras jointly by the Hindus and Muslims. There was fasting and prayers. There was a prayer session at the Jama Masjid after the Friday prayer. A grand rally was held in one of the mosques which was attended by many Hindus as well. Resolutions were ratified and it was decided that a copy of the resolutions would be sent to the Viceroy. A Hindu youth made an impassioned declaration that Hindus shall join the Khilafat Movement.

Aligarh:

A day of plaints was observed with a resounding success. Many Hindus and Muslims kept their shops shut. After the Friday prayer, *Imam Saheb* read affective supplications and prayed for the Caliphate. After that, many of the attendees delivered speeches causing many of those present to become tearful at times. Resolutions in line with the All-India Muslim Conference were adopted. A 77-word telegram was sent to the Prime Minister of Great Britain and Secretary of State for India condemning the recent events.

Bengal:

Khilafat Day was observed successfully in many districts of Bengal. Almost all Indian-owned shops in Calcutta remained shut. After the Friday prayer, supplications were made for the continuity and survival of the Caliphate. In the late afternoon, there was a large gathering of Muslims in the Town Hall which was attended by Hindus as well. Because of the large crowd, there were rallies outside the hall as well. Inside the hall, the meeting was presided by Fazlul Haq. Resolutions were ratified.

Allahabad:

Khilafat Day was observed silently. Shops remained closed. Prayers and supplications were made in mosques.

Delhi:

Every big and small bazaar of Delhi, presenting a somber scene of *hartal*, or a complete shut-down, was raising its voice to say that today we Hindus and Muslims of Delhi actively condemn proposals to change the status of the Islamic Caliphate and the breaking up of the Sultanate of Turkey into pieces. The bazaars around Jama Masjid - Anaj Mandi, Chawri Bazar, Lal Kuan, Chandni Chowk, Sadar Bazar, the clothes market – were all closed. Prayer sessions were held with much humility and submission in all the mosques. The plaints and sighs of the large gathering resounded for some time. Then those at the gathering bowed their heads and engaged in prayer. Later, a rally was held in which nearly 100,000 Hindus and Muslims participated. Many speeches were made marked by the speakers' free and fearless demeanors. Swami Shraddhanand and Mr. Asaf Ali also spoke.

Bombay:

Muslims observed Khilafat Day and Day of Prayer by fasting. Hindus participated too. All the wholesale markets remained shut. All the shops in Bhindi Bazar, Nall Bazar, and Crawford Market remained shut. Slaughterhouses also remained shut. Despite the Deputy Municipal Commissioner's and the Superintendent's insistence, the butchers flatly refused to open the slaughterhouses. The Friday prayer was held at Jama Masjid at 1:00 p.m. Two hours before the prayer, people had started assembling there and all the roads were blocked. There were nearly 50,000 men in the mosque. Volunteers were organizing the assembly. After the Friday prayer, a special prayer was said for the worldly powers of the Caliphate. After that, a rally was held in the mosque. Mian Haji Jan Mohammad Chotani, president of the Khilafat Committee, presided over that rally, the resolutions of the All-India Muslim Conference were ratified, and it was recommended to the president that copies be wired to Mr. Prime Minister, Secretary of State for India, Viceroy, and Governor of Bombay. There was a vote of thanks for Mahatma Gandhi. Many of the Hindu attendees performed the *Mahadev Bhog* form of prayer.

In a similar fashion, there were reports of the situation, rallies, and resolutions adopted in Maunath Bhanjan, Kathor, Moradabad, Basti, Darbhanga, etc. In Basti, Advocate Babu Daulat Ram Asthana was a passionate attendee. There is also mention of similar events in Kheta Sarai, Mirzapur, and other places.

Khilafat Committee and Mahatma Gandhi

The first meeting of the Khilafat Committee was held in Delhi on November 23, 1919. After the All-India Muslim Conference held in Lucknow, British Prime Minister Lloyd George had given a heart rending speech at a gathering of the Lord Mayor from which it was inferred that the Prime Minister of the British Empire was going to renege on his promises. This speech riled the Muslims and soon after a conference of the Khilafat Committee presided by Mr. Fazlul Haq (Bengal) was convened in Delhi with much pomp and splendor. Mahatma Gandhi also attended this conference. Special arrangements were made for his presence at the conference and the crowd was so deep that it would take two hours to traverse between Chandni Chowk and Jama Masjid. The attendees to this conference were only the representatives of the Khilafat Committees of various provinces, although Mahatma Gandhi had been invited because of the magnitude of his position among the people. There were also some Hindu elders in attendance who had been sent by some Muslims as their representatives. The Hindus who had come from Sindh, Rangoon, Bengal, Bihar, United provinces, etc. had been sent on behalf of the Khilafat Committees of those provinces. There were some Shia gentlemen in attendance as well.

Maulana Mohammad Ali's Release and Congress Convention in Amritsar

In December 1919, Maulana Mohammad Ali and Maulana Shaukat Ali were released from Betul jail. Around the same time, the All-India National Congress Convention was being held and concurrent with it the Khilafat Conference. Both brothers were invited by Congress and arrived at the convention straight from jail. Maulana Mohammad Ali gave a long speech that was very passionate and forceful. To quote Maulana Abdul Majid Daryabadi, the attendance of Maulana Mohammad Ali made it feel as if all the Muslims of India were in attendance, since through his knowledge and wisdom, adherence to Islamic faith, fearless quest for the truth, selflessness and sacrifices, he had become the leader of all Indian Muslims. After his release from Betul jail, every railway station he passed through gave him a grand welcome. From Amritsar he was invited to Delhi, and when he arrived in Delhi, there was a swarm of people to receive him. These kinds of grand crowds and conventions underscored the point that the Muslims were in this with their hearts and souls. Now the Muslims believed that the downfall of the central Islamic Caliphate, defeat and breakup of the Arabian Peninsula, and the destruction of the entire Islamic world was the doing of Britain and the Muslims should get together with their Hindu brothers to establish a united national democracy free of the influence of Britain. This could result in crushing the pride and strength of Britain.

All-India Muslim League Convention

On January 9, 1919 the All-India Muslim League Convention was held. The president of its reception committee was Dr. Mukhtar Ahmad Ansari. He gave such a comprehensive, pithy, and courageous presidential address that all of India's attention turned toward the convention. But between the lines, the same sentiment of loyalty was evident, even though it had glimpses of rebellion as well. He stated[15]:

---

15 *Ruidaad Karravai Darul Uloom*, vol 99, pp 3192

"Gentlemen! Today we have gathered here in very delicate times. The Great War in which the nations of the East and the West were involved and that theater of hostilities and conflicts has come to an end, but despite that one war being over, it is the beginning of our anxiety. Some very important matters are going to be decided now. And it would not be without basis to say that the Peace Conference's final decisions shall decide for a long time the reason why the history of the existence of humanity should be written.

"For the Muslims, this is particularly a period of disquietude. This situation that is in front of us today in a history of 1300 years, which has not been without its ups and downs, has never been faced by Muslims before.

"The British government has always exerted the claim in their international affairs and relations throughout the world that <u>because the King of England rules over the largest number of Muslims in the world</u>, the British government particularly deserves attention. But it should be remembered that with every right there is a duty. The time has come for <u>the Muslim subjects of this great country to demand</u> that the royal ministers, whose hands hold the reins of the fate of Britain, fulfill those duty of theirs which are required of them related to the Muslims of India."

Then, condemning the destruction of Islam's worldly powers since the nineteenth century, Europe's deceitful policies, the plunder and looting of Islamic empires, and the artful ways in which the government justified the actions of the White race nations, he stated:

"The series of Islamic empires that once stretched unbroken from the shores of the Atlantic Ocean to the borders of the Chinese Empire is now in tatters and remains in name only. In Europe, to the north of Black Sea, Romania, Greece, and Macedonia too have one after the other left the hold of the Muslims. In Africa, Morocco, Algeria, Tunisia, Tirablus, and Egypt and similarly the Caucasus and Central Asia have ceased to be Islamic states. The 1907 compact between Russia and Britain, which included the establishment, permanence and freedom of Iran, on examination now reveals that its significance is nothing more than a political joke. The poor Bedouins of Arabia and Africa are being cajoled to abandon their nomadic lives in the desert for the dancing harlots of mirthful brothels.

"Today we are seeing that Turkey too, which has for centuries picked up the sword to defend the honor of Islam, is in the same danger and it won't be surprising if it too is broken up and distributed. These are extremely anxious times for the Islamic world."

After that, he discussed the Ottoman Caliphate briefly but comprehensively.

"It is a recognized event in history that in 922 AH (1516 AD), the last Caliph of the Abbasid dynasty Mohammad Abbasi, who was in Egypt, with the consent and permission of the Islamic populace, transferred the position of the Caliph and the spiritual powers of Islam to the Ottoman Sultan, Selim the Resolute. The outward emblems of this glorious position, the sword and mantle of Prophet Muhammad, were also given

in the custody of the Ottoman Empire's first Islamic Caliph and he brought these blessed articles with him to Istanbul. Muhammad Abbasi too assumed residence in Istanbul. From that day on, the Sultan of the Ottoman Empire assumed the titles of Islamic Caliph, Sultan of the Muslims, and Hadimul-Haremeyn (The Servant of The Two Holy Cities, Mecca and Medina), and till today the world's Muslims revere the Ottoman Sultans as their spiritual leaders and the successors to the Messenger of Allah, Prophet Muhammad. Not only in the respected shrines of Mecca and Medina, but everywhere in the world where Islam is followed, in the sermons of Friday and Eid prayers, benedictions are said for their dignity and their victories and conquests. The Sharif of Mecca himself, when he received the edict from Sultan Selim, without any debate or disputation, bowed his head in acceptance and gave the order that the name of the Sultan of Turkey be included in the supplications as the Islamic Caliphate. From that day till now, no Sharif of Mecca has deviated from this practice of veneration for the Ottoman Caliphate. Sharif Hussein himself considered the Ottoman Sultan as the legitimate Caliph and Servant of the Noble Sanctuaries of Mecca and Medina and kept acknowledging his loyalty to him. For a while, the Sharif of Mecca could not refute the spiritual sovereignty of the Sultan of Turkey, but during the European War, for his false self-interest and selfish desires, he raised the banner of rebellion against the Islamic Caliph, whose Caliphate he had previously accepted for himself as well as for all of the Islamic world. This rebellion was not only a violation of ethical laws but of Islamic faith and the spirit of religious education itself, and the Prophet's clear and concise rulings were violated."

Following that, it was demonstrated through Quranic verses and *Hadith* that if someone rebelled against or turned away from the Caliph, war was obligatory against them. About the authority of the Caliph over Islam's holy places, it has been written that:

"The Islamic Caliph's first and foremost duty is the protection of the holy shrines. The correct and real essence of protection can be nothing else but that the Sultan has complete and irrefutable control over the holy shrines and these shrines be kept safe and secure from any intervention by non-Muslims.

"All of the Islamic world's unshakeable faith and settled word is that from the time of Sultan Selim till now, the Ottoman Empire has fulfilled its duties toward the holy shrines of Islam with most excellence.

"The veracity of the claim by the Muslims that no one other than they have the right to decide who is the true Caliph has already been settled by the British government in an announcement. The clear and concise words that Lord Robert Cecil used on November 29, 1917, in response to a question from Mr. King in the House of Commons, are reflected in the following excerpt.

> *'His Majesty's Government has never deviated from the opinion that the matter of the Caliphate is such that it can be settled only by the opinion of the Muslims.'*

Dr. Ansari went on to forcefully refute that faith in the blessed Islamic Caliphate is an obstacle to nationalism and Hindu-Muslim unity. He stated:

"It is our unshakeable faith that a true Muslim will be a true nationalist. If we express solidarity with the Muslims of Turkey and Iran, we have proved with our actions that we also stand in solidarity with our compatriots, and those of them who are in other countries are no less. That pursuer of truth, Ahmed Mohamed Cachalia, was a Muslim of India itself who kept fighting in South Africa for a long time and kept on fighting till the end for our rights as a truthful deputy to that brave heart standard bearer Mr. Gandhi."

This presidential address lit up the hearts of the Muslims, and the pro-British newspapers and people argued over it for a long time. But that notwithstanding, the one conclusion that can be drawn from this address is that the Muslims had the yoke of slavery to the British around their necks. And now they had started to ponder the struggle to get out of the hold of this kind of thinking.

After that, a convention of religious scholars of Bengal was held in Chattogram under the presidency of Maulana Azad Subhani, which has been mentioned earlier. It was the first time that the Islamic scholars, including Maulana Abdul Bari, stepped into the political arena by participating in the League.

In that convention of Muslim League, whose presidential address by Dr. Ansari has been presented earlier, it is observed that the first resolution was one of loyalty to the British government followed by a protest against it regarding the occupation of Jerusalem and Najaf al-Ashraf by British forces. One proposal that was accepted was that the announcement made by His Majesty's Government that the matter of the Islamic Caliphate can be settled only by the Muslims themselves should be borne in mind.

The English Plot in Arab Countries

In India, the Muslims were bringing their anxiety and restlessness to the forefront along with their loyalty to the British government, and were organizing rallies and submitting petitions. And the English weren't heedless of these happenings. They wanted to push a deceptive narrative regarding public opinion. Consistent with that narrative, and as a result of their plotting, a delegation of Palestinian people under the leadership of Sheikh Sulaiman Taji Farouqi was convened and presented itself to *Malik al-Hijaz* (Sharif of Mecca). Addressing Sharif Hussein, he stated:

> *"We have traversed a difficult path and coped with the hardship of a voyage not only to bless our eyes with the vision of the founder of the Islamic government, the builder of the empire who will be the first Arab emperor in the history of the world, whose head holds the wreath of credit for bringing the Arab nation to life, awakening the Arabs from their slumber, and breathing a new spirit of valor and honor in them.*

> *"The building that the Holy Prophet (peace and blessings of Allah be upon him) laid the foundation of, and which was destroyed by alien Ajami hands, may the Almighty keep your honor safe and well for saving it from falling down. In fact, we took this long and arduous journey to*

impress upon his honor that the people of Palestine, who are among the finest of the creed of Prophet Muhammad, who have love for you in their hearts, and who are willing to die in order to comply with your orders at all times, earnestly pray that our neighboring nations who freed us from the hands of the Turks in the name of peace and justice, God forbid do not entangle us in the same trouble again."

Around the same time, the Sharif of Mecca published a manifesto in *Al Qibla*, a newspaper with an Arabist and Islamist ideology, the translation of which is as follows:

"O'Lord, I praise thee and give thanks for your infinite presence, the gift of your unlimited blessing, and for the last Prophet of divine mercy, peace be upon him. In the past days I have received numerous letters in which I have been addressed with the honorific of a ruler and leader of believers. There is no doubt that this is among the special features of my respectable nation, but since this honorific and title is synonymous with word Caliphate, the discussions about which have been repeatedly published in my proclamations in this newspaper Al Qibla itself, therefore it is my request to these honorable gentlemen to address me in their letters with the same words which the Arabs of Iraq, Yemen, Aleppo, and Syria have used to express their fealty to me. The blessings of God Almighty and All Powerful give me hope that the people's thoughts and expectations from me are true and are fulfilled, and in any case, the divine help be with us and them."

This was the game being played by the English. They could not refute the Caliphate, and that is why they were projecting the dream of making Amir Habibullah the Islamic Caliph while simultaneously suggesting the same to the Sharif of Mecca. The manifesto of the Sharif of Mecca is a prime example of the art of desire and of hypocrisy.

When a man came to see Maulana Mahmud Hasan in an Arabic attire during the time the foundation stone of Jamia Millia Islamia was being laid, he remarked that he hated that attire because it was the attire of traitors.

▌ The Paris Peace Conference

The Peace Conference in Paris had started doing its work from January 24, 1919 when matters of the world in general and of Turkey in particular needed to be decided. Prior to the start of this conference, the League of Nations had not yet been established. The president of the conference was the French Prime Minister Monsieur Clemenceau. The conference involved diplomats from 32 countries and nationalities. The five major powers (France, Britain, Italy, the U.S. and Japan) controlled the Conference, although it was dominated by the "Big Four" with Japan playing a minor role. Proposals were made to establish various sub-committees as well.

The representation of nations other than the major powers in these sub-committees caused some resentment among the delegates from other nations. Belgium demanded that it have two representatives in the League of Nations and labor committees and one representative in the ports, riverways, reforms, and reparations committees. The Brazil representative demanded representation in the League of Nations' committee. Canada said that a permanent seat among the major powers in the Council of the League of

Nations as a representative of the smaller nations was more important and necessary for them. Serbia demanded the same representation in every committee as Belgium. Greece and Czechoslovakia asked for their representatives to be in every committee. Portugal said it should have a representative in the reform and corrections committee. Romania asked that their representatives be taken into the ports and ocean ways committee of the League of Nations. Siam stated that it was deeply associated with the matters that were going to be decided in the committees. China asked for a seat at the League of Nations and stated that 150,000 of its men were in the British forces present in France.

In reply, Monsieur Clemenceau stated that in the war there were a total of two million soldiers from the five major powers and hundreds of thousands of them were killed, and as such they were more entitled to determine the future of the world. But regarding the League of Nations, he deemed it proper to give representation to smaller nations as well to get a more unified peace and security.

India was considered an integral part of Britain and was not mentioned at all. This was the Peace Conference on which the Muslims of India had pinned their faith as well, where the power of making decisions was being given to the powerful. And rewards were being solicited. Monsieur Clemenceau had shrugged off the smaller nations with the argument that super powers had sent two million soldiers to the battlefield and lost hundreds of thousands. The argument was that if they could win wars without needing anyone's help, then why should they care about the Hindu and Muslim slaves in India. However, as will be shown later, for a long time the Muslims had the thought wrapped around them that demands could be made of the Peace Conference.

The delegation of the Palestinian people and the announcement by the Sharif of Mecca were enough to sow deception. Along with that, the English were inciting the Shia and the Ahmadiyya communities to voice their opposition to the Khilafat Movement. To entangle the minds of the people and to create an ambiguity about the matter of Caliphate, they had encouraged their faithful servants to cast it as a controversial one.

A proposal to establish the League of Nations was presented by Mr. Wilson, the American President. The details had already been concocted. The intent was to conquer the world but it had to be legitimized through the League of Nations as an endeavor for peace and justice. Allama Iqbal has exposed the secret of this reality in these couplets:

Let's get to the heart of the matter
The pains of the world are new

I don't know much more except some shroud-thieves
Have formed an association to distribute graves

Mr. Wilson was a professor of the philosophy of law. In 1912, he was elected President of the United States from the Democratic Party. In the war of 1914-18, he was initially inclined to remain neutral and intervened to try and end the war. In November 1916 he was reelected President and in April 1917, in an address to a special joint session of the United States Congress, he spoke of the need for the United States to enter the war to "make the world safe for democracy."

On January 8, 1918, in a speech to the United States Congress, he articulated his famous Fourteen Points to bring peace and security to the world. But he was unable to get his Fourteen Points accepted by the Allied at the Peace Conference. Below are selected excerpts from his first speech at the Peace Conference.

> *"I may say without straining the point that we are not representatives of governments, but representatives of peoples. It will not suffice to satisfy governmental circles anywhere. It is necessary that we should satisfy the opinion of mankind...It is a solemn obligation on our part, therefore, to make permanent arrangements that justice shall be rendered and peace maintained...Is it not a startling circumstance, for one thing, that the great discoveries of science, that the quiet studies of men in laboratories, that the thoughtful developments which have taken place in quiet lecture rooms, have now been turned to the destruction of civilization...In coming into this war, the United States never for a moment thought that she was intervening in the politics of Europe or the politics of Asia or the politics of any part of the world. Her thought was that all the world had now become conscious that there was a single cause which turned upon the issues of this war. That was the cause of justice and of liberty for men of every kind and place."*

Was Mr. Wilson deceiving the world or was he being deceived? This debate is irrelevant to our discussion but his statements above are quite interesting in light of America's current attitudes. In any case, Lloyd George, Clemenceau and others verbally endorsed Mr. Wilson's speech; what else could they have done?

5

Petitions from the Loyalists to the British Crown

Meeting of the Firangi Mahal Society of Supporters of Islam

In early February of 1919, the *Anjuman Muid-al-Islam* (Society of Supporters of Islam) of Firangi Mahal had a meeting presided by Maulana Abdul Bari *Saheb* in which it was decided that from the perspective of Islamic decrees, there was no Caliph but the Sultan of Turkey, and from the perspective of Sharia, the Islamic canonical law, in the matter of the Caliphate, other than the Muhammadan nation, the opinion of a non-Muslim has no effect. Wherever the Muslims had raised their voices in this matter, they had always been strictly consistent with the Sharia, and this meeting ratified that stance. It was also decided that the society agreed with the proposal that a decree relating to the powers of the Caliphate be drafted in consultation with legal advisers and signed by the religious scholars of Arab and Islamic countries, and sent to the attention of the Governor General and the Secretary of State for India. This would make it evident that the thoughts expressed by Islamic societies were consistent with Sharia, and if any person issued any orders contrary to these they would not be considered compliant with Islamic law and the government should not have any misconceptions. The resolution passed in this meeting was as follows:

> *"This meeting, recognizing our submission to religious tolerance and expressing our loyalty to His Majesty's Government, asserts that the affiliation of Islamic countries in general and Islam's holy shrines in particular, which includes Constantinople with the seat of the Islamic Caliphate, is a mandate set in stone from an Islamic perspective. Therefore, in the spirit of this Islamic mandate, this assembly beseeches His Majesty's Government with all its might to use its access to and influence on the Peace Conference for the purpose of restoring to the Honorable Sultan, with his precedent rights over them, the countries that were removed from his empire in this war. Otherwise, without this restoration, any peace cannot satisfy the Muslims.*

The same expression of loyalty and the same expectation from the British government that it would use its influence in the Peace Conference in favor of the Muslims to fulfill their promises as in Dr. Ansari's presidential address to the reception committee of the All-India Muslim League Convention are evident here. And with these expectations, the same restlessness, anxiety, and search for a path forward remained conspicuous at the forefront.

Petition of London-Based Gentlemen

The same modus operandi was adopted in London by His Highness Sir Agha Khan, Right Honorable Sir Amir Ali, Mr. Muhammad Marmaduke Pickthall, Mr. Abbas Ali Baig, Mr. Abdullah Ibne Khan Bahadur Yusuf Ali, Mr. Rafiq,

Mr. MAH Ispahani, etc. as well. Along with 30 other gentlemen, they gave a memorandum to Mr. Balfour, Foreign Secretary in the British government, to which he gave quite a dangerous response. In the memorandum was written:

1. *We the undersigned Muslim subjects of His Majesty respectfully wish to present this petition to all of His Majesty's Government that we have read with much worry and apprehension the proposals that have been presented in various newspapers by some irresponsible parties regarding the future of Constantinople. These proposals are of the sort that suggest taking Constantinople from the hands of its present rulers and giving it into governance by some Christian governments or some Christian empire. Therefore, we consider it our duty to inform you at our earliest that doing so would imply a breakdown of the principles on which the Allied entered the war and it would cause not just the Muslims of India, but the Muslims of the entire world to develop emotions of anxiety and restlessness.*

2. *In the past four centuries, a grand revolution has taken place in Constantinople and now it is an Islamic city in every regard. The entire city is filled with Islamic institutions and every corner is filled with Islamic monuments. Most of its inhabitants are ethnic Turks who are Muslims by faith, something that was recognized recently in the House of Commons.*

3. *Recently, the Prime Minister declared that "the Government of Turkey shall remain in place and Constantinople shall remain the capital of all its territories." Muslims, who have helped the Sultanate with physical and moral support, are now hopeful that the*

same principles of union and freedom shall be applied to Turkey as to the European nations. If a different treatment is meted out to Turkey, then it will have a very adverse effect and the Muslims will feel that while they adhered to those lofty principles in remaining loyal and fighting shoulder to shoulder on every occasion, they got nothing in return and Turkey was not treated according to these principles merely because it was an Islamic Sultanate.

4. *In Asia, from the northern border of Syria to the Aegean and Black Seas, and to the southern border of Azerbaijan, there is an estimated population of 19 million people who are Turks in ethnicity and Muslims in religion. The region of Thrace has the same ethnic makeup. The population there is made up mostly of Turks. With utmost respect, we request that this entire Sultanate, including Constantinople which is its capital, be allowed to stay in the hands of the Turkish nation, as per the declaration of the Prime Minister.*

The religious scholars, in particular Maulana Mahmud Hasan, had more insight and foresight in these matters, considered the English their biggest enemies, and held no hopes from them. But this was the transitional period of the Khilafat Movement and the time was about to come when one could say that:

The time has come for the unveiling of truth, a common sight it will be

Silence was the veil of which, that secret will be revealed

Reply from the Secretary of State for India

Toward the end of February 1919, the Secretary of State for India replied to some of the proposals of the Muslim League sent to him, whose text was as follows:

> *"In the matter of the Caliphate, His Majesty's Government's views are the same which it has expressed repeatedly and they are based on the opinion that this matter is of the kind which needs to be decided by the Muslims alone without intervention from others. I would like to take the opportunity to strongly refute the suggestion, made by the Muslim League in one of their resolutions, that the government has reneged on its promises related to the holy places. In the days when His Majesty's forces were occupying the lands where the holy places are situated, not only were these promises kept word for word, but means were adopted, and are being adopted, that in our time occupying those lands no harm comes to the holy shrines. In the end, I consider it necessary to also say that the opinions of the Indians and Muslims relating to the matters that will be decided at the Peace Conference are looked upon with much respect by His Majesty's Government and it gives permission to the Government of British India to direct the representatives of His Majesty at the Peace Conference to consider these opinions.*

The Muslims had another opportunity for a fresh deception. They were disappointed, of course, that they were not given representation at the Peace Conference, which they had demanded.

The British Government was intoxicated with arrogance. As we have shown earlier, the Muslims were content to express their loyalty everywhere and present petitions, but banning gatherings, imposing section 144 of the penal code (unlawful assembly), or fear-mongering and harassment at gatherings by machine gun toting English soldiers had become an everyday affair. Despite that, branches of the Khilafat Committee had been established in every province and within the provincial committees in districts. There were hardly any towns or villages where voices were not being raised for the cause of the blessed Islamic Caliphate. Even the sycophants of the government and the eternal slaves were forced to verbally support the call for survival of the Islamic Caliphate and security of the holy places, and they would use intricate methods to drum up support for the British government's charade of keeping their promises. They would often reiterate that there was nothing to be gained from unnecessary agitation and the nation would only be hurt by that. They would either say that the British government should be trusted to keep their promises or that we should only pray. The day was not far when this dust and trash was going to be washed away in the flood of the people's passions.

Jews and Palestine

As mentioned earlier, by promising the Jews a homeland in Palestine, the English won their support in WWI. The British government set up a Royal Commission to look into this matter, but it was only for show. The Jews were confident that a decision would be in their favor, and there were many reasons for that. One was the influence of the Jews in America and the important role they played in its presidential elections.

Second, by giving the Jews a homeland in Palestine, the British could entangle the entire Arab world in a never ending war so that they would never have the opportunity to organize and make conscious decisions. When the Israeli government was formed, a former American President had said, "This means that a constant war will go on." The confidence that the Jews had can be gauged from a press wire that was broadcast on March 2, 1919: "The Jews have announced they are confident that the demands they have presented at the Peace Conference, in which they have expressed a desire for a Jewish national government to be established in Palestine, will be accepted. Details are yet to be completed but success from a Jewish point of view is apparent. When the Jewish delegation had left the conference room, Mr. Balfour sent them a message congratulating its members on their success."

The French representative at the conference, Mr. Tardieu, said in a statement that France did not object to Britain establishing a ruling authority in Palestine through the League of Nations.

Comments in Newspapers

The comments in newspapers at the time, which continued till April, have been included here since describing the details of each and every event would be difficult.

> *"We see that there is no big city in India where everyone from the scholars of Islam to the ordinary citizen has not paid attention to current affairs. As a result, the meetings organized by the scholars and academics in Lucknow, Calcutta, Delhi, Moradabad, Bareilly, and many other cities followed by Hyderabad, Sindh, and Bombay, have proven that the Muslims of India are talking about the*

issues of Caliphate, survival of Turkey, and the holy places with one voice. The resolutions presented and passed at the Bombay meeting involved discussions on, besides the matter of Caliphate, topics that included Mecca, Medina, Jerusalem, Najaf al-Ashraf, Karbala, Kazmain Sharif, Baghdad, survival of the Sultanate of Turkey, and Constantinople remaining in the hands of the Turks. There was consensus that all these places should remain under the Turkish Sultanate and the Peace Conference should give consideration to the Arabian Peninsula and the holy places, the boundaries of which have been clearly defined in Islamic jurisprudence, to remain under the authority of the Turkish Sultanate. Since the Sultan of Turkey is the Prophet's Caliph, and because the British Empire is the largest Muslim empire, it is imperative for the British ministers to try on a permanent basis to maintain political relations between the British Empire and the Islamic Sultanate and to strive for unity and agreement based on principles of faith and trust.

"In all of these movements, prominent Muslims of Bombay participated, such as Maulvi Rafiuddin, Barrister Maulvi Abdul Raouf, Mr. Muhammad Mian, Mr. Rahmatullah Karimbhai, Syed Muhammad Yusuf Isfahani, Mirza Ali Muhammad Khan, Mr. Badruddin Abdulla, Mr. Abdul Husain Janjaria, Maulvi Abdul Munam (preacher, Jama Masjid Bombay), Honorable Mr. Sharif Devji Kanji, Mr. Hadi Tayyabji, Mr. Muhammad Hasan, Mr. Syed Ghulam Muqba Muhammad Rafi, and Mr. Haji Abdul Karim. The meeting in Bombay was presided by Mian Jan Muhammad Chotani. A significant and important resolution was presented in this meeting asking for the

Muslims of India to let their opinions and emotions known to the Peace Conference, and that the best way to do that would be to send a representative of the Muslims.

"In the meeting of the scholars of Sindh, Maulvi Khair Imamuddin was presiding. In that meeting too, resolutions of a similar nature were presented and the discussions were very passionate. A telegram was sent to His Honor The Viceroy, asking that the government withdraw their troops from the Arabian Peninsula."

Later in the article, there is mention of the loyalty of Muslims and praising His Honor, the Viceroy, he is asked to give representation to the Muslims at the Peace Conference.

"If we take the word of His Excellency Mr. Montagu that arrangements are being made for the security of our rights at the Peace Conference, there is no doubt that all of the world's Muslims will bow their heads with respect in front of the British Crown that it upheld till the very end the justice and equality for which it fought this war. If that is not the case, the Muslims of the world will be right in saying that the Allied said one thing but did another."

The Thought of Taking a Delegation All Over the World

At a conference in Bombay, a proposal was accepted to convene a general convention of the Indian Muslim community in Delhi to have a discussion on all current affairs and put together a delegation that would present itself to His Honor The Viceroy to impress upon him the sentiments of the Muslims. Just then,

Maulana Abdul Bari, Nawab Zulqadr Jang, and Dr. Ansari presented a proposal to take a delegation of Muslims to all the Islamic nations in order to gauge and observe the general conditions and sentiment of the Muslims there. The objective was also to get a consensus among the Muslims and put pressure on the Peace Conference. This delegation could not be put together, but the same conclusions can be drawn from this effort, i.e. the Muslims were in a state of deep anxiety and had expectations of justice from the Peace Conference.

Nadwatul Ulama Lucknow's Proposal

Nadwatul Ulama at its Belgaum conference accepted the following proposal.

1. *"This conference of Nadwatul Ulama, which is a representation of the religious scholars, considers it their religious duty to state that according to the rules of the religion, it is necessary that all the holy places of Hijaz, Jerusalem, Karbala, Najaf al-Ashraf, etc., with which the Muslims of the world have religious affiliations, should remain under direct control of an autonomous Islamic authority."*

2. *"This conference of Nadwatul Ulama is thankful from the bottom of their hearts for the end of the war and for the blessing of peace and security once again and hope that the British government, under the shadow of which 100 million Muslims live, will particularly use the reasons and bases that would express the sentiments of the Muslims at the Peace Conference in a true and clear way and full consideration be given to the interests of Muslims so that the world may have a lasting peace."*

Darul Uloom Deoband's Attitude

The distinguished scholars of Deoband's Darul Uloom, with their insight and vision, declaring the English to be their enemy, had been carrying out a protracted practical struggle for the survival and security of the Islamic Caliphate and freedom for India. Maulana Muhammad Qasim Nanautavi, along with his religious mentor, Haji Imdadullah Muhajir Makki and hundreds of his supporters and helpers were resolute in this struggle and had wagered everything on it. The century's foremost leader, Shaykh al-Hind Maulana Mahmud Hasan, was still in prison in Malta. All eyes were on Maulana Muhammad Qasim Nanautavi and Deoband alone could do justice to the expression of these sentiments.

The Khilafat Delegation and Mahatma Gandhi

By 1918, Gandhiji had overshadowed the politics of India. He had selected those people from whom he wanted to draw support. As a consequence, he went to meet Maulana Abul Kalam Azad in Ranchi but the government did not allow the meeting. He was in constant contact with the Ali brothers. When Maulana Mohammad Ali came from Chhindwara to Rampur for two weeks, Gandhiji immediately came to Rampur to meet him. He was constantly visiting Maulana Abdul Bari in Firangi Mahal. That was how Gandhiji worked – he would select a few top people and would endeavor to make them like-minded. Hence, later on when he started the non-cooperation movement on a grand scale in India, he picked Pandit Motilal Nehru, Hasan Imam, and CR Das. Hasan Imam could not fully join him because, despite agreeing on principles with

Gandhiji, he was not willing to give up his law practice, but he did give his daughter to this cause, while Motilal Nehru and CR Das shook the English up by their roots.

A poem on Hasan Imam was published in the *Zamindar* dated February 20, 1922 under the pseudonym *Janab Muslim*. This was actually Maulana Zafar Ali Khan's pseudonym, who was in Montgomery jail at the time.

> *That morning is no morning, that evening is no evening*
> *A string of fresh calamities is not a message pleasing*

> *Someone was pulled to the gallows post, someone put under the*
> *sword*
> *These are the arrangements of the rulers, reprisals they are not*

> *Who is it that is not captive of the English these days?*
> *Is it not Abul Kalam Azad, or is it not CR Das?*

> *With surprise a friend of mine said to me*
> *That Hasan Imam is not included among the free*

> *Why is it that when they are no less freethinkers?*
> *When defeat is not among the active preparations?*

> *If cooperation is forbidden for an insignificant like me*
> *Then why is it not forbidden for top leaders like thee?*

> *Not used to prisons these leaders of the country*
> *An Imam is not included among the beads of a rosary*

The incarcerated and prisoners of the English were released through a royal decree. Maulana Mohammad Ali was released along with others at the end of December 1919. A few days later, on January 1, 1920, Maulana Abul Kalam Azad was also released.

Gandhiji had earlier expressed his full empathy and support for the Khilafat Movement. On January 20, 1920 a meeting was held in Delhi in which Lokmanya Tilak and other Congress leaders promised their full support to the stance of the Muslims. Lala Lajpat Rai (Punjab), Bipin Chandra Pal (Bengal), and many others also came together and there was no difference between the Hindus and Muslims on the matter of the Caliphate, which was a huge achievement. The proposals that had been accepted regarding sending a delegation to the Viceroy and the Peace Conference, at the time regarding the matter of the imprisonment of Maulana Azad and the Ali brothers, were revisited and it was decided to send this delegation anyway.

A delegation was put together and Maulana Mohammad Ali drafted a memorial which was signed by a number of prominent leaders. In "India Wins Freedom," Maulana Azad has written[16]:

> *"The delegation met the Viceroy. I had signed the petition but I did not join the delegation. This was because I felt that the matters had gone beyond petitions and delegations."*

According to Maulana Azad's account, in reply to the memorial, the Viceroy said only that if a Muslim delegation wanted to go and present the viewpoint of the Indian Muslims to the British government, the government would provide all facilities to such a delegation. But he expressed his inability to personally do anything in this regard[16].

This was the first setback for the Muslims and all the hopes that the Muslims, who were loyal to the British government, had pinned on His Excellency the Viceroy's stated support and blessings were shattered. Some people started to despair at these futile endeavors.

But false hopes and ineffectual wishes nurtured over centuries never leave one's side. The delegation that was put together was led by Maulana Mohammad Ali, had as its members Syud Hossain, Maulana Syed Sulaiman Nadvi, and Abul Kasim, and its secretary was Hasan Muhammad Hayat. Syud Hossain was with Bombay Chronicle at the time and was later appointed independent India's first ambassador to Egypt. The secretary, Hasan Muhammad Hayat Punjabi, was a distinguished alumnus of Aligarh, where he was popularly known as 'Lord Hayat'[17]. Later he took up residence in Bhopal.

Activities of the Khilafat Delegation

The Viceroy had stated previously that the delegation would reach London so late that it was unlikely it would get an opportunity to say what it wanted, but Maulana Mohammad Ali was intent on delivering an ultimatum. On February 22, 1920 members of the delegation reached Venice, from where Maulana Mohammad Ali immediately sent a telegram to the Secretary of State for India and to the Prime Minister urging

---

16 Maulana Abul Kalam Azad, "India Wins Freedom," pp 8-9

17 "Mohammad Ali: A Few Pages From His Personal Diary," Compiled by Maulana Abdul Majid Daryabadi

that the delegation should be given a full and fair hearing before any decisions were taken. The telegram also thanked Mr. Montagu for arranging a welcome for them in Venice, about whose illness they were very sorry to hear.

Because Mr. Montagu was ill, his place was taken by Mr. Fisher, with whom the delegation had its first meeting. Maulana Mohammad Ali, passionately stating the religious significance of Caliphate and the religious jurisprudence basis for the control of the Islamic holy places, presented the following demands.

1. *The Turkish Caliphate should be maintained.*
2. *The holy places, i.e. Mecca, Medina, Jerusalem, and all the holy shrines should be under the control of the Caliph, as they were before the war. In such an event, the Muslims too will be happy that their loyalty was rewarded with maintaining the same position for the Caliphate while securing respect for the holy places and shrines in the Arabian Peninsula.*

Maulana Mohammad Ali's command over the English language was apparent in this speech. Moreover, he was an exemplary orator. He presented his stance very elegantly, but the foundational principles of his arguments were also apparent. For example, he stated:

"Our mission is of a double character. It is our duty to represent matters to His Majesty's Government because we are his subjects; and it is our duty to represent matters to the Caliph, who is the Commander of the Faithful. Both of these duties we would like to observe."

After that, Mr. Fisher gave a procedural response in which he gave them some hope and raised some despair. Regarding a meeting with the Prime Minister, he said:

> *"I hope that before you return to India you may have an opportunity of meeting the Prime Minister and of laying your views before him. As you know, a Conference is taking place at the present time. The Prime Minister is meeting the statesmen of the Allied countries and many important issues are being discussed. Mr. Lloyd George's time is very much occupied, and I cannot promise you that he will be able to see you, but I hope that he may be able to do so."*

Maulana Mohammad Ali, as was his habit, disregarded this snub and went on with what he had to say. He maintained this habit all his life. In the Karachi Trial as well as in compelling Jawahar Lal Nehru for a religious debate, he never failed to maintain his doggedness even at the height of his passion.

Meeting with Mr. Lloyd George

Although Mr. Fisher exerted the power of his high position in stating that he could not promise that Mr. Lloyd George would be able to see the delegation, why would the head of the empire not meet a delegation of his "loyal subjects" who had sailed across the seven seas to ask for their due in return for their loyalty and service? Maulana Mohammad Ali was the same way in front of Lloyd George as well. He kept on insisting on his religious duty. Lloyd George refuted all his positions with a logical argument. Still, he kept on insisting. He presented the viewpoint of the Muslims with much audacity. After all, he was a man of action in that sphere.

The beauty and elegance with which he presented the Islamic basis of the Caliphate and the demands of the Muslims were unmatched and perhaps no one else could have done justice. There is no doubt that he delivered the demands of the Muslims righteously, but how could the English let go of the opportunity to destroy the Muslim world that it had acquired so diligently and covertly over a century! When I read Maulana Mohammad Ali's forcefully reasoned and eloquent speeches, I remember a famous fable in which a religious scholar went to the emperor of the land and advised him to disband his army and to spend that money for the greater good of his people. What is the use of keeping an army? To take someone else's land or to cause bloodshed was the greatest sin. The emperor was a simple man and asked what would happen if someone attacked him? Maulana said he would be responsible for that. The emperor disbanded his army. When the neighboring emperor found out, he attacked. The emperor pleaded with Maulana to fulfill his promise and save his kingdom. Maulana loaded books of Quran, *Hadith*, and Islamic jurisprudence on a number of camels and took them to the attacking emperor. He welcomed the Maulana and met him with respect and honor. Maulana *Saheb* started his speech, saying that bloodshed and conquering the land of others were forbidden and those who do that shall be punished with hell. And in his admonition, he referenced a long sequence of quotes from the Quran, *Hadith*, and sayings of saints and repeatedly tried to impress upon the emperor the fear of God. The attacking emperor kept on listening to Maulana with respect. After a while, he asked to be excused so that he could go and conquer this country, and he would hear the rest of what the Maulana had to say at leisure when he got back. He instructed his courtiers to spare no effort in keeping Maulana comfortable and entertained. Maulana ran back to the emperor who had been attacked, who asked with fear in his voice what had happened. Maulana said to him, "There is no harm in losing only your land; the other one has lost his faith."

Disappointed with Lloyd George, Maulana Mohammad Ali started holding conferences with the British public and making speeches to smooth the process. He went to Paris and won French support for his position. With his legendary linguistic and scholarly excellence, he was replete with logical arguments. He also met with people from the Arabian Peninsula and tried to convince them to accept the authority of the Caliph. They would swear that they were not against the Caliph, but they were like the Kufis in Karbala whose tongues were with Hazrat Imam Hussain, but their swords were against him. Amir Faisal and Amir Abdullah were two sons of the Sharif of Mecca. They had both been enticed with promises of a crown and throne. The Sharif of Mecca had been shown dreams of becoming the Islamic Caliph. And all of them were on the payroll of Britain; they were not the kind who could be persuaded by logic. Amir Faisal had a statement published in support of the Caliphate, but this was sheer hypocrisy.

Maulana Mohammad Ali and his companions, after all their efforts which remained futile, returned to India in early October 1920. From the time they left, there was a suspense among those who were not familiar with the true purpose of the delegation. The late poet Akbar said in his witty style:

> *Sitting on the rugs of the mosque I can only pray*
> *Blessed be the sight of fairies to Sulaiman in Paris*

And Allama Iqbal says:

Do you not have knowledge of history?
That you have started to beg for Caliphate

If we do not purchase with our own blood
To the Muslim such sovereignty is a disgrace

I do not feel as much ashamed of being wounded
As in asking others for salve to heal my wounds

It can be said that nothing was achieved by that delegation, but the way that the Muslims were skirting the issue, it needed the jolt of a setback like this so that the ominous and humiliating fancy of Britain's "loyal subjects" could be expelled from their minds. There were, however, a number of great losses from that failure. First, India was missing the esteemed leadership of someone like Maulana Mohammad Ali at a delicate time. Second, there was a particular kind of bad name that was incurred by them. As soon as the delegation returned, the English, whose spies had known that accounts were not strictly kept during their travels, rustled up their pawns to demand the accounting from Maulana Mohammad Ali. After all, for a person of the unrestrained stature of Maulana Mohammad Ali, how was it possible to keep a detailed account of the expenditure? Lord Hayat was a carefree man from Aligarh, but it was his job as secretary to keep the accounts. Maulana Mohammad Ali, as the leader of the delegation, was busy with so many other things that he could not have kept the accounts even if he wanted to, and neither was that his responsibility. But he was the one asked. The answer Maulana Mohammad Ali gave was, "I will give an accounting only to God on

Judgement Day." The response was, "What if He doesn't ask and forgives your sins without any accounting? You have to give the accounting to us." The traitors to the community and loyalists to the government were emboldened. They started to spread all kinds of rumors. The way in which this accounting was compiled and all the clarifications that Syed Sulaiman Nadvi gave on behalf of Maulana Mohammad Ali reflected the low morals of some in the community, and the disrespect it created for this great servant of the community is heart-rending. Syed Sulaiman Nadvi gave statements regarding the kinds of expenditures incurred during the travel, saying that rooms needed to be booked to hold meetings and conferences, how the currency exchange rates were changing all the time, etc. After all the accounting was compiled, the miscreants had to eat crow. The matter ended but did great damage before it was settled.

The words I have used here need explanation to be fair to the community at large. This talk about delivering the accounting was started by a few miscreant elements who used to act at the direction of the government and were protected by it. This did not diminish Maulana Mohammad Ali's stature and dignity by even an iota. The damage and the mudslinging that ensued were due to Maulana Mohammad Ali himself. He had two great weaknesses. One was that he had no control over his tongue. Whatever came to his mind, he would say it, which hurt people sometimes. Many people have written about him and they consider it his virtue. They draw conclusions of his pure heartedness and fearlessness from it. I do not agree with that at all. It was not Maulana Mohammad Ali's virtue that he called the satirist poet Zafar Ali Khan a traitor. And threatened such a statesman as Khwaja Hasan Nizami with "*Khatm-e-*

Khwaajagii," or the conclusion of his distinction. He spoke such inadmissible words in undue praise of Firangi Mahal that they are not fit to be put down on paper, although he had pledged his fealty as a disciple there. In this way, he had set up a front that was opposed to him and they started repeating all the wrong things about him. The second weakness in Maulana Mohammad Ali was that he just did not know how to overlook and forgive. Whenever some issue was raised against him, he would double down on confrontation. And then there was his pen and its biting sarcasm. In contrast, Gandhiji's style was the exact opposite. He would never say anything in his defense and would say that every person was entitled to their opinion about him. Why should he try to change their opinion, he would say. Maulana Abul Kalam Azad was the same way. It is a shame that this great man remained mired all his life in arguments and conflicts, and in defending himself both intrinsically and personally due to these minor weaknesses.

Maulana Shaukat Ali was made of completely different pieces. Very often people considered him less scholarly, but he was very much a consciously sensible and worthy man. His speeches were brief, as opposed to the long ones that had made all of India weary. Even Gandhiji once publicly said that Maulana Mohammad Ali promises to speak for five minutes, but when he gets up to speak, he sits down only after an hour and a half or two. Anyway, because Gandhiji said it, Maulana Mohammad Ali took it in one ear and out the other. Had anyone else said it, he would have been in deep trouble with Maulana Mohammad Ali. Maulana Shaukat Ali was an organized leader. The way he could systematically put together a movement was just a part of him. Perhaps there was no one like him in India. For instance, at the third convention of the All-India

Khilafat Conference, which was held on December 31, 1919 concurrently with and at the same location as the Amritsar Congress convention, the name of Maulana Shaukat Ali was proposed for president by Maulana Abdul Bari and seconded by Maulana Muhammad Dawood Ghaznavi, Maulana Fazlur Rehman (Editor, *Akhuwat*), Honorable Abul Qasim (Calcutta), Seth Haji Ahmed Siddiq Khatri, and Mr. Musa (Rangoon). Maulana Shaukat Ali used to give brief but comprehensive speeches that were extremely effective. On the one hand, we can read the long speech delivered by Maulana Mohammad Ali at the Amritsar Congress convention. On the other hand, take a look at Maulana Shaukat Ali's speech at the Muslim League:

"I had taken a vow that if ever this constellation was in trouble, I would even give my life for it. But when difficulties struck this constellation, I could not do anything. I am to be blamed for this and I am being punished, and will continue to be punished, for this fault. Whatever we have done for ourselves, we have done with our own hands, because we gave priority to the Prophet's way in dealing with the matters of our time. Whatever punishment we got; it was because of that. I speak the truth when I say that we are deserving of much harsher punishment than this. I speak the truth when I say I was deserving of being hanged when all I got was imprisonment. I ask you one question – what betterment did you achieve from this way of doing things? If you are willing to ignore the way of God and Prophet in achieving your worldly power, then you and I cannot be together. What we have to do now is for all the scholars to get together and decide what is our duty from a Sharia point of view. It is not difficult at all to pass resolutions. I had written a line to my brother,

respected Ali, on which I was questioned. The line was that there is no Muslim who does not desire a victory for Turkey. I asked him to ponder this question before he responds: if we have religious freedom, should every Muslim not say that and shouldn't he have the right? We should dispatch a delegation to His Excellency and the Viceroy and convey to them that if the situation remains the same, we have two choices: hijrat or jihad, migration or struggle. Our delegation should also go to the Islamic Caliph and apologize to him for neglecting our duty."

The speech ended with the applause echoing. How brief, comprehensive, and effective. And such a mapping of the situation and a plan going forward that my eyes get moist even today when I read that speech.

It needs to be said about the courage, bravery, ability, and hard work with which Maulana Mohammad Ali fulfilled this duty that he was righteous toward his commitments to the leadership of the delegation. It was a part of him and he managed to rattle the British Ministers, British public, the statesmen of the Allied countries, leaders of the French Government, leaders of Iraq and Arabia, Amir Faisal, etc. There was a fire burning in the heart of Maulana Mohammad Ali. When he could not convince the British Prime Minister Lloyd George and other members of the British government by reasoning with them, he appealed to the British public, took help from those among the English who were his supporters, and argued and confronted those who opposed him. And since Lloyd George's argument was that that Arabs themselves didn't want to live under the Turks and hence should not be deprived of the right to self-determination, Maulana

Mohammad Ali met with Arab leaders and made every effort to convince them to stay in a Turkish federation while keeping their right to self-determination. Syed Sulaiman Nadvi, a master of Arab literature who spoke Arabic with the fluency of a mother tongue, was with him. This was very convenient for Maulana Mohammad Ali but the matter could not be settled with debates and discussion. Driven by its pride in its strength, Britain was working on a well thought out scheme, while the Arabs were tied up in greed for money and power. The Sharif of Mecca, besides being given a lot of money, had been given the promise of making one son the emperor of Iraq and the other of Jordan. In his passion for the cause, Maulana Mohammad Ali could not gauge the situation and remained engaged in these hopeless endeavors and efforts. He also met the top statesmen of Allied countries such as France, but all to no avail. It did have the effect of rattling the conscience of the Allied and Arab countries; the matter was presented in the right form to India, Egypt, Afghanistan and all Islamic countries, and the atrocities of the Allied were exposed.

6

Maulana Azad's Efforts to Bring the Muslims from the Path of Religion into Politics

Allegiance to the Imamate

Maulana Abul Kalam Azad was released from jail in Ranchi on January 1, 1920 and was elected president of the Khilafat Conference in Calcutta. Abdur Razzaq Malihabadi, in his book *Zikr-e-Azad*, has declared this the first Khilafat Conference, but that is not true. The first Khilafat Conference was held in Delhi and was presided by Maulana Abdul Bari Firangi Mahali, and the second Khilafat Conference was held on November 23, 1919 in Delhi, presided by Maulvi Fazlul Haq. This was the third Khilafat Conference, which was held in February 1920 at Town Hall, Calcutta. There, Maulana Azad gave an extensive address on Khilafat, which was published soon after in book form and is still available in many places today.

On the second day of the conference, Maulana Azad laid the foundation of a scheme, about which his confidant Abdur Razzaq Malihabadi has written in *Zikr-e-Azad*:

"The abstract of Maulana's scheme was that the Muslims of India should be organized through the path of religion.

There should be an Imam of the Muslims and they should consider obedience to the Imam their religious duty. This invitation could be acceptable to the Muslims if they can be convinced through the Quran and Hadith that without an Imam their lives are un-Islamic and they will die in ignorance. When a large number of Muslims have accepted this, the Imam should make a covenant with the Hindus and declare jihad on the English. This joint force of Hindus and Muslims will defeat the English. But who will be that Imam? A respected and reliable person will have to be chosen for this position. A person who cannot be bought by the enemy at any price. Along with that, he will need to be prudent and truly comprehend the current situation. It is obvious that Maulana did not consider anyone other than his own self to be more suitable for the Imamate.

"*After that, it was decided that before taking the matter of Imamate public, an internal effort should be started to pledge allegiance to Maulana's Imamate, so that when this did become public, allegiance to the Imam would have been established. This would also put a check on jealousy and envy among the people, and the Muslims would agree on one Imam to free them of slavery.*

"*Maulana announced that the work to gather pledges of allegiance had already been started in other states. He asked me to take the responsibility for UP. I agreed, and he wrote a note in which he appointed me his Caliph and that I was the proxy for taking pledges of allegiance for him. The note was as follows:*

*In the name of Allah, The Most Gracious and
The Most Merciful*

*My brother Maulvi Abdur Razzaq Malihabadi has
pledged his allegiance to this Fakir. He is authorized
and the proxy to take pledges of allegiance and impart
teaching and guidance based on Sunnah on behalf of
the Fakir. Those seeking honest answers and pledging
allegiance to him would be pledging allegiance to the
Fakir. 'Va-al'aaqba lalmutqiin' – The (blessed) End is
for the god-fearing and pious.*

Fakir Abul Kalam, God-willing

Shaaban 4, 1338 AH (probably April 23, 1920 AD)

Malihabadi then writes that Maulana Azad also wrote down
the draft of the pledge of allegiance, which is reproduced
below:

*I pledge allegiance to Hazrat Muhammad, Allah's
peace and blessings be upon him, and to his caliphs and
deputies, and that:*

1. *Till the last moments of my life, if I am able to, I shall
   adhere to the beliefs and actions signified by the words
   "There is no God but Allah, and Muhammad is the
   messenger of Allah."*
2. *I shall, if I am able to, pray five times a day, fast during
   Ramzan, give charity, and perform the Hajj pilgrimage.*
3. *I shall always, in whatever state my life is in, abide by
   goodness, stop badness, and be patient.*
4. *My friendships shall be on the path of Allah, and my
   enmities shall be on the path of Allah.*

5. *And I pledge that in every state of my life, more than my life, my possessions, my family, more than every blessing and every pleasure in this world, I shall cherish my beloved Allah, His Prophet, His Sharia, and His community of Muslims, and shall comply with the orders given in His path obediently as prescribed in the Quran and Sunnah.*

Later on, Malihabadi writes:

"Maulana said to me, 'A Muslim, whose heart is filled with goodness, has given me a large sum of money to carry out my work. From that, 50 rupees per month shall reach you too. For the time being, make Lucknow your base and start the work throughout the province.' Later on, it was discovered that the large sum of money that Maulana referred to was the Rs. 100,000 that Maulana Abdul Qadir Qasuri's son Mohammad Ali, MA had given to him."

According to Malihabadi's words, Maulana also told him of one of his ways of working: holding dinner parties. According to Maulana, "Whatever is spent on dinner parties, it takes many times more money to hold a rally for 10,000 people, but not one of those attending the rally can be relied upon. But with a modest expenditure of hosting ten people to dinner, all ten of them start paying attention to what we are saying."

Malihabadi writes that he tried that formula and found it efficacious.

On June 8, 1920 Shaykh al-Hind Maulana Mahmud Hasan arrived in Bombay after being released from detention in Malta. Malihabadi writes that around the same time, Maulana

Mahmud Hasan came to Lucknow for the first time and stayed at Firangi Mahal. Hence, Abdur Razzaq Malihabadi went there and took it upon himself to convince the two elders, i.e. Maulana Abdul Bari and Maulana Mahmud Hasan, to agree to Maulana Abul Kalam Azad becoming *Imam al-Hind*, the Imam of India, but both of them demurred. An extract from an ambiguous note by Maulana Abdul Bari is reproduced below:

"I inquired of Maulana Mahmud Hasan and he too doesn't appear supportive of it. Maulana Abul Kalam Azad Saheb is prepared and ready. I do not disapprove of his Imamate and am most willing to accept it, provided it doesn't cause differences in the party. Maulana is eminently worthy of it, but if the majority chose even an unworthy person to be a part of the Islamic family, they will find me most obedient and submissive. The truth is that I honestly don't want to launch this movement from my side nor do I want to appoint someone and take the responsibility of this action upon myself. I am but a loyal servant of this collective of Muslims; I do not have any more compulsions toward this movement. Upon you be peace. Slave-fakir, Abdul Bari."

When Maulana Abul Kalam got this letter, he wrote to Malihabadi, "I saw Maulvi Abdul Bari's letter. 'My friends are in pain, and so are we.' Please fold this saga from your mind, and keep on working. The organizations are complete in Punjab, Sindh, and Bengal." This letter from Maulana Azad is dated September 20, 1920.

Malihabadi has mentioned another letter to him from Maulana Azad[18] in which he writes, "In any case, our sphere of action is complete. Punjab, Sindh and Bengal are united in agreement and the work is going ahead at full steam. The wait for their (Maulana Abdul Bari, Maulana Mahmud Hasan, and Maulana Hasrat Mohani) decision was in vain and remains in vain." Malihabadi goes on to write: "However, in September 1920, Maulana ended his Imamate Movement and the importance of the matter abruptly diminished in his mind. Maulana has never mentioned the reason for that." However, Abdur Razzaq Malihabadi has expressed his opinion on the matter, and given his closeness to Maulana, it is worth examining.

> *"But Maulana Mohmmad Ali was an extremely diligent leader and had a very stormy temperament. His influence was rising very rapidly and he was not only opposed to Maulana Azad's Imamate but to Maulana personally. They had a lifelong rivalry as well. Naturally, Maulana Azad, who was extremely perceptive and cool-headed, had realized that confrontation with the Ali brothers would divide the Muslims. The class of modern minded Muslims were also with the brothers. Then, Firangi Mahal was also opposed, and although there was no opposition from Shaykh al-Hind Maulana Mahmud Hasan, the powerful lobby of Deoband did not side with Maulana Azad either. Under these circumstances, it was not wise to push the matter of Imamate to conclusion."*

This was the second failed endeavor. The Khilafat Delegation at least yielded one political benefit; because of it, the Muslims were able to free themselves of a major misconception.

---

18 Abdur Razzaq Malihabadi, *Zikr-e-Azad*, pp 39

And this was a milestone that had to be achieved to get to the next milestone. It took millions of people out of one era and into another. It annihilated false ideas and beliefs. It made the Muslims ready and willing to breathe freely and to strive for complete independence and a perfect struggle. The Imamate Movement remained in vain and Maulana Azad never mentioned this important religious duty again. It appeared that this matter of Sharia rode away on the waves of the Ganga-Jamuni culture of Hindu-Muslim unity, and the many involvements of Maulana Azad didn't give him time to keep up the struggle of preventing the Muslims of India to lead a life of 'ignorance' and 'transgression.' The truth appears to be that the Khilafat Movement did that work directly that Maulana wanted the Imamate Movement to do indirectly. And that is why Maulana didn't pursue it.

There is an interesting incident in this regard. On April 1, 1920 the pro-government weekly *Mashriq*, praying for a long life for *'Aa'la Hazrat Muhii-al-Millat Validain Haamii Al'uloom Nawab Mir Usman Ali Khan Farman Rivaae Mumlikat Aasafia'* on the occasion of his birthday, presented the proposal that *'Aa'la Hazrat Muhii-al-Millat Validain'* be given the position of *'Shaykh al-Islam'* and his deputies be appointed in every province and representatives in every city. In this way, on one hand there will be control over the thoughts of the public, and on the other the voice of the Muslims would be able to reach the government in a more responsible and efficient manner. A befitting reply was given to this ludicrous proposal by the newspaper *Vakil* from Amritsar in its October 24, 1920 edition, which reveals how much the eternal loyalists were exerting themselves to shamelessly and dishonorably sow mental entanglements among the public. But as one French general said, the passion of the people rises like the high tide of a river, to which only God can say enough!

The Emigration Movement

After it was decided that a Khilafat Delegation should be taken to the Viceroy, the delegation went there, and on its return, Gandhiji raised the question of what the next steps should be. A convention was called to be held in Delhi to address this question, which was attended by Maulana Mohammad Ali, Maulana Shaukat Ali, Hakim Ajmal Khan, Maulana Abdul Bari, and others. Gandhiji presented the program for the non-cooperation movement there. The scheme of non-cooperation was to boycott the government in every way: return all government granted titles, completely boycott all courts and educational institutions, resign from all government jobs, and to take no part in the legislative councils that were going to be established under the 1919 reforms. Gandhiji insisted that this was the only way to force the government to take notice and make changes. It was past time for delegations and memorandums.

Maulana Azad writes in India Wins Freedom":

> *"As soon as Gandhiji presented this proposal, I remembered that it was the same scheme that Tolstoy had proposed some time ago...I also remembered that I had proposed a similar program in an article in Al-Hilal."*

It is unfortunate that I could not find that *Al-Hilal* article anywhere nor did Maulana mention or publish that article again, but a short while later, Maulana did issue a religious decree for emigration in which the Indian Muslims were ordered to emigrate from India. Probing this topic deeper will reveal that emigration and non-cooperation were poles apart: emigration meant leaving this country forever while non-cooperation was for those who were firmly determined to stay here. But in the decree that was published in Amritsar's *Ahl-e-Hadees'* July 20, 1920 edition, Maulana has tried to reconcile the two[19].

It has been stated above that after the Calcutta conference, in February 1920, Maulana Azad tried to install himself as the *Imam al-Hind* and made a program to bring the Muslims from the path of religion to politics in this way, which he ended in September 1920 after an eloquent effort and a considerable expenditure. So, launching the emigration movement around the same time doesn't make sense. In any case, let's take a look at Maulana's decree and its reconciliation with non-cooperation. Maulana has stated:

> *"After considering all the Sharia arguments, the current affairs, matters of interest to the community, requirements, and prudence, I am convinced with all my mental perception of the belief that there is no Sharia-based path forward for the Muslims of India but to emigrate. For all those Muslims who at this time wish to*

---

19 This decree has been copied from *Ahl-e-Hadees* on pp 203 of *Tabarrukaat Azad*, Editor: Ghulam Rasool Mehr. But the date the decree was issued has not been entered. In the preamble, Ghulam Rasool Mehr writes only that the decree was issued by Maulana in 1920. In any case, since Maulana was released from detention in January 1920 and the decree had already been published by July 1920, it must have been issued sometime between January and July of 1920.

*carry out the biggest Islamic act, it is necessary for them
to emigrate from India."*

After issuing this decree of the obligation of Muslims, Maulana
has mentioned one exception:

*"Albeit, for those whose presumption prevails that for
the struggle toward their goals and for declaring and
reminding the true word, it is relatively more necessary
for them to stay in India rather than emigrate, or those
who cannot emigrate for Sharia-based acceptable
reasons, or for those who will be delayed due to natural
causes associated with the movement of such a large
populace, then without a doubt those people should stay.
Such people should devote all their strength and power to
follow Sharia."*

In the same decree, Maulana has written about the non-
cooperation movement:

*"Since the convention in Delhi last February till the
meeting of the Khilafat Committee on April 11 in
Bombay, all the efforts to make non-cooperation
acceptable and popular, to the extent that such proposals
were accepted, had the same basis."*

This implied that "neither could all the Muslims emigrate
from India at the same time, nor was that required by Islamic
law." Emigration would continue and so would the presence
of Muslims in India. Just that for those Muslims who remained
in India, it was not legitimate from an Islamic point of view
for them to show any attachment or fondness toward, or give
support or service to, those who were on the opposing side
of this fight.. Those who did would be considered enemies

of Islam by virtue of Quranic text. *"Those among you who cooperate with them shall be considered from among them."*

This was the form that reconciliation between emigration and non-cooperation took. Now the question arose as to how to determine who was to emigrate and who was to stay. For that, Maulana presented the following direction.

> *"It is up to the leaders of the congregations to determine who needs to immediately emigrate and who has such abilities as to do work internally which would be desirable and beneficial, and also where to emigrate and under what circumstances, if that is the determination such that it bears fruits and blessings. Every person cannot decide for themselves about these affairs."*

> *"The sample of the action of emigration that has been left for us as the standard from the conduct of the Prophet is that the prerequisite to emigration is the allegiance to emigration. There should be no emigration without this allegiance. Those who are going to emigrate should first pledge allegiance to it."*

Here one can understand that which we did not understand earlier, i.e. how the contradictions between the Imamate movement and the emigration movement can be resolved. From the above, it is clear that the emigration movement is but a chapter in the book of the Imamate movement. In the end, Maulana gathers all his qualifications for his claims and authority to state:

> *"This is my opinion, my perception, my firm belief, my faith and not a speculation or a political strategy. All of Europe has gotten out from under Islamic rule,*

Baghdad and Syria are gone, but faith survives. It is not Constantinople that we need to save now, but our faith that is on the line. And the purpose is not the survival of the nation but the survival of faith...I have made the final decision. Those seekers of the truth who have trust in me should give me company on the path of Allah...The exact procedure is that those Muslims who feel they have been granted the favor of action by Allah should immediately inform me of their commitment or meet the following gentlemen and get detailed instructions.

1. *Maulvi Abdul Qadir, Lawyer, Qasur (District Lahore)*
2. *Maulvi Mohiuddin, BA, Qasur (District Lahore)*
3. *Muhammad Dawood Ghaznavi*
4. *Maulvi Abdur Razzaq Saheb Malihabadi, Editor Al-Bayan (Lucknow)*

In this way, allegiance to emigration was indirectly allegiance to the Imamate and Maulana was running both movements concurrently. Maulana had so much confidence in his ability that he did not consider it necessary to poll the people of his ilk for their opinions. He wanted to directly take pledges of allegiance from the people; in fact he had already started the campaign for a pledge for the Imamate.

It is generally suggested that the decree of emigration came from Maulana Abdul Bari. The responsibility for the decree was entirely on Maulana Azad. Ghulam Rasool Mehr told me that Maulana Azad's influence in Punjab, Sindh, and the Frontier was so deep before his detention in Ranchi that when he visited Lahore, up to a 100,000 would gather from far off places and would raise the *Naara-e-Takbeer* slogan so loudly and passionately that it would seem that the sky would fall down. Maulana's influence in Sindh is also evident from his letter dated September 20, 1920 that he wrote to Abdur Razzaq Malihabadi regarding the matter of the Imamate movement, which has been mentioned earlier. It was perhaps the effect of this influence that the Mullahs of Sindh emphasized emigration and set off. Among those who left India, there are a few who deserve mention:

1. *Maulana Ahmad Ali of Sheranwala Darwaza in Lahore. He was an erudite scholar, a simple natured man, and a respected elder. He taught the Quran at Sheranwala Darwaza mosque. He used to educate everyone from the horse-carriage and horse-cart drivers and the general public on reading the Quran to instruction and guidance to the scholars on Quranic verses. I had also pleaded my way into the class of scholars and read 10 sections of the Quran under him. I was unfortunate that I had to go home for a few days in the middle of the session on account of my wife falling quite ill and could not complete the lesson. I am very proud of having been his student. He was ordered by Maulana Sindhi to return to India to continue his work here.*
2. *Khan Abdul Ghaffar Khan Usmanzai (Peshawar)*
3. *Sardar Mohammad Aslam Khan (Balochistan)*
4. *Aziz Hindi*
5. *Usman Saheb Bhopali*

Many others, including graduates of colleges such as Iqbal Shaidai (Lahore), Akbar Khan, and Ahmad Shah Khan (Bhopal), and a large number of other migrants headed to Afghanistan.

The English were well aware of the geographical position of Afghanistan, its financial situation, and the scarcity of land and resources there. The way they spent a lot of money in the French Revolution to produce those who were pro-revolution, who would go about assassinating people, creating terror in Europe, and causing the revolution to slow down, they had used their craftiness in the same way to let lose their agents who would show people the decree of emigration and draw their attention toward their obligation to the Sharia-based order to indoctrinate them in emigration. They would show them greener pastures, telling them they would get all sorts of relief when they got there, that they would get rich, and lead a life of comfort.

Zafar Hasan Aibak writes[20]:

> *"One after the other, groups of emigrants started arriving in Jalalabad and from there to Kabul. At first they were lodged in tents but it was impossible to make satisfactory living arrangements for them there. The poor women who were in purdah were extremely inconvenienced. A few rude Kabulites even verbally abused them. Some of them started selling their possessions to buy food, which were bought by the locals at less than half their worth. Not being able to understand the Persian language, their indigence, being in a foreign land and on top of that the absence of any loyal well-wishers: all these were misfortunes that no one can understand other than those who have seen and faced them. Eventually, when the number of the arriving immigrants started growing, they were taken to other provinces of Afghanistan such*

---

20 Zafar Hasan Aibak, *Aap Biitii* (Autobiography), pp 213

as Panjshir, Qataghan, Badakhshan and Turkistan. A few youths went on to Tashkent from Turkistan. Some stayed in Qataghan and Badakhshan but remained unsettled due to financial difficulties. Many of them returned to Kabul."

In Kabul, the Afghans were intensely opposed to the immigrants. Questions were raised about who was a national and who was not. The rulers of Afghanistan could not help but be affected. As a result, one day orders were given for all the immigrants to appear at the police station with all their belongings. When everyone gathered there, a police officer looked at his wrist watch and said that in five minutes, everyone had to decide whether they are willing to be relocated to a certain place outside Kabul or not. That destination was Daldali. There was a college graduate among the immigrants, who also had his eyes on his watch, and as soon as the five minutes passed, he said they had decided not to go there. The police officer had no recourse at the time and the matter was put off. Later, they were ordered to leave Afghanistan. The migrants then decided to go to Iran. When the government of Iran found out, the local newspapers welcomed the migrants heartily. In those days, Iranian newspapers used to come to the office of the newspaper *Zamindar*. An article in one of them said we Iranians were those who had given refuge to Humayun, that our hospitality was world renowned, and we will 'place the migrants on our eyelids,' meaning we will treat them with esteem and honor. *Zamindar* wrote an article in vigorous support of the migrants, in response to which Mahmud Tarzi, the Foreign Minister of Afghanistan, wrote a letter of rebuttal addressed to Ghulam Rasool Mehr received by *Zamindar*. By that time, the caravan of the refugees had left for Iran.

When they were leaving, the Afghans standing at a distance were chanting, "Kill these Indians, they are thieves." But before the caravan could get much further, a letter from Enver Pasha was received by Amir Amanullah Khan advising him not to allow the migrants to leave, otherwise his government would get a bad name within the entire Islamic world. Consequently, the migrants were called back but their distress prevailed and gradually they all returned after losing a lot. Nothing was achieved. Only the doom and devastation of this movement left an enduring lesson for the Muslims of India, that there was no place for them outside their country.

Maulana Azad's sole intention was to take the Muslims away from the path of religion into politics, which they had declared forbidden fruit for quite some time. When the Khilafat Movement directly accomplished that, there was no longer any need for this intermediary solution.

The suggestion that it was Maulana Abdul Bari who had issued the decree of emigration had become so popular that Zafar Hasan Aibak too had repeatedly written in his autobiography that emigration happened because of Maulana Abdul Bari's decree, as if he was its organizer. But this suggestion has no basis. Perhaps the real reason for this misconception is that Maulana Abdul Bari was the accepted leader of Indian Muslims at the time, and be it the common person or the elite, English educated or the religious scholars, they were all so beholden to his dignity that they could not conceive of such a large-scale movement to have come from the side of anyone but him.

Maulana Abdul Bari had placed a lot of restrictions and constraints on the decree of emigration, which made it impossible not to conclude that he had not initiated the decree, nor was he an active supporter of it, and nor had he declared it a duty or obligatory as Maulana Azad had in his decree. In fact, it was on that topic that there was an argument between Maulana Sanaullah Amritsari and Maulana Abdul Bari, but this argument is purely academic since Maulana Sanaullah Amritsari neither gave a decree on emigration nor opposed it, and therefore we shall disregard that argument. However, Maulana Abdul Bari's decree is entered below so that the reality can manifest. First of all, it is imperative that it be clarified that Maulana Abdul Bari did not issue a decree on emigration per se, in the way Maulana Azad had by writing a complete treatise on it, which he referred to in the decree and which is now unavailable.

One of the migrants, Ghulam Muhammad Aziz Amritsari sent a telegram to the Viceroy with the following text: "Since the religion of Islam does not allow us to stay in this country, it is the intent of us emigrants to leave this country very peacefully. Can we expect that you will not put any obstacles in our path?" Along with that, he requested Maulana Abdul Bari for a relevant decree on emigration, to which Maulana replied as follows:

> *"Regarding emigration, I declare that all those Muslims who cannot satisfy the conscience of their heart or their faith here, should follow the orders of Islam and should emigrate from this country to a place where it is possible to have better means for fulfilling their service to Islam and obedience to Islamic law (Sharia)."*

From this reference and context it is understood that Maulana Abdul Bari extended an invitation for emigration rather than declare it a duty or obligatory. In fact, he made it permissible for only those who wanted to emigrate. This was the kind of lawful justification for individual emigration that Haji Imdadullah *Saheb* had given after the failure of the Indian Rebellion of 1857 and for which he got the suffix of *Muhajir Makki*, or the 'Emigrant to Mecca.' Maulana Abdul Bari's 'decree' was published in newspapers in early May 1921, after which some people raised questions based on misunderstandings. Maulana clarified things and dispatched the following write-up to *Mashriq* of Gorakhpur, which was the lead in asking these questions. It was published in the May 6, 1920 edition and reveals the complete reality.

Firangi Mahal, Sha'ban 2, 1338 AH

Respectfully, Peace be Upon You

Some gentlemen have requested via telegram a reply to their inquiry on the matter of emigration. A reply has been given but it wasn't detailed, and for that reason I state these details. I hope you will publish it.

From a Sharia viewpoint, emigration is utilized in two ways. One is emigration from endowments and the other from the homelands. Emigration from endowments is to leave everything prohibited by Sharia and be bound by the laws of Islam. This emigration is eternally legitimate. The other is emigration from the homelands. This is of a few types:

1. *Migration from Mecca to Abyssinia happened twice at the time when there was no 'Dar-al-Islam,' a seat or home of Islam, and so migration took place from the 'place of idolatry and polytheism' to the 'home of the People of the Book' or from a 'place of injustice' to the*

'home of justice.' And if we are to believe in the Islam of the just and fair king of Abyssinia, The Negus, then that migration too was toward 'Dar-al- Islam.'

2. *Migration from Mecca at the time when it was 'Dar-al-Harb,' a land where worship of Allah was not allowed and had to be abandoned, toward Medina which was a 'Dar-al-Islam.' This migration was a duty and was abrogated after the victory over Mecca. In other words, those who bring the faith by way of migration are entitled to this order, not otherwise, to the extent that even heritage etc. does not entitle you to it. According to Imam Razi's statement, this migration shall again become a duty when such conditions return for the Muslims and they have no other resort.*

3. *Migration of the Bedouins to Medina. This was essential to gain equality of rights. This too was abrogated; in fact orders were issued that if a person can pray and fulfill the obligations to Islam in the place they were born, then they do not need to migrate.*

4. *Migration from 'Dar-al-Fasiq-o-Zulm,' a land of immorality and injustice, to 'Dar-al-'Adl-o-Taqvaa,' a place of justice and piety. In fact this migration from a land where there is an abundance of sin is desirable for those who commit such sins as well as those that don't.*

5. *Migration from 'Dar-al-Harb' to 'Dar-al-Islam' is desirable and becomes obligatory in certain conditions, and unnecessarily invoking Sharia while living in 'Dar-al-Harb' is forbidden. We consider India to be 'Dar-al-Islam,' and live here in quest of closeness to our faith and the word of God. For that reason, emigration is not a duty. But when there is no other way but to either emigrate or be mired in difficulties, or there is a willingness to*

> *commit sin, or by remaining in the country, one will not be able to serve God as much as from outside, then in these situations emigration is legitimate. In the current circumstances, if able and talented people emigrate to Kabul or hardworking and industrious people want to leave the country and go there, it is the hope that it will bring more benefit to Islam and they will also serve their beloved nation. From the Hadith we learn of the virtue of migration to Syria in the latter days.*

Zafar Hasan Aibak, an intelligent and passionate young man who was Maulana Ubaidullah Sindhi's right hand, has written in his autobiography[21]:

> *"By declaring India to be 'Dar-al-Harb'* [which is patently false], *Maulana Abdul Bari issued a decree that it was the duty of Muslims to emigrate from here. In response to that, preparations started being made in Punjab and the Frontier for emigration."*

He goes on to write that "Amir Amanullah Khan had hoped that educated Indians of our party would come to Afghanistan through this movement, but what happened was that illiterate peasants joined this movement." Then he mentions their great distress.

Aibak has written that "the amount of shortsightedness that occurred in Afghanistan was matched only by the mismanagement that was evident in India. It did not occur to anyone to write to Amir of Kabul or send someone there to inquire what arrangements had been made for receiving and settling the migrants, nor did anyone think of arranging

---

21 Zafar Hasan Aibak, *Aap Biitii* (Autobiography), pp 209

for the migrants to leave in small caravans a few days apart so that one caravan could be well settled there before the next one arrived. After the decree of emigration, gullible Muslims sold their homes and lands for half their prices, and without thinking of the results and consequences, set out for Afghanistan." Aibak is right about that, but Maulana Abdul Bari is not to blame for it.

Passion and Excitement in India

The Peace Conference of the major powers was going on in Paris and London, and Maulana Mohammad Ali had taken a delegation to London and was working with it there. Here in India, the passion and excitement of the Muslims juxtaposed that starkly. On one side, Maulana Abul Kalam Azad was taking pledges as the *Imam al-Hind* so that he could change the direction of the wind by uniting the Muslims and imposing on them the requirements of Sharia to take the path of politics. He had also issued the decree for emigration and people had even embarked upon it. The people were getting restless with their emotions. There was an abundance of rallies and conferences. But nothing could be achieved with merely arousing emotions and giving meaningless sacrifices. However, to channel the right emotions into practical action, Mahatma Gandhi was working hard to get ready for a full-scale confrontation with his complete non-cooperation plan. The wait was only for the details of the new procedures that the Peace Conference would put out.

Meerut Khilafat Conference

Therefore, on March 23, 1920 the Khilafat Conference was held in Meerut with much pomp and show. Mahatma Gandhi was busily traveling all over, putting all his effort and energy into it. He was meeting every relevant person and participating in every rally as if he had taken it up as his responsibility. He participated in the Meerut Conference as well. There, he relayed the decision of the leaders of Delhi that if the conclusions of the Peace Conference were going to be against the Turks, then we would have to do that much more, and the non-cooperation movement was very much a part of that scheme. Mahatma Gandhi also said that to act upon this scheme, Hindu-Muslim unity was of the utmost importance. This is how Mahatma Gandhi described the scheme:

1. *Renounce all government titles and civil positions*
2. *Resign from all army and police employments*
3. *Refuse to pay taxes and other government imposed obligations*

The outcome of this was desirable, and the non-cooperation movement had not even fully started nor had any political party formally adopted it when Hakim Ajmal Khan wrote the following memorandum to the Deputy Commissioner[22]:

Sir!

The patience and peaceful attitude of the Muslims evident from the start of and during the war is no secret at all. Despite extreme emotional distress, which started with the events of the Ottoman Empire during the war till today, not one of them has reacted in violation of any law in any part of the country and instead have even joined the British forces in the Dardanelles Strait, Syria, Iraq, and other parts of the Ottoman Empire.

---

22 *Mashriq* (Gorakhpur): dated April 18, 1920 pp 15

They thought that their holy places would be safe as was promised to them. But none of them are now in their control in the true sense. Mecca Sharif, which is the holiest of the holy places, and Medina Paak, which is the resting place of Prophet Muhammad, peace be upon him, are not truly in the hands of Sharif Hussein. Jerusalem is being taken from Muslim control and given to the Jews. And all of the holy shrines of Iraq are directly in control of our government. In the same way, the rest of the Arabian Peninsula is also, to a large extent, under British control. Instead of fulfilling the promises that were made regarding Constantinople and Thrace, forces were deployed in Constantinople itself and it has been proposed that the Caliphate forever stay under the shadow of the international cannons of Dardanelles Strait.

The Muslims have till now used all the means that they can think of to draw the attention of the British government toward their demands but no attention has been paid to even the most insignificant sections of their rights and petitions. Under these circumstances, as an insignificant Muslim, as a protest against the treatment of the Ottoman Empire by the British government, I renounce all those honors that have been bestowed upon me by the government. Along with the Kaisar-i-Hind Gold Medal and other medals from the coronation in the royal courts of England and India, which I am sending along to you, from this date I also consider myself retired from the title of Haziq-ul-Mulk and with it I also request that my name be expunged from the list of courtiers. I hope that you will kindly forward this letter to the local government along with the medals, and I will be very grateful for that. Since this matter is of great import to the public, I am also sending a copy of this memorandum to the press.

Ajmal

A storm was brewing in the colleges as well. *Anjuman-e-Himayat-e-Islam* ("The Association for the Support of Islam") of Lahore was the largest association of Muslims in India. It not only had a grand Arabic madrasa and a big orphanage under its auspices, it also had a high school, an intermediate college and a degree college, and a large press associated with it where books were authored and published on a large scale. Informative books from the *Anjuman-e-Himayat-e-Islam* press were distributed all over India. Government funded Muslim education institutions used the curriculum as prescribed by the association. Students from its college quit the university en masse and did not return even under the duress of disciplinary action.

The Grand Convention in Deoband

A grand convention was convened in Deoband on March 19, 1920. The announcement for the convention had been sent to various newspapers such as *Aftab, Hamdam, Paisa Akhbar,* and *Al-Khalil,* which said that followers of Deoband, wherever they may be, should participate in it with sincerity, religiosity, and comprehension. Consequently, thousands of Muslims from cities and villages attended the convention and Maulana Habib-ur-Rehman *Saheb* Usmani, the assistant organizer, despite his ill-health and weakness, gave an extremely heartfelt and sorrowful speech in which he stated that Islam and Khilafat were complementary to each other. He urged the Muslims to shed their sense of impotence since true power was in the hands of God who had helped the weak and helpless against a tyrant such as the Pharaoh. The speech was so forceful and appreciated that a surge of deep emotion engulfed the audience. Even Maulana Shabbir Ahmad Usmani was so affected by the speech that when he stood up to speak after Maulana Habib-ur-Rehman, his voice cracked with emotion and he couldn't say anything. At the end of the convention, it was decided that the following telegram should be sent to His Majesty's Government[23].

"The religious community of Deoband also, like the rest of the Islamic world, expresses to His Majesty its deep shock and profound anguish at the fragmentation of Turkey, from which the Islamic Caliphate has been dismantled piece by piece, and requests the responsible members of His Majesty's Government to immediately repeal the policies that can cause such intense anxiety, have the potential to result in a very dreadful situation, and prove the promises and covenants of the British government to be unreliable. No Muslim individual will be able to see with their own eyes the destruction of their dignity."

Then the audience prayed with much supplication and entreaty after which printed copies of the *dua-e-qunoot*, a special supplication mentioned in the *Hadith*, were distributed. This supplication is recited in situations of deep anxiety and had become a part of these gatherings for many years.

---

23 *Mashriq* (Gorakhpur): dated April 18, 1920 pp 16

March 19, 1920 - Khilafat Day

October 17, 1919 was observed as 'Prayer Day' in all of India at the direction of the Khilafat Committee. Now, at the advice of Mahatma Gandhi, the Khilafat Committee decided to observe March 19, 1920 as Khilafat Day and as a day to prepare the nation for *satyagraha*. Passionate rallies were held in all the major cities, central locations of districts and subdivisions, and even in townships and villages. There was a complete *hartal* or shut down. These rallies were seemingly a precursor to the *satyagraha* movement and were held peacefully and somberly. Gorakhpur's *Mashriq*, in its March 25, 1920 edition, published the following report.

> *"In Delhi, Calcutta, Lahore, Bombay, Lucknow, Bijnor, Mirzapur, Jaunpur, Banaras, Kanpur...Raebareli, Agra, Saharanpur...suffice it to say that not only in India's big cities but even in townships and villages, there was a general strike on March 19th and rallies were held peacefully. In the Bombay rally, Mr. Gandhi stated that the need still exists for more strikes and satyagraha."*

In the same edition of *Mashriq*, on page 17 it is stated:

> *"In Basti town and Pucca Bazar, there was a call for a general strike and all the businesses remained closed. The Muslims spent all day in prayer and worship. Friday prayers were said in the Eidgah in a large congregation. Maulana Saiyad Fakhir Allahabadi led the prayers and moved the congregation to tears with sorrowful prayers. In a passionate speech, Babu Daulat Ram pledged that their Hindu brothers shall stand by the nation's Muslims in their delicate times. Such a grand gathering of lawyers*

and legal professionals of all classes had never been held in Basti before. Maulana Saiyad Fakhir Saheb spoke for two hours. Resolutions from the Calcutta Khilafat Conference were read out. The last message was sent to His Royal Highness through the Viceroy of India. Similar events were reported from adjoining areas such as Ganeshpur and Pansi."

There were myriad other rallies and conferences before and after this. Muslims were expressing their passions and expressing their opposition to the British government by going to these rallies and lending their voices to slogans. And they were awaiting a plan of action. On April 22, 1920 an announcement was made for an Awadh Conference in Faizabad and rallies were announced at various places but the leaders of the nation had now decided to take some firm steps. Consequently, in the last week of April 1920, the following letter from Maulana Abdul Bari was published in *Hamdam* of Lucknow:

Khilafat Conferences have been held and are being held as needed. Muslims should hold these conferences as they deem necessary but there is no need any more to convene them for mere show when not necessary. In fact, my opinion is that Muslims should suspend these events. In particular, it is certainly not proper to convene a Khilafat related conference without express permission from the Khilafat Committee in Bombay. And, in principle, attendance in such conferences is not required. The time has come to work. Don't put your load on others. If convening a conference is needed in any part of the country, then let the local people attend them. One or two regular scholars from elsewhere can be invited, but unnecessarily inviting a lot of celebrities from elsewhere should be avoided. Regarding myself, I have decided that other than situations where my attendance has tangible benefits, I will decline any invitation to rallies that are merely for show...My friends have expressed their desire that I trouble the eminent gentlemen if they so wish. I have obliged so far, but now there is such an excess of services needed that I am unable to. My situation is:

Don't tease O' fragrant spring breeze, blow your own way
All you can think of is to flirt, while I sit here weary

There was a similar turn of events when the Workers' Conference was convened at 11 am on April 18, 1920 at Royal Theater in Delhi presided by Maulana Hasrat Mohani, in which Maulana Ahmad Saeed said in his address that the Khilafat Committee asks the Muslims for neither emigration nor jihad; it only wants non-cooperation with the government to come into action and efforts be made to make progress with the Swadeshi movement, the nationalist self-sufficiency movement.

The president of the conference stated that it was not their purpose to implement any new policy, but to bring to action the proposals enacted by the Khilafat Conference or the *Anjuman-e-Ulema-e-Hind* ("The Association of Islamic Scholars of India"). Indian leaders had passed resolutions for action in the Khilafat Conference and the Swadeshi and non-cooperation movements. The first duty of this conference was to transform those resolutions into a plan for action.

The Rallying Speech of Dr. Kitchlew in Lahore

On March 28, 1920, at the annual fair in Lahore, Muslims held a grand rally presided by Dr. Saifuddin Kitchlew. The rally is significant in that Dr. Kitchlew strongly endorsed the non-cooperation movement with supporting arguments. He stated[24]:

"Jihad is a duty all the time, and in such times when forces are attacking Islam and there is a holy war, it is the duty of Muslims to get ready for jihad. But there are various means for jihad. If you have a sword in your hand, then it is jihad-bil-saif, or jihad by the sword. If you don't have a sword, or cannons, guns, fighter planes and other armaments, then what is your religious duty? Under these circumstances, if an announcement is made that 'Muslims! Rise and kill the English,' and you manage to kill a dozen or two English, what would be achieved from that? You know all about the massacre at Jallianwala Bagh. Under these circumstances, religion doesn't force you to wage jihad by the sword.

The Question of Emigration

With your wife and children, with just the clothes on your body or with all your possessions, how can we just go to another country? We don't have ships or other means. Where can a population of 70 or 80 million go? This too is an impossible task. Then what else remains? A force greater than these two by means of which you

---

24 *Mashriq* (Gorakhpur): dated April 18, 1920 pp 17

can torment the oppressor: 1. Renounce all government titles and civil positions. 2. Resign from all army and police employments. 3.Refuse to pay taxes and other government imposed obligations."

The Grand Convention of the Islamic Scholars of United Provinces

A grand convention of the Islamic scholars of United Provinces was held on April 5-6, 1920 to unite the scholars around the issue of the Caliphate. A large number of scholars and the general public attended. Along with passionate speeches, the following proposals were accepted:

1. *The scholars should immediately take responsibility for influencing public opinion on the issue of the Caliphate.*
2. *Opposing and hypocritical scholars should be boycotted.*
3. *All the resolutions from Khilafat Conference Calcutta and the speech given by Maulana Abdul Bari on the occasion should be ratified and endorsed.*
4. *Maulana Abdul Bari's decree should be published. Its decisions regarding the Caliphate should be acted upon.*
5. *Hakim Ajmal Khan should be congratulated on renouncing his government conferred titles and honors, and national titles of Masih-ul-Mulk and Raees-ul-Mahkma should be bestowed upon him as a mark of appreciation*
6. *This convention urges those scholars who have titles bestowed upon them to renounce the same.*
7. *Scholars should get an oath from their disciples and all Muslims to advocate for the Caliphate in their speeches and their writings with all their might.*

8.   *Recruitment of soldiers should be stopped.*

9.   *Muslims should stay away from elections held under the constitutional reforms.*

10. *The day that the Peace Conference decides on the matter of the Caliphate in a manner which is against the principles of Islamic Sharia should also be the day that we get complete independence from the British government.*

A committee of 24 scholars was also formed with Maulana Abdul Majid Badayuni as its secretary. Badaun was made its central office. The government had gotten quite worried about these conventions and rallies. On the occasion of each one of them, the government had marched its soldiers armed with machine guns, but there was not even a hint of fear among the public. The Nizam of Hyderabad famously said 'Amen' quite loudly when supplications were being made about the Caliphate after the Friday prayer. Khwaja Hasan Nizami too had given information to the government regarding the Nizam's support for the Caliphate, which was mentioned by Maulana Mohammad Ali with surprise. The Nizam was pressured for this and on April 7, 1920 "His Excellency" Huzur Nizam issued an edict with his signature on it, which had the following order after some introductory words:

"In order to keep my dear subjects secure, I issue this order that any convention related to the issue of Caliphate should have the following conditions placed on their organizers:

1.   *Such conventions in which the intent is to present movements, as early as possible copies of the presiding orders should be passed to the government.*

2. *Information about the place and date of the convention should be given in writing at least one week in advance to the governing district or city magistrate as the case may be.*

3. *Accurate proceedings of the convention should be sent without delay to the governing district or city magistrate as the case may be for informational purposes.*

4. *Violation of these directives will be subject to strict accountability*

The days of bowing to the orders of "His Excellency" had passed. Hence the orders were disobeyed. There were arrests and detentions. But the caravan kept on moving forward.

7

Consequences of the Announcement of Loyalty

Situation in Europe and Turkey

Let us now examine the situation in Turkey. But before writing anything else, it appears essential to talk about the geographical position of Anatolia, Thrace, and Smyrna, since people have often expressed their love for these places but few people know what and where they are.

Anatolia

Anatolia is a Greek word which means 'east,' geographically referencing it to some Asian parts of the Ottoman Empire. During Roman times, Anatolia was referred to as Asia Minor. The area of Anatolia is 12,000 square miles. Its maximum length is 700 miles and maximum width 400 miles. The interior has mountain ranges with the largest one being the Taurus Mountains which stretch from the Mediterranean coast to the Euphrates River. Sakarya River is one of its principal rivers. This is also where the philosopher Pythagoras and the epic poet Homer were born.

Anatolia's famous city Ankara is situated 215 miles south-southeast of Constantinople and 330 miles southeast of

Smyrna. Its second largest city, Adana, is a fine and attractive city. A third city is Bursa, where the mosque Masjid Khizra is quite famous. Smyrna is a grand and beautiful city situated on the eastern shore of the Gulf of Izmir. Samsun is a famous port city of Asia Minor (Anatolia) situated on the Black Sea coast. Sinop is a famous city and port in Anatolia. The famous philosopher Diogenes was born there. Cankaya is the name of a majestic hill with orchards and gardens a few furlongs from Ankara. A small town of the same name is situated there, which is a district of Ankara. Ghazi Mustafa Kemal Pasha used to live in Cankaya. Trabzon is a fortified city 900 kms from Constantinople and 140 kms from Erzincan. Ozkoy in the east is also an important railway station.

Thrace

Thrace is a province of Turkey in which famous towns of Adrianople and Edirne are situated. Adrianople has Sultan Selim's tomb and some grand mosques. One area of Thrace is only 60 miles from Rodosto Gallipoli, where the Greeks had dreamt of occupying Constantinople in 1922, the curtain over which had been brought down by the stone-splitting sword of Ghazi Mustafa Kemal.

Greek Attack

The temporary peace accord was creating a stir in the minds of the Turkish nobility and the Islamic world. The ink on the temporary peace accord had not even dried when, on May 6, 1919, at the venue of the Peace Conference, Germany would reject every condition of the peace accord that it considered against its national interests; the newspapers started questioning whether the temper of war was still raging in Germany. It was strange that French Prime Minister Monsieur Clemenceau and the British Prime Minister Lloyd George gave Greece permission to occupy Anatolia. Usually a status quo is maintained after a temporary peace accord till a permanent peace can be achieved. But with Turkey, there was a notion of a Christian-Islamic war. Law, traditions, civility, principles, justice - all were shelved. The English claimed that the Turks were in the minority in Anatolia and that the Turks would get only those areas where they were in the majority, for which only an area with a population of five million was identified. Even if that was the case, although it was a blatant misrepresentation, a referendum was necessary. But they didn't even wait for that and on May 13, 1919, with the support of the Allied fleet, Greek forces landed in the port of Smyrna to wipe Turkey off the map. This was a precious opportunity for Greece and the Allied forces to put out this obstinate fire.

Over in Constantinople, the situation was that those under the aegis of the empire had lost hope and were so meek that they considered the submission of Turkey to be a blessing. The Turkish Parliament showed some vigor and put forth a resolution of protest. But the Sultan dismissed the parliament, made Damat Ferid Pasha the Prime Minister, Ali Kemal the Minister of Interior, and included Adil Bey and Mahmud Ali in the ministry to take the control of the government in his hands. Or it can be said that he handed over the control in custody of the traitor Damat Ferid Pasha. Turkish nobles were being assassinated. Allied and Greek warships had dropped anchor around Constantinople. Officers from foreign countries were occupying all of the key positions. The people were restless. A grand rally was held in Hagia Sophia. Nearly a hundred thousand people were assembled. A British plane was circling overhead. The Grand Mufti, who was an intellectual comrade of Maulana Mahmud Hasan and a supporter of his mission, refused to issue a religious decree to give up resistance at the insistence of the Muslim Caliph. He was arrested and sent to Malta and another Shaykh al-Islam was brought in his place, who was termed a Maulvi of the "Brigade" by the late eloquent of the time, Akbar Allahabadi.

Do you know who this Maulvi of the Brigade is
He is the translation of the British policy into Arabic

Along with the attack by Greece, rebellion against the English spread in the entire Islamic world. Afghanistan has been mentioned earlier. In Iraq, a 100,000 strong army was advancing toward Baghdad. In Iran, rebellion was rising against the covert incitements of the English. Bolshevik Russia, under the leadership of Lenin, was inciting the Islamic world to bear arms against the English everywhere and was providing all possible aid. Enver Pasha and his companions had fled to Europe in fear of the atrocities of the English. Jamal Pasha and many other Turkish nobles were in the same boat. Enver Pasha came to Russia in February 1920, where Lenin convened a Congress of the People of the East in Baku. Enver Pasha participated in this conference. The English were of the opinion that Russia was also inciting the revolutionary parties of Iran to rebellion.

On the other side, matters between Amir Faisal and France were not being settled. France was insistent on demanding submission from Syria and Amir Faisal was asking for full recompense for his treachery. He wanted to be made an absolute king. How could this notion be acceptable to France, which thought that the English were deceiving them of their fair share in the victory? And the tune that the moderators were insistently singing about the friendship between Britain and France failed to impress them. Italy had the same complaint. The English had become the village chief but they were not able to satisfy everyone because their policy was based on deception. There were no takers for the Fourteen Points that President Wilson of America had put forth. The independence of international waters, freedom of human beings, the right to self-determination, etc. - these were all pleasant notions but to cast them in practical terms was to abandon colonialism. Mr. Wilson rued the fact that the reasons why he had intervened in Europe did not appear to be fulfilled. He was not successful at the Peace Conference and eventually returned to America disappointed and despondent. He was so disheartened by his failure that in March 1921 he was politically isolated and subsequently withdrew from politics completely.

For these reasons, the Peace Conference, which was being held sometimes in London and sometimes in Paris, was not reaching any conclusion. On the other hand, British forces occupied Constantinople in March 1920 and put all the Turkish nobles they could find under the sword. The aim of the English was to wipe Turkey off the map. The weekly newspaper *Mashriq* writes in its issue dated March 18, 1920 on page 3:

> *In Constantinople, a grand demonstration has been held related to the matter of the Caliphate. This demonstration was held in the vast grounds adjacent to the Hagia Sophia Mosque. Its purpose and objective was to have a discourse on the contemporary political situation and*

to send a memorandum to the super powers. The rally started after the Friday prayers. The ground has an expanse of thousands of meters and all of it was packed with people. The ground is between the Hagia Sophia and Sultanahmet Mosques, and its 300 summoners to prayers first offered supplications after the Zuhr prayers for the security of Islam. A French woman gave a passionate speech in which she said that the French nation would remain opposed to any such resolution which is against the interests of the Turks. There were speeches by Riza Nur Bey and others, and a memorandum was sent to the Honorable Sultan, the Turkish House of Representatives, and European countries which read as follows:

"Astana is the center of Islamic Caliphate. Smyrna should be transferred to its masters since it is the port city for the southern parts and has been with the Turks for more than a thousand years. Adrianople should be kept with the Ottoman Empire since it is the last of the defensive lines of the threshold. The eastern and western parts of Anatolia have remained in Turkey and its residents are mostly Muslims."

But these proceedings neither could nor did have any effect on the Allied countries and the Peace Conference.

Treaty of Sevres (Conditions for Peace with Turkey)

Eventually, permanent peace arrived in the form of a killshot for Turkey. In May 1920, Allied countries made public the conditions for peace with Turkey which came to be known as the Treaty of Sevres. This treaty laid out the following conditions:

1. *Dardanelles Strait and all other straits will be put under international control.*
2. *The Sultan, in his capacity as the chief of Muslims, will remain on the seashore at the gates of Dardanelles Strait (Golden Horn) under the eye of the English.*
3. *Southern Anatolia, Cilicia, and its capital Adana will be given to France.*
4. *The province of Antalya will be given to Italy.*
5. *Smyrna will be handed over to Greece.*
6. *Cut off from all oceanic routes, Turkey will be given middle Anatolia.*
7. *Arab provinces will be given under the control of England and France.*
8. *A new republic, Armenia, will be brought into existence located in the eastern provinces on the shore of Black Sea.*
9. *According to the promise made by the English to Jewish organizations on November 2, 1917, it was decided that a Jewish nation would be established in Palestine. (The promise made to the Muslims was completely forgotten)*
10. *Turkey's border will remain the same as it is now, but the Commission to be set up for demarcation may amend it as required. According to this, all those parts of Thrace and areas of Constantinople and Asia Minor that have a majority of Turkish population shall be included in Turkey.*
11. *There will be no changes to Turkish rights and privileges in Constantinople, but if the Turks do not faithfully*

> *comply with the terms of the treaty, the Allies will have the power to amend them.*

>   12. *A Zone of the Straits is proposed to control the waters between the mouth of the Dardanelles on the Mediterranean and south of the Bosphorus on the Black Sea. The zone within these boundaries will have no connection to Turkey.*

This declaration of peace caused a stir in the Islamic world to the extent that a European historian writes in a biography of Ataturk that on reading about this treaty, Sultan Vehideddin's face turned red.

8

Mahatma Gandhi's Declaration of War

Mahatma Gandhi's Leadership

Mahatma Gandhi had now presented his entire scheme of *satyagraha* and non-cooperation. He used to say that one should speak the truth, that the basis of every action is truth, to speak what one thought and to do what one spoke and there will be no deception in life. He asked everyone not to hate the English as they were brothers too; but rather to hate the government that had been established over them. *Ahimsa* should be strictly adhered to in actions and violence should not be used in any circumstance. Women should spin the *charkha* wheel and men should weave the *khaddar* cloth. In this way, the Rs. 610,000,000 that goes out of the country to purchase clothes shall be saved and remain in India. There should be no cooperation with the government. Students should drop out of schools, colleges and universities. Lawyers should leave advocacy. Police and army employees and other employees such as those in the government should resign. Gandhiji said that if people act on this scheme, *Swaraj* (self-rule) could be achieved in one year. Gandhi was a wise man. He wanted to change the mood of the people of the country. He wanted to remove the inferiority complex and the sense of being slaves from their hearts Only with this psychological revolution could India move toward the goal of independence. He considered freedom of conscience to be necessary before the country became free. To him, purification of the inner self and purity of the heart were essential. When a person weaves *khaddar*, spins the *charkha* wheel, rejects the pants, coat, and tie, the transformation of apparel would inevitably become prominent in a revolutionary form. With these unique notions, India was shaken. And Hindus started to think of him as an avatar and sought out an audience with him. Gandhi had set the wheels in motion.

Gandhiji had started to wander through the entire country. The sympathy he expressed for the Islamic Caliphate and the sincerity with which he came to the fore with the Muslims had an effect on every word and deed, and very soon he became a recognized and accepted leader of the Indian Muslims.

After winning the war, the government decided to hold celebrations here and there and was busy singing odes of praise at the shrine of the British government. On October 17, 1919, which was proposed as a 'Day of Prayer and Gathering,' it was decided that Muslims would not participate in any celebration of victory or peace, whatever they may call it, and would boycott it. This decision was reiterated in Khilafat Conferences and associated meetings. Maulana Hasrat Mohani, a great man and a selfless leader, repeatedly emphasized this. Mahatma Gandhi too endorsed this decision. He used every opportunity that presented itself to mobilize the nation and stand up boldly against the government. In this way, he was doing a very deliberate and sincere work to bring the mind surrounded by slavery into the atmosphere of freedom and to fill the desolate and deserted settlements of the heart with patriotic love. This was how the nation was coming to know itself. Self-awareness was being created in the nation and as it was coming to know itself, it was also recognizing its leaders. Its state was no longer thus:

I walk a little while with a fellow traveler
I do not recognize yet my guide for the way

The joint meeting held on November 24, 1919 in connection with the second Khilafat Conference (Delhi), presided by Maulvi Fazlul Haq, has been described in newspapers as follows. The nature of this meeting was of utmost importance since representatives of both major communities of the motherland were assembled to deliberate the Khilafat Conference and the matter of the Caliphate. Gandhiji, Swami Shraddhanand, Pandit Krishna Kant Malviya, Dr. Savarkar, Mr. Shankar Lal, Mr. Mohanji etc. are worth mentioning for their presence.

At the appointed time, Gandhi entered the hall. Everyone cheered and gave him a standing ovation. He was welcomed by Khwaja Hasan Nizami, Maulana Sanaullah Amritsari, Dr. Ansari, Seth Abdullah Haroon, Jan Mohammad Chotani, Dr. Savarkar, Khan Bahadur Shah Vilayat Husain, and Maulana Saiyad Muhammad Fakhir Allahabadi. Gandhiji took the chair for the session. The hall resounded with clapping from the audience. So many flowers were thrown at him that all you could see around him were the petals. Poems of Janab Dana and Khaliq were read. After that, Gandhiji delivered a speech in which, mentioning the importance of the Caliphate, he emphasized Hindu-Muslim unity and said that if the hearts of the Muslims were heavy, the Hindus were with them. Then Hakim Ajmal Khan proposed that until the matter of the Caliphate was settled, it would not be possible for the Muslims to join in the celebrations for peace. Swami Shraddhanand seconded the proposal in a forceful speech. Syed Husain, Krishna Kant Malviya, Mr. Mohanji and others also emphatically supported the proposal in their speeches. Gandhiji spoke again and said that no one should join any celebration of peace nor watch the fireworks. It was essential to stay away from these celebrations. He then appealed for contributions to the Khilafat Committee and gave a token paisa to the fund. That was it - the paisa was auctioned and it was bought by Seth Chotani for Rs. 501. Another Rs. 1000 was collected in contributions and Rs. 1500 was pledged.

After that, in another meeting, the public demanded a 'darshan,' an auspicious viewing of Mahatma Gandhi. Gandhiji said that he wasn't worthy of a *darshan*; this was the time for work. Addressing the women, he said they should spin the *charkha* wheel and he would come to have their *darshan* and touch their feet.

Period of Self-Awareness

On May 30, 1920, the All India Congress Committee's meeting took place in Banaras. Lokmanya Tilak passed through Banaras the same day but for some reason did not participate in the meeting. In this meeting, it was decided to demand an amendment to the Treaty of Sevres. The Khilafat Committee also met on the same day and formed a sub-committee to consider what steps to take next. The members of this committee were Mahatma Gandhi, Maulana Shaukat Ali and Maulana Abul Kalam Azad. The committee unanimously decided to wait for the decision of the Peace Conference before taking any major steps.

Mahatma Gandhi, meanwhile, convened a Hindu-Muslim conference on June 1, 1920. The meeting was held with much pomp and show. About three hundred delegates came from all over India and the gathering was about twenty thousand people. Also present were Mrs. Besant, Pandit Madan Mohan Malviya, Sir Tej Bahadur Sapru, Pandit Motilal Nehru, Mr. Chintamani (Editor, 'Leader') and others. Sir Tej Bahadur Sapru advised the Muslims that they should not participate in the *satyagraha* and non-cooperation movements. But the general opinion was opposed to that idea. Since moderates were also present in this meeting, it was difficult for any extremist resolution to pass. There were strong speeches on the need and importance of Hindu-Muslim unity.

An Ultimatum to the Government

On June 9, 1920 there was a meeting of the Khilafat Committee in Allahabad in which it was decided to give the Viceroy a month's notice to resolve the issue of Caliphate, which was a religious issue, otherwise they would be compelled to join the non-cooperation movement. This warning was exactly in line with the principle of *satyagraha*; to work openly, to insist on the truth, to give an opportunity to the opponent, and to inform and then carry out civil disobedience were its basic principles. People may not have understood at that time but Gandhiji had made a firm determination. It was after this that a delegation of the Khilafat Committee was formed which consisted of the following persons: (1) Mazharul Haque (2) Yaqub Hasan (3) Maulana Shaukat Ali (4) Maulana Abul Kalam Azad.

The delegation met the Viceroy of India in late June 1920 and they told him that the issue of the Caliphate was a religious matter for them (the Muslims). Therefore, he should put pressure on the Home Government to make amendments to the Turkish peace agreement according to their demands, otherwise they would be compelled to start the non-cooperation movement from August 1920 onwards.

This was the first time that the "loyal subjects" of the British government gave an ultimatum to their masters, as if they had taken the yoke of slavery off their necks and thrown it away, and stood opposed to the government, challenging it as free men. Now the only thing left was to beat the drums of war. Earlier, on June 22, 1920, Mahatma Gandhi also sent an appeal to the Viceroy of India in which he wrote that he had supported the diligence and sacrifice of the Indian Volunteer Ambulance Corp and other organizations in London and always remained loyal to Britain. Now he was requesting the Viceroy to resolve the matter of the Caliphate as per the wishes of the Muslims. There was still time. Otherwise he would be compelled to be the first person to raise the flag of rebellion. He wrote that it was his opinion that the Muslims had three paths that remained under the present circumstances: a) Jihad by the sword, b) Emigration, and c) Non-cooperation, and that he had recommended non-cooperation to the Muslims.

Pandit Madan Mohan Malviya took the responsibility of motivating the Rajahs to use the *charkha* wheel. Sarala Devi Chaudhurani, who hailed from a family of Rajahs, had learned how to spin the *charkha*. Ratna Devi Bahadur, who sat all night with the wounded of the Jallianwala Bagh massacre despite the curfew, was engaged in spinning the *charkha*.

Mahatma Gandhi wrote a scathing article in 'Young India' on the advice that Tej Bahadur Sapru had given to Muslims to not participate in the non-cooperation movement.

As far as the matters of the massacre of Jallianwala Bagh and the atrocities in Punjab were concerned, there was a unanimous demand from the leaders of India that the officers found responsible should be immediately transferred. But the Viceroy refused to accept this and was supported by Mr. Montagu, the Secretary of State for India, which perhaps exacerbated the sadness and anger.

On the other hand, the demeanor of the Muslims was transforming. There was prolific use of *khaddar* apparel and Gandhian cap. The tradition of wearing long kurtas and pajamas was being seen among the college students as well. In a blind wave of enthusiasm, some 18,000 men had emigrated from India in July and August. Whether the decree to emigrate was right or wrong has to be decided by the Islamic scholars, but it did express the deep emotions of the Muslims. It is not easy to leave one's homeland and possessions and be exiled to another country.

Explosive Times are Approaching

August 1 was approaching. Khilafat Committee had made an emphatic and vigorous appeal to all the people of India to make the day successful. On July 28, 1920 Gandhiji called on all the people of the country to start the non-cooperation movement on August 1, 1920. Gandhi said that till the Rowlatt Act was repealed and the Treaty of Sevres amended, their campaign would continue.

August 1, 1920 "Zero Hour"

The zero hour was approaching. There was immense tension in the country. On August 1, 1920 the battle of the non-cooperation movement was to commence. Everything was at stake and Gandhi was going to call out to the country to raise the anchor and sail.

Come what may, we have set the boat afloat

Expressions of loyalty, the acceptance of British subjecthood, and the age of petitions, delegations and begging were embellishments that were going to be shelved to oblivion; India was about to become a battlefield of conflict. The Muslims were about to become the leading cavalry to confront the noble and the ignoble British government. These were the same Muslims who until recently were included in this dust-biting government.

August 1, 1920 came and was welcomed with much pomp. All of India woke up. Pledges were taken. Numerous rallies were held. Oaths were taken to even sacrifice lives for Mother India. Emotions of devotion to the Ottoman Caliphate were at their peak.

The day started with Mahatma Gandhi himself returning the special distinctions, medals, and honorifics granted to him. He wrote to the Viceroy in a letter[25]:

It is not without a pang that I return the Kaisar-i-Hind gold medal granted to me by your predecessor for my humanitarian work in South Africa, the Zulu War medal

---

25 'Young India', August 4, 1920

granted in South Africa for my services as officer in charge of the Indian volunteer ambulance corps in 1906 and the Boer War medal for my services as assistant superintendent of the Indian volunteer stretcher-bearer corps during the Boer War of 1899-1900. I venture to return these medals in pursuance of the scheme of non-cooperation inaugurated today in connection with the Khilafat Movement. Valuable as these honors have been to me, I cannot wear them with an easy conscience so long as my Mussalman countrymen have to labor under a wrong done to their religious sentiment. Events that have happened during the past one month have confirmed to me the opinion that the Imperial Government have acted in the Khilafat matter in an unscrupulous, immoral and unjust manner and have been moving from wrong to wrong in order to defend their immorality. I can retain neither respect nor affection for such a Government.

He also wrote that the bloody drama of persecution and tyranny that played out in Punjab was an additional factor for this action. In this letter too, after writing in detail about his past loyal services to the British government, Gandhi wrote that he could no longer remain loyal.

The day of August 10, 1920 came, the draft of the peace treaty was to be signed without any amendment, and the Turkish representative, Tewfik Pasha, signed the treaty with the same trembling hands with which he had received the draft of the treaty. The peace accord was completed without any amendments to the Sevres Treaty. The special articles penned by foreign intellectuals, India's protest, opposition of Egypt and Afghanistan, all proved ineffective. How well the Poet of the East has said:

Without the staff of Moses, God's word to him would be baseless

The English were arrogantly presumptuous that they would trample the unarmed Indians under their feet. Now Maulana Mohammad Ali's fiery speeches were beginning to rage in the midst of the whirlwinds in the company of Gandhiji like stormy waves. After failing in London and Paris, Maulana Mohammad Ali had sent a telegram expressing his devotion to the Muslim Caliphate. And now the battlefield was ready and he was telling the Muslims that the British colonial policy was the cause of their downfall. India was the largest capital of the British. If the British were ousted from India, then the world of Islam would get rid of the heavy load of stigma from their chests. That was the only way to confront the British and revive the Islamic Caliphate. Maulana Mohammad Ali's knowledge and virtue, his style of speech, the splendor of his words, and most of all his heartache and grief all together instilled a sentiment of perseverance in the hearts of the common people as well their leaders, and they felt that a falling wall could be strengthened by the independence of India. Maulana Mohammad Ali used to say that the *charkha* is a cannon whose shells fall directly on the hearts of the English. He was a preacher of emotional sentiments and Gandhiji, who was now firmly determined, stood up resolutely to fulfill the commitment he had made. He received rousing welcomes at the railway stations in Punjab, Sindh, Madras, etc. Gradually, students started leaving schools and colleges, lawyers started separating from courts, titles and honors started being returned, and people started resigning from jobs.

The Viceroy of India made fun of all this. He thought he could uproot this movement with arrows of ridicule and derision. In a statement, Lord Chelmsford described these activities as "the most foolish of all foolish schemes" and said that this movement based on frivolous advice was truly insane, impractical and dreamy. Time proved that Lord Chelmsford had made a terrible miscalculation. They considered the sea to be calm even though there was quite a storm brewing there.

Religious Decree for Non-cooperation from 500 Islamic Scholars

During that period of turmoil, scholars from all schools of thought had gathered on the same platform. For instance, distinguished Islamic scholars of India Mufti Kifayatullah and Maulana Ahmad Saeed from Deoband, Maulana Sanaullah Amritsari, Maulana Abdul Hakim Gayawi, Maulana Mohammad Ibrahim Sialkoti, and Maulana Syed Muhammad Dawood Ghaznavi from Ahl-e-Hadees, Maulana Saiyad Muhammad Fakhir Allahabadi and Maulana Abdul Majid Badayuni from the moderate class of scholars, Maulana Abdul Bari Firangi Mahali and Maulana Salamatullah *Saheb* Firangi Mahali from the old center of Islam in North India, Maulana Azad Subhani, Allama Syed Sulaiman Nadvi and Maulana Abul Muhasin Muhammad Sajjad Haider Bihari from the Barelvi movement, ignoring their differences and factionalism of many years, were all working shoulder to shoulder for the Khilafat Movement. Maulana Sanaullah *Saheb* and Maulana Saiyad Fakhir *Saheb* were prominent in every conference and rally. Maulana Hafizur Rahman Wasif writes on page 44 of his essay "A Commentary on the History of Jamiat Ulema":

"In November 1919, a powerful group of scholars from all parts of India came together on the occasion of the Khilafat Conference. After concluding the meetings of the Khilafat Conference, all the scholars present held a meeting which only these scholars attended. At the motion of Maulana Abul Wafa Sanaullah, and seconded by Maulana Munir-uz-Zaman and other scholars, the distinguished scholar Maulana Abdul Bari Saheb was chosen to preside and the proceedings started. There was a consensus among all present that a party of scholars should be established and its name would be Jamiat Ulema-e-Hind. It was decided that this organization would encompass all of India. Hence, all present accepted membership of the party immediately and Jamiat Ulema-e-Hind was established."

At the motion of Maulana Sanaullah, and seconded by many others, Mufti Kifayatullah was selected as the temporary president of the party. It is apparent from this that all scholars of Islam were united and in agreement in their participation in the Khilafat Conference and gave it all kinds of support.

Maulana Ahmad Saeed was made the secretary. The following gentlemen who were present were deemed its members:

1. Maulana Abdul Bari Firangi Mahali
2. Maulana Salamatullah Firangi Mahali
3. Maulana Abul Wafa Sanaullah Amritsari
4. Hazrat Pir Muhammad Imam
5. Maulana Asadullah Sindhi
6. Maulana Saiyad Muhammad Fakhir, *Sajjada-Nashin* Daira Shah Ajmal
7. Maulana Maulvi Muhammad Anees

8. Maulana Mohammad Ibrahim Sialkoti
9. Maulana Syed Kamaluddin
10. Maulana Qadeer Bakhsh
11. Maulana Taj Muhammad Sindhi
12. Maulana Muhammad Ibrahim Darbhanga
13. Maulana Khuda Bakhsh Muzzaffarpuri
14. Maulana Maula Bakhsh Amritsari
15. Maulana Abdul Hakim Gayawi
16. Maulana Muhammad Akram
17. Maulana Munir-uz-Zaman
18. Maulana Muhammad Sadiq
19. Maulana Muhammad Dawood Ghaznavi
20. Maulana Syed Ismael
21. Maulana Muhammad Ubaidullah
22. Maulana Azad Subhani

This is not a complete list of the scholars but only of those who came to attend the Khilafat Conference and laid the foundation of Jamiat Ulema-e-Hind there. Maulana Abul Wafa Sanaullah and Maulana Muhammad Dawood Ghaznavi extended an invitation for the first meeting of the party in Amritsar.

On December 6, 1920, a meeting of the Jamiat Ulema-e-Hind was held in Calcutta presided by Maulana Taj Muhammad Sindhi, and on December 8, 1920, bearing the signature of 500 scholars, a religious decree endorsing the non-cooperation movement was issued. This decree was written by Maulana Abul Muhasin Muhammad Sajjad Haider Bihari.

Jamiat Ulema-e-Hind's first working committee was convened in Delhi on February 9-10, 1922, and its members were:

1. Maulana Mufti Muhammad Kifayatullah
2. Maulana Abdul Halim Siddiqui
3. Masih-ul-Mulk Hakim Ajmal Khan
4. Maulana Shabbir Ahmad Usmani
5. Maulana Abdul Majid Badayuni
6. Maulana Mazharuddin
7. Maulana Abdul Qadir Qasuri
8. Maulana Hasrat Mohani
9. Maulana Ahmadullah Panipati
10. Maulana Azad Subhani
11. Maulana Abdul Qadeer Badayuni
12. Maulana Mohammad Ibrahim Sialkoti

Lokmanya Tilak

Before the appearance of Gandhi in the sky of Indian politics, Lokmanya Tilak was the country's recognized leader. Maulana Hasrat Mohani was his disciple. Gandhi would regularly declare that he was not a political man but a religious one. When Gandhiji accepted the presidency of the All-India Home Rule League, after Mrs. Besant left, he declared that he was entering politics for the first time. In contrast, Tilak considered himself a political man. His guiding principle was that India's independence should be achieved by any means necessary. For that reason, he believed that the bloody events of Punjab and the deep emotions that arose from the Khilafat Movement should be used in the Montagu-Chelmsford Reform. July 23, 1920 was Tilak's birthday. On August 1 at 40 minutes past midnight, he suddenly passed away. The mourning that took place in India at Tilak's death was unprecedented. When his ashes were brought to be immersed in the Ganges River, I was a student at Allahabad University. All of us students, both Hindus and Muslims, had gone to the banks of the river, barefoot and our heads uncovered. On his death, Gandhiji wanted to take part in his funeral when some people objected. Gandhi declared that a patriot of the nation has no caste. And Gandhiji, Maulana Shaukat Ali, and Dr. Kitchlew gave a shoulder to his bier. Hasrat read a poem on the banks of Ganges, whose refrain was:

> *Why should we not mourn in India today,*
> *Tilak has left this world*
> *The strong Tilak, the virtuous Tilak,*
> *the leader toward freedom Tilak*

At that time, the question in front of all of India was who was going to lead them. The complete answer to that question was soon to be had by all of the nation in such a way that all the hearts would cry out in unison.

Special Session of Congress in Calcutta

From September 4-9, 1920, a special session of the Congress was held in Calcutta. Lala Lajpat Rai, who had just returned from the United States, was appointed president of the meeting. The session was convened specially to discuss and debate the issue of the Caliphate and for Congress to abandon its traditional course of action and now step into the field of direct action and non-cooperation. Prior to this meeting, Gandhiji, Maulana Mohammad Ali and Maulana Shaukat Ali had made extensive tours of India and prepared the country for embarking on non-cooperation. There was great excitement among the people for this meeting, 5000 delegates came from all parts of India to participate in it, and there was a gathering of more than 100,000 people. On the way, Maulana Shaukat

Ali had drafted a proposal for non-cooperation with Gandhiji in the train. This proposal aimed at non-cooperation with the British government on all fronts. In particular:

1. Government courts and all government meetings should be boycotted.
2. Children should be taken out of government schools and colleges and those schools and colleges that receive government assistance, and independent and self-sufficient institutions should be established for them.
3. Military, clerical staff, and members of labor groups should refuse working in Mesopotamia.
4. Members should resign from all the councils.
5. Foreign textiles should be completely boycotted.

At the same time, on September 7, Muslim League held its meeting. Muslim League also supported non-cooperation, but after Khilafat Committee and Jamiat Ulema-e-Hind entered the fray, they softened their advocacy. It should also be remembered that the Muslim League of the time did not oppose Congress. The Khilafat Conference too, presided by Abul Kalam Azad, was convened during the same days. It was that presidential address that Maulana Azad used to give shape to a forceful book for all people on the matter of the Caliphate.

At the meeting of the Congress and the Khilafat Conference, the proposal of non-cooperation was approved with enthusiasm. However, in the Congress session, Mr. Muhammad Ali Jinnah alone raised his voice in opposition to it. In any case, in the special session of the Congress, a green light was given to the Khilafat and non-cooperation movements. Till then, Mahatma Gandhi had managed with his impressive individual influence and backing of the Khilafat Committee. Now Mahatma Gandhi unleashed his new program on the nation.

The government was rattled by the nation's enthusiasm and the numerous rallies, processions, and Gandhiji's widely recognized leadership. It issued a warning that the people should refrain from participating in these movements else force will be used against them. The government also announced that the indulgence shown toward Gandhiji during the protests against the Rowlatt Act will not be extended now. The answer Gandhiji gave to this was to publish the various modes of his entire program and invite the nation to surge forward.

Finally, in August, under the leadership of Gandhiji, the Gujarat Political Conference was held solely to deliberate on the matter of the Caliphate. Non-cooperation was opposed there but a resolution in favor of non-cooperation passed with 1855 votes for it and 823 against. There was unanimous consent among the Muslims to vote for the resolution, with the exception of Muhammad Ali Jinnah, who opposed the resolution and voted against it.

In those days Gandhi used to write lengthy articles to explain his views. He wrote that English culture should be abandoned and Indian culture should be adopted, and the only means to do that was with independent education. Consequently, on October 18, 1920, Mahatma Gandhi laid the foundation of an independent university in Gujarat, the Gujarat Vidyapith.

On October 27, 1920 Mahatma Gandhi published an open letter to all the British living in India, in which he described his services, justified the current initiative, and urged the

British to understand the situation and give the right advice to the government.

Nagpur Congress

The annual meeting of the All-India Congress was held in Nagpur on December 26, 1920, presided by C. Vijayaraghavachariar. The British government had, at the same time, made a program for Prince Arthur, the Duke of Connaught, to tour India. He was coming to inaugurate the Legislative Council, and to deceive India into believing that the British had fulfilled the promises they had made and set the country on the path to a proxy government. Gandhiji proposed that the Duke be boycotted and after the proposal was passed, he wrote a letter to the Duke of Connaught in which he stated with arguments why he was compelled to boycott him. In it, it was made clear that no humiliation of the Duke was acceptable but it was the avoidance of the system of government, a change in which was necessary for truth and justice, and which was beyond the authority of the Duke. Gandhiji always used to say and teach that our fight was not with the British but with the government and its system of governing, which is not based on justice and equality.

At the Nagpur Congress, Gandhi wrote the proposal for non-cooperation in English, the opening words of which were:

"Since, in the opinion of the Congress, the Government of India has completely lost the confidence of the country, the people of India have decided to establish Swaraj (self-rule) in India."

The translation of this proposal was read out by Maulana Mohammad Ali in this session of the Congress. Here too, Mr. Jinnah remained active in opposing the proposal for non-cooperation, but, as the rural saying goes, "What is the value of a hand-fan in a windstorm?" Mr. Jinnah did not find even a single supporter and the proposal was accepted.

After the non-cooperation resolution was passed at the Congress' special session and again and again at its annual conferences, Gandhiji became the Commander-in-Chief of this non-violent jihad; behind him was the full force of the nation and its political institutions such as Congress, Muslim League, Khilafat Committee, Jamiat Ulema-e-Hind, etc. India had arisen with one voice for its independence and the restoration of the Caliphate.

After the decision of the Nagpur Congress, Srinivas Shastri, who was the best speaker in India, withdrew from the Congress. He told the newspapers that after the non-cooperation proposal was approved, it was not possible for him to attend the Congress meetings, and in the same vein, there was no room for other moderates in the Congress. India was now a battlefield. And where was the room for peace, flattery and divination in this bloody battle?

Gandhiji, Maulana Mohammad Ali and Maulana Shaukat Ali toured all of India. Wherever they went, they were welcomed with passion and respect, huge crowds showed up, and grand rallies were held. Gandhi never spoke for more than five or seven minutes but Maulana Mohammad Ali did not speak for less than two to two and a half hours. He used to cry and make others cry. From time to time he used to recite Quranic verses in such a way that the title of Maulana became completely apt for him. As a result, the fear of being imprisoned by the British government and even the fear of being shot to death vanished from the minds of the people. Even the villagers who were scared of the constable's face now came out in the field with open chests. In front of the police and the army, slogans of *Naara-e-Takbeer, Allah-o-Akbar,* long live Hindu-Muslim unity, long live Mahatma Gandhi, long live Maulana Mohammad Ali, and long live Maulana Shaukat Ali would pierce the sky. When someone went to jail, their family members would be congratulated as if he had done the family proud. Lucknow, Ajmer, Aligarh, Allahabad, Madras, Bengal, Delhi, Assam, Punjab - the entire country was toured. On one hand there were slogans of *Bharat Mata Ki Jai* and *Naara-e-Takbeer*, which were being chanted by both Hindus and Muslims, and on the other hand there was the government response of an endless stream of seizing and capturing. All the students of schools and colleges, who were excelling in education and sports, came out and presented themselves for arrest, and went away rejoicing.

Peace Assembly

The government, on the one hand, expanded the number of arrests, and on the other, came up with a plan against the non-cooperation movement using the princes and landlords, which was to establish 'peace assemblies' from the district level to the provincial level. In order to prove that these assemblies were public bodies, all its appointed members were non-government people, who were the same landlords and taluqdars. These peace assemblies held that the scheme run by Gandhiji was bound to create violence, which would lead to the people being devastated and ruined, thereby justifying their benevolent government in its efforts to establish peace. Their advice was that people should remain away from Gandhiji's non-cooperation movement. I too had the chance to glimpse an introductory scenario of this but it would be appropriate to mention another incident before narrating it.

Mahatma Gandhi had persuaded the Muslims to join him in the non-cooperation movement. Now, in order to shake the whole of India, he thought it necessary to bring three particular men to his side. These were Motilal Nehru, Syed Hasan Imam, a barrister from Patna whose patriotism was legendary, and Mr. CR Das, a barrister from Calcutta. Getting Motilal Nehru was easy. His son Jawaharlal Nehru had returned from England after passing the law exam and was the only son of Motilal. He was ardently working to take the country to freedom and gave it his all, and his influence was accepted in the entire family.

Syed Hasan Imam's law practice brought in Rs. 50,000 - 60,000 per month. He told Gandhiji that he agreed with the movement but he could not leave his law practice. However, he gave a signed blank check and volunteered his daughter to work for the movement. Maulana Mohammad Ali worked hard on CR Das. He was the *Hatim Tai* of his time, the pre-Islamic Arab chieftain known for his generosity. His income too was around Rs. 50,000 - 60,000 per month, but he had a debt of Rs. 500,000. After much cajoling, Maulana Mohammad Ali persuaded him to leave his law practice and join the movement but on the condition that the debt be paid soon. And the debt was paid soon, because the simple and humble CR Das sold off his house. When Gandhiji came again, he stayed in the same house and CR Das was living there too, but as a tenant. Such were the great sacrifices that the nation gave.

Allama Iqbal told me in Lahore that it was a great success for Gandhiji that he was able to bring CR Das into his fold as CR Das had a very high spiritual status.

Allahabad District Congress Conference

Allahabad District Congress organized a conference under the presidency of Maulana Mohammad Ali. I too had the opportunity to attend this conference as a member of the public. The conference venue was surrounded by British troops. But were they there to intimidate or to provide peace and security? Nobody even noticed the troops. Maulana Mohammad Ali came dressed in an 'abaa, a long cloak. He received many ovations from the attendees for his presidential address. Lala Lajpat Rai was also present and gave a very influential speech. Mahatma Gandhi was there too. In those days, he used to wear a white *khaddar* dhoti and kurta and a cap which is known as the Gandhian cap today. All he said was that he too believed that employment in the army was illegitimate. And he had the entire audience repeat that employment in the army was illegitimate. Maulana Mohammad Ali had said in his inaugural address that people have highly praised him but he is not a humble man, that he drank all those compliments but he wants to hear another compliment and that is that he is a great friend of the Hindus. When Pandit Motilal Nehru got up, he had a piece of paper in his hand. He was reading it and giving a speech in his charming manner. Pandit Motilal was very eloquent, an excellent orator, and fluent in Persian. Contrasting the impersonal and authoritative style of the erstwhile administration to the courteous disposition at the time, he said that in the past, when the Collector *Saheb* wanted to summon someone, it would be written *"hukum naama banaam...,*" or that 'the order is in the name of so and so,' and that the person should appear in the presence of "*ii.n jaanib,*" or 'I, on this side.' Now look at this epistle, it says "*janaab-e-man,*" or 'Dear Sir,' and is signed off with "*niyaaz-mand Kalaktar,*" or 'Your obedient servant, Collector.' The audience was delighted with this anecdote. We could not see Pandit Jawaharlal Nehru since he did not get up, although I remember Maulana Mohammad Ali saying that, "Brother Jawaharlal has given up smoking foreign cigarettes and is chewing betel nut instead." Pandit Motilal gave "Peace Assembly" the name "Slave Assembly," but the Peace Assembly later proved to be quite atrocious.

Return of Maulana Mahmud Hasan and the Activities of Jamiat Ulema-e-Hind

Maulana Mahmud Hasan departed Malta on March 12, 1920 when he was still in custody. After staying for 18 days in "*Sayadi Bashar*" and nearly two months in "*Vais*" in government custody, he arrived in Bombay in late May of 1920 and was released. He was always trailed by the government's CID agents. In Malta, he would appear front and center among his close advisors, sitting on a carpet with a sash on his turban and a rosary in his hand. In Bombay as well, a Maulana Rahim Bakhsh visited him and advised him in a very well-wishing manner to spend the rest of his life in the remembrance of Allah and also advised him not to visit the office of the Khilafat Committee and instead go directly to Deoband. Arrangements had also been made for his onward journey.

When Maulana stepped off the ship, many of the nation's leaders were present to welcome him. The sky was resounding with the slogans of *Allah-o-Akbar*. The procession started with great pomp and splendor and he went directly to the office of Khilafat Committee, where he was given a grand welcome and the title "Shaykh-al-Hind" by the leaders of India, which has become a part of his name. The Khilafat Committee of Bombay also presented him with a letter of thanks. After a two-day stay in Bombay, Maulana left for Delhi and stayed there at Dr. Ansari's house. From there he left for Deoband two days later. On the way, the people of Meerut presented him with an address. Maulana Syed Muhammad Mian writes on page 210 of the Volume I of *"Ulama-e-Haq"*:

"There was a crowd of people at every station on the way. When he reached Deoband's station, the crowd was massive. People from towns and villages had come to see him."

Later, on page 211 he writes:

"The hearts of Muslims were awaiting calmness and assurance. The arrival of Hazrat Shaykh ended this wait. Now the steps of the Muslims were the most swift and confident. Every person was smitten by the movement and eager to give it their all...A small number of people who were opposed to him were in a state that when an important person from that group died, even if that person had earlier been extremely influential and popular among Muslim scholars and the common people, the situation at the time would be that it would be difficult to find men other than specific members of the household to join the funeral and perform the funeral rites and burial. There would be no choice but to take the bier in a motorcar (God forbid)."

This was the state of emotions of Muslims at the time. These were the reasons that the *Pesh-Imam* of Jama Masjid was compelled to return his honorary title of *Shams-ul-Ulama*.

With the arrival of Maulana Mahmud Hasan, the acrimonious rivalries that may have been hidden in the hearts of the people evaporated. India's Muslims had found a leader, a recognized and widely accepted leader to whom they bowed their heads and whose directives were worthy of their compliance.

Shaykh-ul-Hind had contracted the pernicious ailment of arthritis when he was in Malta. The painful conditions of captivity must have been unable to affect the heart and mind of such a devoted man, but he could not help but show the effects on his body. When he reached Deoband, it was not even possible for him to sit and get up, let alone walk around. But, in that condition, he would go on to lead the movement, make the difficult effort of journeys, and attend meetings.

Hazrat Shaykh was not only the spiritual leader of understanding, insight, knowledge and grace, but also asceticism and piety, nationalism, purity and worship. He was also a disciplined man. The combination of this ascetic lifestyle, spiritual leadership, and physical activism was reminiscent of the bygone days.

Second Annual Conference of the Jamiat Ulema-e-Hind

The first meeting of Jamiat Ulema-e-Hind on December 28, 1919 in Amritsar was presided over by Maulana Abdul Bari. Congress Conference presided by Pandit Motilal Nehru, Khilafat Conference presided by Maulana Shaukat Ali, and Muslim League Conference presided by Hakim Ajmal Khan were also held there concurrently. Demands for the restoration of the Caliphate were being made everywhere. The second meeting of the Jamiat Ulema was held in Delhi on November 19-21, 1920. It was presided over by Shaykh-ul-Hind out of respect for the wishes of all the community scholars and was accepted by him to spread his message to the entire community, although his health was deteriorating at the time. His presidential address was a summary of truths, the basics of which are given below:

1. The worst enemy of Islam and Muslims is the English, and non-cooperation with them is obligatory.

2. Protection of the Muslim community and preservation of the Islamic Caliphate are purely religious demands and if brothers in the homeland ask for sympathy and support in these regards, it is valid and they are entitled to it.

3. If, in the present time, the use of artillery, guns, and airplanes could be justified for the defense of the masses from their enemies, and despite the fact that these things did not exist in the early days, then there should be no doubt about the justification for demonstrations, display of national unity and unanimous demands, because in the present time, for the people concerned with these things who don't have cannons, guns and airplanes, these means are their weapons.

Regarding Hindu-Muslim unity, his golden words from the speech are given below[26]:

---

26 *Ulama-e-Haq*, Volume II

"There is no doubt that the Almighty Allah has made your compatriots, the nation's most populous people (Hindus) to, in one way or another, support you in achieving such a noble cause of yours. I consider the unity and harmony of these two sects to be very useful and fruitful. Considering the delicacy of the situation, the efforts being made by the elders of both parties for this are very valuable in my heart, because I know that if the situation were opposite of that, it would make the freedom of the country impossible forever. Here, the hard claw of the administrative government will keep tightening its grip day by day, and if a faint picture of Islamic power has survived, it will be wiped from existence just like the wrong words in our misdeeds."

After that, he gave the scholars of the community a mandate to walk the straight path of God that they had received in light of Quran and Sunnah, to bring back to the folds of their congregation through wisdom and good sermons those who have separated from them, and if this leads to confrontation, use counseling as the best resort.

Establishment of Jamia Millia Islamia

Aligarh Muslim University has always been in the eyes of the leaders of the nation and at every opportunity people have tried to get the support of the students and teachers of the university. At that time, Aligarh was the cultural and etiquette capital of India's Muslims. Its support was invaluable at a time when the Islamic world, the Islamic Caliphate, and the holy places were in grave danger. More importantly, a part of the movement was the boycott of schools, colleges and universities, and so there was bound to be an effort to make the students of Aligarh quit their university and join the non-cooperation movement. The students themselves had decided that they should deliberate on this important matter and enter the field of action. Maulana Abul Kalam Azad was invited by some of the student leaders there and delivered a speech in Aligarh Union. He said, "We have come here knowing that you have bowed your head before the law of truth and you want to know what are the rulings of Allah and His Messenger in the present situation. First of all, I would like to ask you, who is the scholar of India who, in your view, has the authority to inform and invite you to apply the divine commandments in the light of the Quran and Sunnah on the present situation, and to inform you and invite you to action. That is why I will not say anything today. Go and think, and give me an answer tomorrow. Tonight there will be the deep desolation of the night, the Almighty, and you. Search your conscience at that time, take an account of things around you, and form a thoughtful opinion." With that, he adjourned the session. The next day, there was a gathering again, and the students said they considered him the greatest religious authority and scholar of India. Then Maulana said that since they considered him authorized and asked him questions, he would say that non-cooperation with the government was as obligatory as prayer, fasting and duties of Islam, and called upon them to get out from inside the walls of college and boycott college education.

Surprisingly, the ground that was prepared with this effort and endeavor did not yield any results and the desired end was not achieved. Dr. Sir Ziauddin Ahmad was then the Pro-vice-chancellor of the university, and in every way the university's responsible administrator. Dr. Ziauddin had published a statement in the newspapers in support of the protection of the Ottoman Caliphate and the Holy Land. But how could he have supported the non-cooperation movement? He cleverly and cunningly aired his propaganda and the result was that Maulana Abul Kalam was accepted as the independent Imam of India but his edict, like the edict of the Turkish Caliph of the Muslims, remained ineffective.

Maulana Mohammad Ali and Maulana Shaukat Ali were the heart and soul of Aligarh. They were Aligarians. Maulana Abdul Majid Daryabadi has praised Mohammad Ali for an incident in which he gave attention to a lowly clerk or a cook in the presence of an officer of the university, and has attributed it to Mohammad Ali's Islamic spirit. But this Islamic spirit was in fact in the veins and in the entire being of the Aligarians. Mohammad Ali and Shaukat Ali used to regularly go to Aligarh, and this was an ordinary incident there.

Mr. Towle, the Principal, was coming from one side and a low-level employee from the other. First, Mohammad Ali sprang toward the employee, said *"assalamu alaikum"* and hugged him before turning to the Principal and saying, "Good Morning, Mr. Towle." This was an added charisma of the education and training of this institution. Maulana Shaukat Ali was a Collector in the Opium Department. He used to come to Aligarh on his breaks, and when it was time for him to leave, the students would gradually take all his things away, as if it were an organized conspiracy. Someone would take his blanket, someone else the quilt, and so on. And money would not stay with him and all of it would get spent. In the end, Maulana Shaukat Ali would make a round of the hostel rooms in the company of a few students, complaining that "the rascals looted me," and asking for donations of four or eight annas for him to make his fare back. This was a game that was played on his every visit. It was a must for both brothers to participate in the annual Sir Syed Day celebrations. Maulana Mohammad Ali was known for his non-serious playful mood there. He used to play a very intelligent and interesting role in the "*Jehl-e-Murakkab*" there. People may not remember or understand *Jehl-e-Murakkab* or "Ignorance of one's ignorance," - it was kind of a light-hearted gathering in the evenings where the discourses were intelligent but laced with humor and mischief. In this way, both brothers were extremely welcome and popular in Aligarh. The meeting of the Aligarh University Foundation Committee that was held in Kanpur, in which there was stiff opposition to Maulana Mohammad Ali, had all of Aligarh behind the Maulana.

The brief story behind the incident was that the Aligarh University Foundation Committee's intent had already been to acquire from the government such a university for the Muslims of India which fulfilled their needs. The demand of the Muslims was that the university should be for all Indians in which Islamic schools and colleges were affiliated to it. The government was not agreeable to that. A local style Hindu university had already been established in Banaras. The Muslims stuck to their persistent demand. Toward that effort, a delegation was formed whose president was Maulana Mohammad Ali and that evening he held a meeting in which he wished the body to agree that the delegation be given full authority to set up its conditions. In those days Maulana Mohammad Ali was considered a supporter of the government and had very good relations with the top British officers.

That was enough to make Muslims suspicious. A group insisted that whatever the delegation decided, they should bring it to the Foundation Committee and get it approved. Maulana Mohammad Ali asked if people did not trust him anymore. The answer given was that in principle it was necessary for the final decision to be made by the Foundation Committee. So, during the night session, the group of Maulana Abul Kalam Azad, Maulana Hasrat Mohani, Right Honorable Sir Amir Ali, Khwaja Ghulam-us-Saqlain and Nawab Viqar-ul-Mulk came up in opposition. When the resolution was presented, students of Aligarh were present to cause commotion and uproar on behalf of Maulana Mohammad Ali. Khwaja Ghulam-us-Saqlain had delivered a fiery speech a day earlier. On that day, he remained absolutely quiet. Right Honorable Sir Amir Ali perhaps saw his imminent membership of the Judicial Committee of the Privy Council at risk of being declined. Maulana Hasrat Mohani was not a great speaker. Nawab Viqar-ul-Mulk was highly respected. He was old by then and hard of hearing. He was considered very religious, sincere, and wise. Mohammad Ali showed him a proposal which he agreed to and remained silent. Now Maulana Azad was left. When he stood up to speak, various calls and whistles started to create chaos. But there was a call for quiet and Maulana read such an apropos couplet that the audience was silenced. With the full force of his oratory, he opposed the resolution. Maulana Mohammad Ali won by two votes. And right then, the call for morning prayers was heard. After the prayers, there was a continuous flow of people into the residence of Maulana Azad. Now they were upset about the resolution. Mohammad Ali had kissed the hands of Nawab Viqar-ul-Mulk as soon as the resolution passed. Now he too came to know the real reason. In his newspaper *Al-Hilal*, Maulana Azad wrote a scathing article under the title "Companionship at Midnight," filled with sarcasm and criticism of Mohammad Ali. Hasrat Mohani wrote a poem on Mazharul Haque, whose name means 'Manifestation of Truth,' first verse of which was was:

> *His name is 'Manifestation of Truth,' but*
> *a follower of falsehood he is*

Allama Shibli wrote a poem criticizing Khwaja Ghulam-us-Saqlain for his opposition to the resolution as a co-member of the delegation.

> *"You are only a co-member of the delegation,*
> *don't be beside yourself with excitement"*

Then the resignations started. First, Mazharul Haque resigned from the delegation, in response to which a laudatory article was published in *Al-Hilal* under the title "With Mazharul Haque." Then Ghulamus Saqlain submitted his resignation. Finally it was Nawab Viqar-ul-Mulk's turn. In a lengthy article published in *Al-Hilal*, he stated that the draft of the resolution that Mohammad Ali showed him was not the one that was passed. On reading it, he had wondered why we complained about the mutual disagreement among the Turks. And, although that draft had not been a very good one, it could at least be tolerated. That is why he had remained silent. In the end he apologized to the people, said that he was old and hard of hearing, and that the incident had proved that he could be deceived. For that reason he was now giving up public service and would lead a retired life.

The article caused quite a stir in all of India. Commenting over it, Maulana Azad wrote that on passing of the resolution,

Mr. Mohammad Ali had kissed the hands of Nawab *Saheb*. In fact, given Nawab Saheb's elder status, it would not have been unwarranted if Mohammad Ali had kissed his feet. But now we know what the true reason was.

The delegation disbanded. Mohammad Ali's stock fell and Maulana Azad became a hero of the Muslims. Mohammad Ali regained his position in the community and cast off the label of government loyalist through his display of exemplary sacrifices, unparalleled audacity, boldness, and Islamic passion. But the rift of distrust that had been created between the two leaders could never be mended. And that was a big deficit for the community.

9

The Movement at its Zenith

New India

January 1921 arrived in India and along with it the intoxicating notion of freedom. The people were invited to give the ultimate sacrifice at the gallows post in the direction of total independence. At the appeal of Deshbandhu CR Das, 3000 students went on strike at colleges. Thousands dropped out of college. National College was established in Calcutta on February 4, 1921. In Bihar, the foundation of Vidyapith was laid. In Patna, Ahmedabad, Bombay, Banaras and Delhi, National Colleges were opened. In Bengal, Gujarat, and Bihar, National Universities were established.

In November 1920, Nadwatul Ulama Lucknow ended the government subsidy of Rs. 500 per month. At the time, although Syed Sulaiman Nadvi was the administrator of Nadwatul Ulama, but Habibur Rehman Khan Sherwani, an important member of the board of directors of Nadwatul Ulama, was a staunch opponent of the non-cooperation movement. The expenditure of Nadwatul Ulama was Rs. 1000 per month then, out of which only Rs. 450 per month was left coming from Nawab Bhopal. Even in those circumstances, the passing of a resolution to stop the aid was a sign that those who were not concordant with the non-cooperation movement had lost their position and influence.

In November 1920, elections were held under the 1919 Reforms. Congress totally boycotted the elections, and although a number of for-hire candidates who were sycophants of the government ran in the elections, very few from the public voted. The campaign to set up educational institutions was ongoing. As a result, due to the effort of Rajendra *Babu*, a college was established on Patna-Gaya Road, and he was appointed Principal. A number of highly meritorious professors at government-run colleges resigned and joined this college. The syllabus was the same as other colleges and there was no difficulty acquiring capital for the college.

> *See how we have collected twigs for our nest*
> *But know also that we desire to set fires too*

In a similar trend, 250 students of Patna Engineering School said farewell to their studies and approached Barrister Mazharul Haque to give them accommodation. Mazharul Haque was one of the top barristers. He lived a life of utmost comfort and luxury. He had a grand house in which he used to live and was also building a second majestic mansion. But the situation was different now.

When Motilal, CR Das, Rajagopalachari, Vithalbhai Patel, Mohammad Ali, and Shaukat Ali had left the comfort of their homes and sacrificed everything to enter the field of action, how could Mazharul Haque stay back? He left his luxurious and comfortable home with all its accoutrements and went to live in a garden on Danapur Road in Patna with all the students. A friend of his had a small house there, in which he started to live. Gradually some thatched hutments made from palm leaves came up there. The boys were brimming with passion. They were enduring all kinds of discomfort and difficulties living there. A *charkha* workshop was also set up. Cows were kept. Mazharul Haque used to live among the students. He used to teach them. He ate the basic food they ate. Sometimes they had to get by on just chewing some gram nuts. Most of the students were Hindu, but by then, the distinction between Hindu and Muslim had disappeared. The boys too treated him like their father. It was that place which was named Sadaqat Ashram later, acquired a lot of fame throughout all of India, and to which people pilgrimage for a view even today. By God, what a beautiful sight it was. Jamia Millia Islamia, Vidyapith, Sadaqat Ashram, Madrasa Calcutta, and who were the teachers there - Maulana Mohammad Ali, Babu Rajendra Prasad, Mr. Mazharul Haque! Straw mats to sit on and basic grains to eat.

Along with that, watchmen were posted at liquor stores. People were now weary taking liquor sales licenses, and embarrassed too. Boycott of foreign clothes had started; in fact foreign clothes had been burned. Everyone was wearing the coarse *khaddar*. *Charkha* was being spun everywhere. Simplicity, selflessness, mutual love, unity, truth, determination for freedom of the homeland, and strong non-violence were the swords of Gandhi's followers.

By the time April passed, Pandit Motilal Nehru, Rajagopalachari, Vithalbhai Patel, and Rajendra Prasad had said farewell to their law practices. These people were famous in their professions throughout India, and had incomes of Rs.50,000-60,000 per month.

A unique and heartwarming aspect of this scene was the Hindu-Muslim unity. Many Hindus used to chant the *Allah-o-Akbar* slogan. Islamic scholars, with the desire in their hearts to sacrifice their lives, were spewing fire from their lips, and had declared non-cooperation a jihad against the British. And they not only issued religious decrees but were also inviting the rope and the gallows post for themselves.

Foray into Aligarh

With great ease and determination, the Ali brothers stormed Aligarh in October 1920. They had thought that all they needed to do was go there, and all the students would get behind them. But they had misjudged the politics of the British and the fabrications of Dr. Ziauddin Ahmed. Mohammad Ali was not successful in this, the story of which is that Dr. Sir Ziauddin Ahmed set his stooges who booed in derision at Mohammad Ali in the Union Hall. The custom at Aligarh was that booing was allowed on one of their own, but there should be silence for a visitor. But here it was not a matter of an entertaining speech, but of a decision. Maulana Mohammad Ali left dejected, but a large group of students were supporters of the movement. Even though not everyone was ready to act, a movement arose later among the students, another session was organized, and Maulana Mohammad Ali was invited back. Maulana Mohammad Ali came but he was sad and spoke for only five minutes. He said that he had come to Aligarh thinking it was his own but now he was being evicted from it. This affected the assembly and the students showed their determination and courage for non-cooperation. One of these students was Zakir Husain, later to become Dr. Zakir Husain, President of the Republic of India, who had recently been appointed Assistant Lecturer at the university. The result was desirable and an atmosphere was created that already existed but was not apparent. And Maulana Mohammad Ali called on the students who could come with him then, went to the Old Boys' Lodge with them, and started residing there. Old Boys' Lodge was not owned by the College, but by the alumni, yet they were ordered to leave. Around 150 students, with their belongings on their head, marched out of the institution behind Mohammad Ali chanting *Allah-o-Akbar*, and a national Muslim university under the name Jamia Millia Islamia was established in Aligarh. Maulana Mohammad Ali assumed residence there. Initially, Maulana Mohammad Ali was its Principal, and, as was his habit, gave speeches from morning till the evening. Later, Khwaja Abdul Majid *Saheb* was appointed Vice-Chancellor. In this way, through the courage of Mohammad Ali, an independent university came into existence, which is presently doing very useful work. With this revolution in Aligarh, and after that throughout the country, national colleges and schools started to open. There was perhaps no district where at least one school was not opened. This was the objective of non-cooperation. Consequently, those institutions that used to receive government aid were boycotted.

Maulana Azad's Foray into Madrasa Aliah Calcutta

In the same way that this movement was about English medium schools and colleges, it was also about those madrasas, the seminaries, which received government aid. Among all the madrasas, there was a magnificent and famous one known as Madrasa Aliah Calcutta which ran on government aid.

When Maulana Abul Kalam Azad was under detention in Ranchi, he had established a national educational institution there. Now he came up with a plan to close the Madrasa Aliah Calcutta, which had quite a bit of influence on the Muslims of Bengal and all of India, and to establish a national madrasa instead. Due to the influence of Maulana's personality, about 250 students agreed and funding was also procured. Maulana was concerned about recruiting good teachers and eventually, Hazrat Maulana Hussain Ahmed Madani agreed to take charge. From this it can be deduced what the eminence and glory was of a national madrasa. Whatever work Maulana did, there was always this sort of greatness in it. The 250 students that had left the Madrasa Aliah following Maulana Azad's fiery speech found a temporary home in the madrasa that was opened for them in Calcutta's famous, grand and majestic Jama Masjid (Masjid Nakhoda).

On December 20, 1913 Mahatma Gandhi inaugurated this national Arabic madrasa. The speech that Maulana Azad gave on that occasion is important from the aspect of being given at the inauguration of an Arabic religious madrasa. First, getting Gandhiji to lay its foundation stone. Second, this speech was complete proof of how the atmosphere was then, and how much love and acceptance Muslims had for Gandhiji. Parts of this speech have been entered below[27]:

> *"Mahatmaji! The class of students that is in front of you and whose eyes are glued to you is that class which left the grand building of the Madrasa Aliah Calcutta and its magnificent hostel (where all necessary accoutrements of living in luxury and comfort were available), merely*

---

27 *Khutbat-e-Azad*, Sahitya Akademi Press, pp 378

to fulfill the orders of Allah and for their status as true Indians. This is the class that has endured many difficulties on the path of non-cooperation, including hunger and thirst."

After that, Maulana mentioned the case where one section of the community is seeking sustenance through government education while a system of Arabic madrasas are only keeping the flame of true knowledge burning. In the end he said:

"I drew your attention to this matter for the reason that only a jeweler can discern the right gems and I know that you can discern the right gems of sincerity and devotion."

The speech that Gandhiji gave in response to this is extremely important. It gives a sense of how sincerely he was committed to the divine Caliphate. Addressing the students, he said:

"I am very pleased to see you all. You must be steadfast in your intentions, whether you step forward or step back. Islam is in danger right now. The Caliphate has been destroyed. The holy shrines have been seized. India's sovereignty has been defeated in Punjab. It is your duty to be committed to these tasks and to perform the duties that you owe to Islam and India."

Gandhiji asked the teachers to give religious education to the students which will make them true Muslims and true Indians. The sole purpose of starting national madrasas was to prepare such people who would reject slavery and give their lives for freedom. He said he knows that Islam teaches its adherents to love mankind and that he would instill in the teachers and students of this madrasa the spirit of Hindu-Muslim unity in which the issue of the Caliphate and *Swaraj* were at stake, and he, as an active Hindu, would say that the security of Islam was ever as important to him as that of Hinduism.

From this brief speech by Gandhiji, the following things are clear:

1. Gandhi too gave priority to the matter of the Caliphate. This is evident in his every statement and every speech.
2. Caliphate and *Swaraj* had been deemed two objectives of the nation and had been tied together to form the same process i.e. the protection of Islamic countries and holy places was possible only when the power of the British to colonize and the chains of slavery over India were broken.
3. India was moving slowly but with sure-footed confidence toward complete independence.
4. By declaring Hindu-Muslim alliance necessary, a practical struggle and a passionate endeavor had been launched for the achievement of this complete independence. The principle behind this alliance was that in religious practices, the two shall remain within their respective principles, but in matters relating to the nation, they shall put their heads together.

It is not possible to recount all the means by which the non-cooperation movement spread from district to district. What Janab Shah Muinuddin Ahmad Nadvi has written on page 221 of his book "Hayat-e-Sulaiman" should be considered true for every district:

"After the Nagpur Congress, the whole of India resounded with the non-cooperation movement, and Azamgarh in

UP became its major center. Branches and panchayats of Khilafat Committee were established throughout the district. Trials almost ended in courtrooms. Drinking alcohol ended and liquor stores completely disappeared. Nobody was taking liquor sales licenses any more. A national school had also been established. Darul Musannefin Hindustan, a writers' academy, had become the source of reference for many influential leaders of the country. The credit for the organization in Azamgarh goes to Sayyid Saheb and Maulana Masood Ali. Sayyid Saheb, i.e. Syed Sulaiman Nadvi, mostly took part in state and all-India level activities and would usually participate in the important meetings of Congress and Khilafat Committee. In those days, all the prominent leaders would stay at Darul Musannefin. Maulana Shaukat Ali, Dr. Ansari, Pandit Motilal Nehru, Pandit Jawaharlal Nehru, Mrs. Sarojini Naidu - Darul Musannefin has had the honor of hosting all of them. For Pandit Motilal Nehru and Pandit Jawaharlal Nehru, Darul Musannefin was a regular guest house. When the two used to tour eastern UP districts for Congress work, they would make Darul Musannefin their headquarters. And they would stay there for many days in a row."

The Story Behind the Procurement of Rs. 10 Million

On March 31, 1921, in the Bezwada Working Committee of Congress, Gandhiji appealed for the collection of Rs. 10 million within a fixed period of time. With his finger on the pulse of the nation, he wanted to hit two targets with the same arrow. First, the Congress would be able to acquire decent funds for its expanding work, and second, it would have a psychological effect on the government. Gandhi already had a great influence on the nation and had acquired a lot of trust from the people of the country. In order to put more impetus behind the appeal, and considering that the public was extremely passionate, Gandhi set the deadline of December 31, 1921 for the collection of Rs. 10 million. And how could there be any difficulty meeting the goal when Gandhiji himself had appealed, especially when many big businessmen were handing signed blank checks to him. And by December 31, 1921, all Rs. 10 million were collected.

In this regard, it is worth mentioning that the British strongly opposed this effort and tried their best to stop the money from being collected. Due to Gandhiji's great self-confidence, he was not distressed by this at all. In this context, the following excerpt on page 237 from *Aap Biitii* (Autobiography) Vol I by Zafar Hasan Aibak, a resident of Kabul, will be of interest:

"From the news we got from the newspapers, it was evident that it would be impossible for Gandhiji to be successful in this. There was about a week till the annual meeting of Congress in December 1921 when we learned that Rs. 100,000 remained to be collected for the target of Rs. 10 million. It was obvious that the target of Rs. 10 million would not be met by the appointed date. For that reason, Qibla Maulana Saheb (Maulana Ubaidullah Sindhi) decided to ask Russians for some financial help... Maulana requested the Russian Ambassador on behalf of the Kabul Congress Committee to ask his government for financial aid and to get him an answer before the last week of December 1921. Russia agreed to send

the remaining Rs. 100,000 to the All-India National Congress through the Kabul Congress Committee. Maulana informed the Congress about this but two days before the appointed date, news reached that the target of Rs. 10 million had been collected. Maulana informed the Russian Ambassador that the money was no longer needed and that the Kabul Congress Committee thanked him for the offer to help."

It should also be known that Maulana Obaidullah Sindhi had formed a Provisional Government of India in Kabul and a branch of the Indian National Congress, and had informed all the revolutionary parties of India on behalf of this Provisional Government that when India is attacked, the people of the country should not resist these attacks but facilitate the killing of English people in every way and not support them with money and men. They should keep disrupting the railways and telegraph facilities. To publicize Indian news, Jamal Pasha had arranged for the publication of local newspapers translated into Persian.

The *Khaddar* Scheme and Boycott of Prince of Wales

On July 18, 1921 Gandhiji presented a scheme in the Working Committee that was accepted unanimously with the exception of Maulana Hasrat Mohani, who was opposed to it. Instead of *khaddar*, he had started the *swadeshi* movement, and had even opened a *swadeshi* clothing store in Kanpur. There, night and day, he would give lectures to every passerby, opposing *khaddar* and in support of *swadeshi*, with references to statistics of usage. Hasrat Mohani commanded a lot of respect in Congress and among all kinds of people for his firm stance, exemplary courage, speaking the truth, intoxication with the idea of freedom of the country, clear mindedness, and many other ethical and spiritual qualities. People would silently listen to him. But all these efforts proved futile.

On July 31, 1921 a bonfire of foreign clothes was lit for the first time in Umar Sobani's park in the locality of Parel in Bombay. With great pleasure and delight, people brought foreign clothes and fed it into the bonfire. The leaping flames were crying out in their voice that all the accessories of slavery were being consigned to fire. After that, having a bonfire of foreign clothes became a common practice. There was no city or town where this practice was not held.

Mahatma Gandhi's Nationwide Tour

Maulana Mohammad Ali and Maulana Shaukat Ali were constantly touring with Gandhiji and grand rallies were held everywhere they went. The crowds were huge. Maulana Mohammad Ali's speeches would stir a lot of passion; Gandhi's greatness was touching the sky. There were almost daily rallies in all the cities. Thousands of people would gather to listen to speeches by local leaders. All the people were willing to give the highest sacrifice. The entire nation was intent on rebellion. Only those who saw these scenes could assess their true impact. Now the Khilafat and *Swaraj* movements had melded into one. There were meetings of Khilafat Committee and Jamiat Ulema-e-Hind as well and they were full of energy and passion. But now, the restoration of the Caliphate was deemed to be by way of *Swaraj*, and the entire nation's sights were set on freeing the country from slavery. The stature of

Congress was rising day by day, although other parties were passionately engaged as well and it was because of them that this environment had been created. They were increasingly taking on the role of promoting and helping.

As stated earlier, Sir Syed Ahmad Khan proposed a two-nation ideology in 1918 on the premise that the poverty of Muslims could only be removed at the mercy of the British government, and devised a scheme to keep the British as the ruler of India for as long as possible, arguing that if the British left India, the Hindu majority would prevail over the Muslim minority and destroy the future of Muslims. That is what the Aligarh Movement was. It has also been stated earlier that the Khilafat Movement was like a lightning strike on the harvest stack of Aligarh. Maulana Mohammad Ali's personality was adorned with great virtues such as religiosity, piety, knowledge and grace, his elegant composition skills in English and Urdu, his skill in the art of poetry, his forceful eloquence, his sincerity and self-sacrifice. And he had become an undisputed leader of India soon after his release from detention. When he made a whirlwind tour of India with Mahatma Gandhi, slogans of 'Long live Maulana Mohammad Ali' were chanted everywhere along with slogans for Mahatma Gandhi. Both Hindus and Muslims would chant slogans of *Allah-o-Akbar*. Maulana Azad has written in "India Wins Freedom":

"And then came the period of long tours of India to prepare the country for the non-cooperation movement. Gandhi intensely toured the country. I used to be with him on most of the tours. Mohammad Ali and Shaukat Ali would also be with us."

If the purpose of this writing is that Maulana Azad alone was truly with Gandhiji on all his tours and that the position of Mohammad Ali and Shaukat Ali was of occasional company, then that would be in contradiction to observation and history. There are still people around who observed that period. I, myself, had quit the University of Allahabad in 1920 and joined this movement and was constantly taking part. The truth is that Gandhiji's tours particularly included the committed Ali brothers with him. Maulana Azad toured as well and would address large crowds, sometimes before or after Gandhiji and sometimes along with him. Maulana's greatness too was reaching into the skies.

10

The Response of the Government

Karachi Trial

On September 19, 1921 a meeting of Khilafat Conference was held in Karachi presided by Maulana Mohammad Ali. As usual, there was a lot of passion and excitement in the meeting. Besides distinguished scholars and leaders of Islam, there were also Hindu leaders and members of the public in attendance. In the meeting a proposal was presented to make it illegitimate from an Islamic viewpoint to join the British army because doing so could force a Muslim to shoot at another Muslim, the punishment for which is hell according to the Quran. In addition, Muslim soldiers had also been compelled to join a war that would facilitate Islam's holy places to fall in the hands of the enemies. The significance of this proposal can be gauged from the fact that it was proposed by the presiding member. One of the reasons for this could be that Maulana Mohammad Ali may have been eager to speak on the topic. Therefore, he delivered a very long and passionate speech, using all his eloquence and quoting verses from the Quran and *Hadith*. He not only declared the employment of the army as religiously illegitimate but also strongly urged all the listeners to do their best to resign from the service of the army. The rule of thumb is that if a presidential proposal is on a non-controversial issue, it is not seconded and there is no debate on it. Only a vote takes place. But following Maulana Mohammad Ali's presentation of the proposal, Maulana Shaukat Ali, Dr. Saifuddin Kitchlew, Hazrat Maulana Hussain Ahmed Madani, Maulana Nisar Ahmad, Pir Ghulam Mujaddid, and Jagadguru Shankaracharya also gave passionate speeches and strongly seconded the proposal. The proposal was approved unanimously.

It is not known if Mahatma Gandhi was consulted on this proposal. Those who work to bring about a rebellion in the armed forces, their ways and means are completely different from others through which they bring about revolution. And aggression is their basic principle. All this is done secretly and by putting one's life on the line. But post-war despondency was prevalent. It was as if people were tearing their flesh with their own teeth. Maulana Hasrat Mohani told me about an interesting incident in this regard. In those days, rallies were happening in every village, town and city almost every day. One such rally was held by those soldiers who had fought in Hijaz and Jerusalem as part of the government forces and who were being bestowed with medals, honors, and, in some cases, with land grants by the government. These people had not spared anything to give the rally its splendor and display, and were all sitting in the front row. Maulana Hasrat told me that Farhatullah Baig was also in attendance. When he got up to speak, he commenced with a couplet of his, which he read boldly, emphasizing the words 'now' and 'support,' staring at the people sitting in the front row from one end to the other:

> *They come now as if they support non-cooperation*
> *These bastards come after devastating the Haram*

In any case, this proposal rattled the British government. Whither the thought of subjugation and servitude, it soon became obvious that the people of the nation had entered the arena of rebellion with a do-or-die attitude. The sycophants of the government were washed away in the tide of these emotions. They were nowhere to be found, sitting at home saving face. They did not have the courage to enter the arena or say one word in public. The Khilafat Conference in Karachi was the last nail in the coffin of the British government. This proposal greatly strengthened the heroic and courageous determination of the people to achieve independence and the British realized it was time to pack their bags. The declaration by the Islamic scholars based on verses of Quran and *Hadith* and by Jagadguru based on the Hindu religion that serving in the armed forces was illegitimate and forbidden was no small matter. After that, the rallying cry in every city, town, and village was:

Pack your bags, the rule of foreigners is about to go

In our Basti district, the firebrand orator Babu Ram Davan Singh, who was then the president of Basti district Congress, was famous for shouting this slogan and giving passionate speeches. This Gandhian man of action was not one to stand behind. "I also say that military service is forbidden," he declared. All of India resounded with this rebellious slogan.

After the Karachi conference, Maulana Mohammad Ali resumed his usual tour of India with Mahatma Gandhi, was arrested at the Waltair railway station, and later charged with promoting rebellion in the army and inciting violence among the public.

The government arrested all those people too who had given speeches at the Karachi Khilafat Conference, i.e. Maulana

Shaukat Ali, Maulana Hussain Ahmed Madani, Jagadguru Shankaracharya, Dr. Saifuddin Kitchlew, Maulana Nisar Ahmad, and Pir Ghulam Mujaddid. Maulana Mohammad Ali was also accused of giving a rebellious speech at Karachi Eidgah and for spreading hatred against the government.

The caravan of freedom fighters entered the courtroom in this manner[28]:

> *"The first to enter was Maulana Mohammad Ali with the Quran Shareef in one hand and a bottle of ink in the other. Maulana Shaukat Ali entered behind him, laughing and gesturing with unfeigned delight in response to the ardent and sincere gazes and passionate salutations. Behind him, Maulana Hussain Ahmed Madani came in with consummate dignity and sobriety. Jagadguru came in looking determined and vigilant with a staff in his hand. After them, Dr. Saifuddin Kitchlew and Maulana Nisar Ahmad entered, talking to each other and smiling, and responding to salutations with gestures. Behind him came Pir Ghulam Mujaddid, smiling and reciting verses of the Quran Shareef. Everyone kept standing till all the leaders had taken their seats."*

This was a preliminary hearing to determine if sufficient evidence existed against the defendants to proceed to a trial. The government's confoundedness was evident from the following account, which is quite interesting:

---

28 *Siirat Mohammad Ali* ("Biography of Mohammad Ali"), Raees Ahmed Jafri, citing an account of the Karachi Trial by Abdul Qadir Beg, MA, LLB (Alig)

"Barbed wire had been installed in the compound surrounding the hall and armed police and soldiers stood on guard. There were 150 Indian and 150 British soldiers in the compound. A machine gun had also been installed on the northern side of the hall. Those who came into the hall to watch the proceedings were mostly lawyers, barristers, and students."

Now neither Muslims nor Hindus were going to be intimidated by these bullying tactics and empty threats. The accused refused to take part in the court proceedings and did not question the witnesses. These witnesses were CID officers who presented excerpts from the speeches and the court eventually handed the case over to Sessions Court for a trial.

Proceedings of the Sessions Court

When the trial started in the Sessions Court, everyone remained silent while Maulana Mohammad Ali entangled with the judge and emphatically insisted that if God's law contradicted the law of the British government, he would be obedient to God and ignore British law. Anyone who called himself a Muslim should abide by the rules of the Quran. If he violated any verse of the Quran then he is not a Muslim etc. etc. He gave a full sermon which was absolutely out of place and irrelevant. Once Maulana Mohammad Ali admitted that he had tried to dissuade Muslims from serving in the British army, the confession was complete. Now there was no need to have a long discussion before the judge about what the teachings of Islam were in this regard and what had been taught by the last divinely ordained prophet, Prophet Muhammad, peace be upon him.

Suffice it to say, this verbal battle continued for a while. The judge kept trying to stop Maulana Mohammad Ali, who was determined to prove that according to the Quran and *Hadith*, employment in the army was forbidden for a Muslim. It came to the point where the Judge kept repeating that this was irrelevant while Maulana Mohammad Ali refused to yield and delivered the whole sermon, and finally the helpless judge became quiet.

The court sentenced Jagadguru Swami Shankaracharya to one year imprisonment and the rest to two years imprisonment. This verdict acted like gasoline on the fire raging against the government and all of India became a fiery blaze. Instead of causing any fear or despair among the people, it emboldened them further. The situation was such that people wanted to find an opportunity to face a bullet. It was the same for the thousands of students who had quit college and entered the arena.

The Afghan Bogey

Before that, Maulana Mohammad Ali had gotten entangled in the storm of an "Afghan bogey." The story behind it was that what the newspapers at the time had called a "bogey" was actually a scheme of Maulana Mahmud Hasan. This scheme was that Afghans and tribals would attack India, the many underground political parties with their headquarters within India would rise up in jihad, the country would be freed, and a united democratic national government would be established. This is evidence of historical significance. It shows that Shaykh-ul-Hind's movement included the great leaders of India and the honorable members of the government in exile. Maulana

Mohammad Ali was also among them. The Viceroy knew everything. The Viceroy also had copies of the proceedings, actions, and correspondences related to these matters, which the traitors of Islam delivered to the government to derive benefits. There was no shortage of people like Anis Ahmad, Allah Nawaz, Maulvi Rahim Baksh etc. The Viceroy showed all these documents to Tej Bahadur Sapru and Pandit Malviya. The patriotism, sincerity, and selfless service of Tej Bahadur Sapru and Malviyaji were recognized by the whole country but Tej Bahadur Sapru considered direct action against the government to be harmful for the country. He considered the Jallianwala Bagh incident to be an act of wrongdoing by an individual and did not hold the government responsible. Malviyaji had done very active and passionate work in the matter of Jallianwala Bagh but he thought it would be good if peace was achieved with the government. For these reasons, the Viceroy sought them out for selfish purposes. There were all sorts of people on the English side. After Lord Chelmsford's oppressive and cowardly policy, Lord Reading, a man of tolerant temperament, high morality and an understanding nature, was made Viceroy. Lord Reading laid his net as soon as he arrived. By this time, the whole of India was in a state of disarray and had boldly entered the arena of resistance. The display of guns, rifles, and machine guns by the government had no effect on anyone. The government's violent and strict policies had also failed. Lord Reading's desire was to somehow extinguish this fire. For this, he was intent on using the snare of trickery as a means to salvation.

His first attempt was to somehow bring Mahatma Gandhi under his control. The British order had not yet understood Gandhiji. Until then, they had been testing this extraordinary human being on a normal level. The other effort was to give the movement and its leaders a bad name. Hence, in order to strike two birds with one stone, Lord Reading first tried to meet Gandhiji and attempted to manufacture the understanding that it was Gandhiji who had requested the meeting.

Raees Ahmed Jafri has quoted a detailed statement of Maulana Mohammad Ali in his biography of the Maulana. From that we find out that Malviyaji wrote to Mahatma Gandhi saying that he was unwell, otherwise he would have come himself, that he would like to meet Gandhiji, and that if Gandhiji were unable to come to Allahabad, he would come to see him. In this way, when Gandhiji went to Allahabad, he met the Viceroy there at the latter's request. The go-between was Malviyaji. This meeting went on for 15 hours over six days. Lord Reading offered to help get India its independence and restore the power of the Turkish Caliphate. All he desired in return was that the non-cooperation movement remain free from violence. This was nothing he needed to ask for since the non-cooperation movement was founded on non-violence. But there was a secret buried in that request.

The government had promoted a rumor against Maulana Mohammad Ali that a man sent by the Shah of Afghanistan had come to him and that he wanted to facilitate the occupation of India by Afghanistan. Maulana Mohammad Ali states, "At this, certain esteemed Hindu gentlemen had distressed Mahatma Gandhi, asking why he trusted the two brothers so much, saying that they never wanted *Swaraj*, and that all they wanted was to bring the rule of Afghanistan over India."

Malviyaji and Dr. Sapru showed Mahatma Gandhi "a few authentic and false excerpts taken out of context" from

Mohammad Ali's speeches, "which had been provided to them by the Viceroy with the intent to create mistrust between us." On hearing this, Mahatma Gandhi considered it necessary to issue an appropriate statement, saying that "acting within Mahatma Gandhi's non-cooperation movement, it is not our intent to achieve *Swaraj* through violent means. But our speeches have had the wrong effect on some of our friends. So, we express our regret for using words that could have led to the wrong conclusions."

The Viceroy showed Gandhiji the excerpts that Sapru and Malviyaji had already shown him. On seeing them, Gandhi said that his intent was to have the brothers issue a statement so that no one has the pretext to be discontent about this matter. The Viceroy said that it would be very good, that the government had decided to prosecute the Ali brothers, but that if such a statement was issued, there would be no reason to prosecute them. Gandhi replied that it was their job to prosecute; he had no interest in that. There was an urgent need to publish a statement and, in any case, it was their duty whether the government prosecuted them or not.

Consequently, the above mentioned statement of Maulana Mohammad Ali was shown to Dr. Sapru and Pandit Malviyaji and published in newspapers. But before issuing the statement, and rightly so, Maulana Mohammad Ali expressed his desire to look at those excerpts. Gandhi agreed and telegrams were sent to Lord Reading and Pandit Malviya. Lord Reading remained silent but Malviyaji sent those excerpts.

Maulana Mohammad Ali states, "As soon as I read the excerpts, I remarked that some of them were misunderstood, misinterpreted, or misinformed, while some of them were downright being given the wrong meaning. There was not a single quote that proved the intent to incite violence." Yet, to dispel any doubts or suspicions from the hearts of his homeland, the statement was issued.

As soon as the statement was published, the government loudly spread the rumor all over India that Maulana Mohammad Ali had apologized, otherwise he would have been prosecuted. The thought was that this would cause the nation to lose trust in Mohammad Ali. But that time had passed. People were certainly surprised, but they understood the plot.

Lord Reading tried to take full advantage of this statement and his meeting with Gandhiji. While speaking at Chelmsford Club, he implied that it was Gandhiji who had sought the meeting with him. On the other hand, there was an indication that Mohammad Ali had apologized to avoid prosecution. Maulana Mohammad Ali writes, "As soon as my hasty brother Maulana Hasrat Mohani read this speech, he wrote to me a letter stating that if Mahatmaji had informed me before publishing this statement that the Viceroy had pardoned me on this condition, then there was no one more cowardly than me. And if he had not informed me of this, then there is no one more unfaithful than him. But my zealous brother did not understand that there might be a case where Lord Reading was giving the wrong summary of the meeting."

Maulana Mohammad Ali writes further, "In any case, when I read the Chelmsford Club speech, I was enraged, and I asked Mahatmaji if I had his permission to reply to it. It was a Khilafat meeting. I was presiding. The presidential address was to be something else, but after that, I only tore Lord Reading's veil of misrepresentation. I hardly gave a harsher speech than that in my entire life."

This was followed by the trial in Karachi. After the verdict of the trial, Maulana Mohammad Ali became more of a hero. Although many people were sentenced, most of the mention was made of Maulana Mohammad Ali, because firstly he was the leader of India's Muslims at that time and secondly, the proposal at the Khilafat Conference in Karachi that was the basis of the trial was made in his presidential address.

This was the time when the people of India had put everything on the line for their freedom. Rallies were held every day. And in these rallies, volunteers would appear from who knows where, who would set up gatherings inside and outside these rallies and sing poems of all kinds. Troupes would gather and outside the conference hours, they would entertain the attendees. This rallying cry had reached every home:

Said the mother of Mohammad Ali to him
Son, sacrifice your life for the Khilafat

Shaukat Ali is also with you
Son, sacrifice your life for Khilafat

There were many more couplets in the poem, all ending in the verse "Son, sacrifice your life for Khilafat." Alas, I wish someone separate from the literary and literary criticism point of view, and more from the perspective of service to history, had collected all these couplets. It would have shed a bright light on that period. A heartfelt poem from the aftermath of the Karachi trial was found and is as follows:

The convicts of Karachi are saying
For two years each, we are going

Blessed are your silken clothes
Blessed are your cotton and muslins

Congratulate us for our blanket pieces
For two years each, we are going

Blessed are your palace residences
Blessed are your pillows and poster beds

Congratulate us for sleeping on the ground
For two years each, we are going

Blessed are your milk and pudding
Blessed are your biscuits and butter

Congratulate us for our dry breads
For two years each, we are going

These were such affectionate emotions, expressions of such veneration, love and intrepid determination; they narrate stories of disregard for the clutch of law. These poems were read and people would cry uncontrollably. There is a famous town in Bijnor district called Kiratpur. In Kiratpur was the house of Mirza Abdul Latif Baig who was the president of Bijnor District Congress Committee. A district conference was held in Kiratpur which was presided over by Mirza Abdul Latif Baig himself. I was also there. This conference took place before the Ahmedabad Congress and after the verdict of the Karachi trial. Mirza Abdul Latif Baig was a man of a great heart and mind. A few days before the Kiratpur conference, witnessing these scenes of crying and wailing, he said to me that he was not in favor of all this and that it was a sign of weakness. It was said in passing and I forgot about it. A few days later, at the Kiratpur conference, a troupe of singing volunteers came from somewhere. First, they went around town from house to house, singing in the most pleasing way:

> *Here comes the season for the charkha*
> *Mothers and sisters, spin the charkha*

I had written down the entire poem, but it is a pity that I don't have it anymore. I only remember this couplet. After that, outside the conference, the poem of the Karachi verdict stated earlier was sung. When the conference started, at the participants' request, the president gave permission for that poem to be read during the proceedings. By God, what a scene it was! The participants were restless, and the most moved was Mirza Abdul Latif Baig. He was weeping bitterly and his whole face was wet with tears. Later I asked him, "Mr.! What happened to that admonition of yours?" In a very sad tone he replied, "I had lost control."

This was not a unique situation. The state of the entire country was like that. There were arrests every day. People happily went to jail. In some places, lorries would be parked to take them to jail, and so many would rush to get inside that the police would have to stop them saying there is no more room. It was exactly like this:

> *The pleasure of the crime increases after the punishment*

Attitude of the Government

The attitude of Viceroy Lord Chelmsford was oppressive and tyrannical. He thought he could threaten and instill fear in the people to get his way. He would show off his army of Englishmen, machine guns, and rifles, and when the people were not intimidated by them, he would carry out innumerable arrests, long sentences, and all kinds of harsh treatments in prison. Prisoners were sent into solitary confinement for small infractions. Those who had been sentenced by the court to rigorous imprisonment were made to ground bamboo plaster walls. During summer, the prisoners would be locked inside barracks, and during winter, the door of the barracks would be kept open. The blankets and coarse cloth used in beddings were infested with fleas. In the food served, bread was half-cooked and wet, to make it heavier and pass the ration requirement. The leftover flour would be sent to the administrators' homes. *Masoor Dal* lentils were served at 8 am and eggplant mash at 5 pm, often with insects floating in it. Newspapers were banned and if any made it inside, there would be such a raid as if the offenders were murder or dacoity suspects.

However, there were some officers who were testing the depth of emotions of the prisoners to gauge how strong the freedom movements were in India. They would either challenge the prisoners or let them roam free. For instance, the Collector of Lahore had assumed the tactic of challenging them. Lala Lajpat Rai sent 50 graduates (and don't forget, a graduate in 1920, not today) to volunteer jail time. In a challenging tone, the Collector said, "Very well, send them to the English Quarters." "English Quarters" was the jail's most comfortable section, where fine food was served, because it was where the

English prisoners were kept. The next day, Lalaji volunteered another 50 graduates. The Collector again gave the same order. The idea was to test the depth of this movement. The third day, another 50 graduates arrived. Now the Collector was nervous and fearful, but he gave the same order to take them to the English Quarters. When another 50 graduates arrived the fourth day, the Collector felt defeated and said, "India is making a sacrifice, and if India goes on making this sacrifice, we shall have no objection to leaving India."

Prisoners were handcuffed as well. That is why when Maulana Saiyad Muhammad Fakhir 'Bekhud' Allahabadi, *Sajjada-Nashin* of Daira Shah Ajmal, was arrested, he wrote a poem in which there was a couplet:

In my wearing these fetters, there is not the least bit indignity
The ways of my ancestors are the traditions of the Holy Prophet

The Women

The women too had entered the arena at the beginning of the movement. The first among the Muslims to step forward was *Bi Amma*. In her lap, such valiant men and courageous defenders of Islam such as the Ali brothers had been nurtured. *Bi Amma* was a very pious and devout woman. Her sons were very young when she became a widow. It was only her perseverance and determination that, even under the circumstances, she facilitated such an education and imparted such an Islamic training that even after going to England and becoming such excellent orators and writers of English, they resolutely stuck to Islamic tenets. *Bi Amma* was quite old by the time she entered activism and even people like Malviyaji called her *Mata*. She used to take part in rallies and after the

Karachi convictions, she started working full-time for the movement. Mohammad Ali's wife used to wear a *burqa* and she too started working for the movement after the Karachi verdicts. She used to go to all the rallies and even gave speeches. Maulana Hasrat Mohani had a daughter. He was not in favor of *burqa* and his wife and daughter would attend rallies wearing *chador*, the long shawls. Under their influence, many Muslim women shed the *burqa*. They would lead processions and raise heartrending slogans.

As far as Hindu women were concerned, it was a special mission for Gandhiji to take them out of *purdah* and encourage them to work for the nation. This had a deep impact. Women of all ages came into the movement and many of them went to jail as well. I heard two songs sung in a women's procession in Lahore which were very interesting. The gist of one was that the stove and housework be damned, let's go listen to the lecture. In the other, the postman was addressed and repeatedly asked if a letter had come from a person who had gone to jail in sacrifice for the nation. For example:

> *O'postman, O'postman, pray tell,*
> *has any letter come from Agha Safdar?*

This would be followed by asking the same for other prisoners. This was also a special and heartening scene of Hindu-Muslim unity.

To sum up, this was the situation in India, and the caravan of India's freedom, under the leadership of Gandhiji and oblivious to hardships and difficulties, was persevering toward its destination. All the Muslim scholars and leaders of India had rallied behind Gandhiji and were giving it their all for amendments to the Treaty of Severs, restoration of the Caliphate, and achievement of *Swaraj*.

A Few Examples

India's courage and perseverance and the repressive actions of the government can be gauged from a few incidents reported in the newspaper *Zamindar*.

On December 15, 1921 Maulana Abdul Razzaq Malihabadi, editor of the newspaper *Paigham* of Calcutta, was sentenced to two years rigorous imprisonment in Calcutta.

On December 19, 1921 Manzar Ali Sokhta was arrested in Allahabad, and on the same day, Maulvi Abdul Rehman, secretary of the Khilafat Committee, was arrested in Calcutta. A large number of people took an oath that they would wear *khaddar* and donate to the Khilafat Fund every month.

It was reported on the same day that Pandit Hanuman Prasad gave a statement in which he said that the orders of Congress were received by Platoon 17 stationed in Basra and many soldiers agreed to leave the employment of the army. The platoon was returned to Karachi, where these soldiers resigned.

In Lahore, eight-year olds were patrolling the streets of Dabbi Bazar, shouting slogans that service in the army was forbidden. The police beat them with batons.

On December 20, 1921 a surety bond for Rs. 2000 of Allahabad's daily newspaper 'Independent' was confiscated. On the same day, Pandit Madan Mohan Malviya's nephew Shri Krishna Kant Malviya was arrested.

On December 22, 1921 around 500 volunteers came out in Calcutta and 253 of them were arrested.

On December 25, Murtaza Ahmad Khan wrote a poem on the Turkish woman, Fatima Khanam, whose militant deeds were becoming very popular. It's last couplet was:

Dishonorable men of the nation, it is a teaching moment
The gentler sex is resolutely riding into the battleground

On December 22, 1921 the trial of Lala Lajpat Rai, Pandit Santanam, Dr. Gopi Chand, and Malik Lal Khan started in Lahore's Central Jail. When the government's lawyer, Mr. Herbert, said that the court should not have mercy on any of the four and that it should give as much punishment as it has in its authority, Pandit Santanam said, "Amen." Mr. Herbert said that when Lala Lajpat Rai in his message, which was written on December 3 at 5 am and signed by Lalaji, stated that we knew that this meeting would be banned and we would be arrested, then how can it be said that he was not aware of this order. Lala Lajpat Rai responded, "But who says we were not aware of this order?" Pandit Santanam added, "We knew that a mad dog was present and it was possible that it would bite us."

On December 22, 1921 Lala Roop Lal, Secretary, Congress Committee, City of Amritsar, was sentenced to six months rigorous imprisonment and a fine of Rs. 1000. Also, there was a hearing in the case against Syed Birjees, Congress Secretary, Firozpur. In Jalandhar, Lala Lajpat Rai was sentenced to one year hard labor and in Lahore, 20 volunteers refused to disperse and were arrested. The answer given by the public was that for two hours they marched through streets where they were forbidden to, chanting slogans. On December 22,

1921 as well, Magistrate Major Ferrer, announcing a sentence against Lala Badrinath, editor of the daily *Swaraj*, under Section 124 of the Indian Penal Code, said, "I am indicting this man under Section 124 of the Indian Penal Code of India. Looking at his behavior in court, I have come to the conclusion that he is like a mad dog and nothing can stop him from spreading poison except imprisonment. I sentence him to three years of hard labor."

On December 20, a case against Maulana Mohammad Shafiq, Muhammad Abdul Wudood, Babu Jatadhari Prasad, and Babu Vindhyadhari Prasad Verma was presented in the court of the District Magistrate. Only nine lawyers had been allowed inside. At 1 pm, there was the call for the afternoon Muslim prayers. The court refused permission for the men to go outside and offer prayers. But Maulana Mohammad Shafiq and Muhammad Abdul Wudood offered prayers right there in the courtroom. 500 volunteers roamed around the city, ringing bells and asking people to assemble in the compound of the courthouse. Babu Tarkesari Prasad, secretary, was arrested.

On December 25, Head Constable Muhammad Akbar, who had testified on behalf of the prosecution three days earlier, entered a plea that his testimony had been given under undue duress and pressure, presented his resignation in the office of the Superintendent of Police, and said that his conscience did not allow him the damnation of employment in the British government for a minute longer. He was given a sentence of three months in prison under Section 29 of the Police Act.

Two boys, Mohammad Azam and Abdul Aziz, aged 18 or 19, were charged with propagating *khaddar* and sentenced to one year of hard labor.

In the editorial article of the December 26, 1921 issue of *Zamindar*, the following was written:

> *"Since the day of the arrest of Pandit Motilal Nehru and other leaders, the movement has received a great deal of support. Petition after petition are being received in the local office of the Congress. And a large number of the citizens of the city are coming to enroll as volunteers. On the day of the arrival of Prince of Wales, there was such an impromptu total strike in the city, the likes of which had never been seen under the skies of Allahabad."*

The students of Presidency College Calcutta presented a resolution to stage a protest against the government's tyranny and injustice by going on a total strike from December 15 to December 21, 1921. The sons of Honorable Sir Vinod, Mr. Justice CI Ghosh, Dr. Sarat Pasak, and Rae Bahadur Jonibi Bahadur voted in favor of the resolution. *Zamindar* wrote in a commentary:

> *"The sons of Pandit Madan Mohan Malviya and Dr. Sapru have already actively participated. Now observe the style of the sons of these supporters of cooperation with the government."*

On December 22, 1921 the humorous poet Ahmaq Phaphundvi was arrested. Calcutta's 10,000 porters stopped work.

On December 24, 1921 Prince of Wales was to arrive in Calcutta. A complete boycott was advertised and the streets of the city were completely deserted.

On December 26, 1921 Maulana Habib-ur-Rehman Ludhianvi was arrested at his home at 8 am. Afraid of the reaction of the

Maulana's relatives and of the people at the arrest of such a big leader, the Deputy Superintendent of Police himself came in a car with a large number of policemen, but Maulana refused to sit in the car and asked that he be handcuffed and taken as an ordinary volunteer. The Deputy Superintendent then handcuffed the Maulana and led him away.

A few volunteers were arrested in Jagraon and a crowd of 10,000 welcomed them. On January 3, 1920 Krishna Kant Malviya and Govind Malviya were arrested again along with their friends. On January 8, 1922, to stop the recruitment of volunteers in Willingdon Square in Calcutta, a European Commissioner, a subordinate Indian officer and a sergeant raided the place. Following that, thousands of volunteer candidates and 400 recruited volunteers marched, from which 169 were arrested.

On January 20, 1922 in Aligarh, a sub-inspector ordered volunteers to disperse. The leader of the volunteers, Abdul Hamid Khan replied that just as the sub-inspector was such a devotee of this government of hypocrites, how could the protesting volunteers show even the slightest disobedience to religious matters and divine commandments? At this the policemen started to hit the volunteers with the butts of their guns, kick them with their boots, and beat them with batons. Abdul Hamid Khan asked the volunteers to sit down and read the following couplet:

May the enemy not be fortunate to be killed by your sword
May the heads of friends be safe to brave their daggers

The crowd raised nationalistic slogans and sat down. The sub-inspector dragged the volunteers by their legs, on their stomach, and palms grazing the ground, but they showed no sign of pain or anger. A volunteer, Sadiq Ali, was even pushed into a cauldron of boiling oil in a shop, causing his body to be badly burnt. Those volunteers who became unconscious from the beating were taken to the police station. But neither did anyone run nor did they retaliate in any way (such incidents were common).

On January 6, 1922 a group of 24 volunteers led by Pandit Prem Prakash and Master Daya Ram took to the streets in Amritsar shouting slogans. A large contingent of armed policemen and Gorkha soldiers arrived and mercilessly thrashed them with canes and batons. Pandit Prem Prakash was seriously wounded and he fainted, but other groups of volunteers continued their march.

On January 18, 1922, on releasing Maulvi Manzoor Ahmad *Saheb*, a preacher at Jamia Millia Islamia, from jail, the Magistrate smiled and said he had received orders from the Deputy Commissioner that they did not want to keep him in jail beyond the three and a half weeks he had spent there. Maulvi Manzoor Ahmad replied that he didn't care if he was kept in jail or released, and that he had hoped to spend a year or two in jail.

Customers could not be found at liquor stores any more. There was a constant vigil at the liquor stores by Congress volunteers. On January 23, 1922 the surety bonds of Akali Press and Siyasat Press were confiscated.

On the arrest of Maulana Abul Kalam Azad, Zafar Hasan Khan sent the following poem from Montgomery Jail, which was published in the January 19, 1922 edition of *Zamindar* under the pseudonym *Muslim*:

I too would break abstinence with home-made wine
Provided it has the sweetness of Hijaz mixed in it

Bring me the fiery wine that would warm my blood
Coterie cherishing bartender, may you live long

There was light in the gathering where the candle melted
Why wouldn't our prayers be answered if tenderness
was in our hearts

Look at the pleasures of infidelity so your blood
may become heavy
Do your ablutions with the blood of your heart so
that you may pray

Abul Kalam came after being held captive in jail
So long-held relationships would become secluded secrets

Maulana Abulkalam Azad gave the following message after his arrest.

Maulana Azad's Message

The night of waiting was very dark but the morning of hope is also so alluring and life-affirming. Pity on those who still do not stir. Come, let us fold the bed of negligence forever. Take the holy name of God and depart on the last leg of the journey to our destination. The path is clear and the destination is coming to the fore. In a few days of courage, patience, sacrifice, and steadfastness, we shall finish a journey of centuries.

Wayfarer, with your parched lips, do not be weary
Now you have taken the fountain of survival

"Oh you who believe! Persevere in patience and
constancy. Vie in such perseverance, strengthen each
other, and be pious, that you may prosper"
(Quran, 3:200)

Fakir Abdul Kalam, December 10, 1921

Letter From a Father to his Son

God is Great

Blessings my dear son Ataullah Khan,

May Allah enhance your life and destiny

After prayers for progress, a long life and dignity, let it be clear that congratulations are in order. It truly gives me happiness that God Almighty gave me a son like you. Stay true to your word and religion. Let your feet not slip from under you. You shall certainly be successful, God willing. Convey my congratulations to and blessings for those friends who are in jail, because they too are my sons and brothers. May God help you and all the workers of the Khilafat. Amen.

From Chaudhry Habibullah Khan

Raees Sahadar Township, District Etah
December 25, 1921

11

Greco-Turkish War

Greek Occupation of Smyrna

After the Great War, the most powerful country in the world was Great Britain. They were the greatest political bosses globally. The world was running on their orders. Therefore, the injustices in Turkey and the oppression of the Turks were rightly blamed on Britain. There was a conference of the superpowers going on in Paris. The name Monsieur Clemenceau may be found in places in this regard, and some other voices may be heard, but in any situation, all of them were instruments of the English i.e. Britain. All that happened was what Britain decided. Mr. Wilson's great points were noted down on a piece of paper merely to deceive him. A strange thing that happened at the time was that before permanent peace was achieved, something that had not been put into the temporary peace accord was accepted by the Peace Conference and Greece was given the right to occupy Smyrna and have dominion over Anatolia. At the Paris conference, Lloyd George, Monsieur Clemenceau and Vittorio Orlando sat down to decide the fate of the world. Monsieur Clemenceau hated Turkey and was at the forefront of all matters. On May 6, 1919, at the suggestion of Monsieur Clemenceau, the Peace Conference allowed Greece to occupy Smyrna, and on May

13, 1919, with the support of the Allied Fleet, the Greek army marched into Smyrna.

It is a strange coincidence that on May 13, 1919 the Greek army landed at Smyrna under the shadow of the British and Italian ships and on the same day, Mustafa Kemal left for Anatolia as the Inspector General of the Anatolian army. As it happened, when the Greek troops were landing on the shores of Smyrna, a high speed car left the coast for an officer to make a call to the Turkish Governor of Smyrna. The commanding officer told the Governor that Britain had ordered that Smyrna and the province of Aydin be handed over to the Greeks. If lightning had struck near the feet of the Governor, he would not have been so alarmed as he was when he heard that order. His head was bowed. Perhaps he was thinking about what to do. The Governor raised his head and started to speak. Smyrna should be handed to Britain, France, or Italy, but not to Greece. The commanding officer replied in a haughty tone, "This is a decision of the Supreme Council of Allies and is irrevocable." The governor was forced to hand over the charge. The Caliph of the Muslims Sultan Vehideddin had already issued a command not to interfere in Smyrna, with which he was obligated to comply. The Turkish Parliament, which had been protesting, had already been dismantled and the British stooge Damat Ferid Pasha had been given total power. Meanwhile, on the seashore, around 100,000 Greeks were amassed, the most prominent among them the priest accompanying the invading forces. As soon as the Greek soldiers came ashore from the ships, he raised his cross and bellowed that this was a Crusade, Smyrna and Aydin belonged to Greece, and Muslims should be expelled. This call from the padre filled the Greek soldiers with passion and hate, and they got riled. What could the Governor have done?

There is neither permission to suffer nor to plead
To die of seclusion, that is the wish of my captivator

Otherwise the Turkish Governor and the brave Turkish soldiers in his barracks would have at least shown the essence of swordsmanship, whatever the result may have been. On the other side, the Turkish public was fired up. The iron willed Muslim of Anatolia could not allow himself to endure this humiliation as long as he could breathe. Common people gathered in mosques and raised passionate slogans that Smyrna belonged to the Turks. They were ready to play with fire but they were not ready to be Greece's slaves or handover their country to someone else. Hence, a delegation was put together which went to meet the Governor and sought permission to put up resistance. But the Governor could not do anything. He gave a half-hearted response that the leader of the Muslims, the Caliph, had ordered that there be no resistance.

When the gardener started a fire in my nesting garden
The leaves on which I rested my head fanned the flames

Alas, I wish Sultan Vehideddin had not been so deprived of a sense of honor and zeal - the blood of so many innocents would not have been shed in Anatolia. These stories of atrocities and terror, which will continue to haunt the scholars of human culture on the pages of history till Judgement Day, would have remained incomplete. The black mark that it left cannot be washed off by any soap.

If, on this side, Sultan Vehideddin was ready to bow his head to every order of the Allied countries, then on the other, the

Muslims of Anatolia were still insistent on showing their courage and perseverance in the shadow of the minarets of mosques. Revolutionary groups sprang up all around. Irregular militias began to form. Sultan Vehideddin was afraid that the Allied countries would get upset and he decided to take Anatolia out of the fire and put it on ice.

The Caliph always had faith in Mustafa Kemal. It is a coincidence that on the day the Greek forces landed in Smyrna, the Sultan dispatched Mustafa Kemal to Anatolia as the Inspector General of the Anatolian army. Mustafa Kemal was pondering the issues and thinking that nations could not be destroyed when governments and armies lose a war. Germany, which was the real opponent of the Allied countries in WWI, oblivious to its defeat in the war, was holding its head high, rejecting the Allied countries' terms one after the other, and sending messages after messages, for which the leaders of the Allied countries were burning the midnight oil to study. The demands reached the point where the Allies put their troops on alert, but Germany was not even afraid of this empty threat and the confrontation steadily continued. Here in Turkey, plans were being made to ransack and devastate the entire country; there was no other way. Those who had been in power and were responsible for pushing Turkey into war were either absconding or underground.

From the beginning, Mustafa Kemal was opposed to joining Germany in the war. His military acumen was telling him that in the end Germany would be defeated. But the declaration of war was done by the War Minister, Enver Pasha. And when this had happened, the military skills and self-confidence that Mustafa Kemal exhibited on the battlefield proved that confining him to the rank of Major was a short-sighted solution to the matter at hand.

After considering the matter in its entirety, Mustafa Kemal decided that the only way was to assemble the remaining Turkish forces in Anatolia and start the war again. Given the plan of the Allied countries, which had become apparent since before the Treaty of Sevres, there was no other way. He had just started strategizing on how to get to Anatolia when the Sultan appointed him the Inspector General of Anatolian forces. This was a gesture of unforeseen support for Mustafa Kemal.

Mustafa Kemal's Statesmanship

The fluent demonstration of deliberation and extreme diligence, determination, insight, and patriotism by Mustafa Kemal can all be summed up to say that he was a great man. He turned a spark into a volcano and gave life to a dead body. Mustafa Kemal departed in his full regalia with medals as the deputy to the Sultan. When he had left, Damat Ferid Pasha said to the Sultan that by making Mustafa Kemal the Inspector General of the armed forces of Anatolia, the Sultan had given him the opportunity to incite a rebellion there. The Sultan realized his mistake and immediately sent his men to convey the order to Mustafa Kemal to return immediately, but he had disappeared quickly, nowhere to be found.

Mustafa Kemal, in his capacity as a deputy to the Sultan, sailed in a dilapidated boat-like ship, arriving in Smyrna instead of Samsun, with his five traveling companions. There, the officers of the Allied army thought he was their man. From the seashore he traveled straight to the Telegraph Office and stayed there for four days, sending telegrams to Turkish army officers at various places, asking them to come to Anatolia with their forces.

On May 19, 1919 Mustafa Kemal reached Samsun. The English were occupying the place, and he escaped from there too. He went into the interior of the country and engaged in inciting rebellion. Then he went to a town near Smyrna and stayed there for a few days. There he received information about the barbaric atrocities of Smyrna and he doubled down on inciting rebellion. The English learned about his activities and they issued an order for his arrest. Mustafa Kemal left for Amasya. There he convened a consultative meeting. Amasya was not occupied by the English.

The Meeting in Amasya

In Amasya, Mustafa Kemal convened with Rafat Bey, Ali Fuat Bey, and Rauf Orbay. The four of them, in the face of tragic, shocking, and hopeless circumstances, unanimously agreed to the following actions:

1. Prepare an organized army for resistance in Smyrna, instead of irregular militia groups.
2. Incite rebellion in all cities, towns, and villages.
3. Give military training to all the volunteers.
4. Procure money, weapons, and provisions.
5. Split the resistance efforts in Anatolia into three parts:

   a. Resistance in the eastern part would be the responsibility of Kazim Karabekir.
   b. Western Anatolia would be the responsibility of Ali Fuat.

   c. The charge of the central area would be with Mustafa Kemal himself.

6. Establish a central government, unaffiliated with the government of the Sultan, for coordinating resistance efforts in the entire country.

7. Consult with the true representatives of the nation to form this central government. This was critically necessary. Integrate the various small organizations and committees that had been set up for the purpose of resistance into one unit, after the establishment of which concerted efforts could be made to save their country and they would have the rightful claim to address the world.

Looking at these significant and forceful decisions, it can be estimated what mettle and tenacity constituted the personalities of Mustafa Kemal and his associates. They did not know the meaning of hopelessness, as if they were the essence of this couplet of Allama Iqbal:

> *God asked if I found His world to my taste*
> *I said no, He said then lay it to waste*

The Condition of the Turkish Army and Greek Atrocities

When Greek forces landed in Smyrna, the XVII Corps of the Ottoman Army was there under the command of Nadir Pasha. There were also two regiments of the 56th Division under the command of Lt. Col. Hürrem Bey, one of which was stationed in Aralik under the command of Ali Bey.

Before going to Smyrna, when Mustafa Kemal was secretly conspiring in Constantinople to go to Anatolia and organize resistance, Asmat Pasha, Rauf Orbay, and others joined in. They and many others rushed to Anatolia after Mustafa Kemal left, and no resistance had been begun till the consultative meeting in Amasya, before which nobody wanted to go against the orders of the Sultan. This gave the Greeks all the opportunity to carry out their barbaric atrocities. They came ashore in Smyrna from the west and wanted to go to the city of Ozkoy in the east, which was an important railway station. However, Ali Bey, whose forces were secure, put up a stiff resistance against the Greeks and inflicted heavy losses on them. Now the Greeks dispersed throughout the country and worked toward fulfilling their mission. Preparations started for war. During this period, Greek forces entered the villages and carried out massacres on a large scale. They would set fire to villages where Turks were living. They burned many villages down to ashes.

Based on his individual responsibility, Ali Bey confronted the Greek forces on their arrival. There is an incident from May 28, 1919. Before that, there had been no resistance against the Greeks, but nationalist forces were organizing themselves in Somak, Hasar and Salihli. On June15, 1919 Col. Kasim Bey took temporary charge of the 61st Division at Balikesir. Later, he was given the charge of two northern areas which included Ayvalik, Soma, and Akhisar. Many patriots were getting the army ready. Cemal Pasha left Smyrna under a false name and on the evening of June 15, 1919, the brave Ali Bey's forces ambushed the Greek in the dark and decimated the Greek forces at a place called Pergamon. Forces from Balikesir and Bandirma also came to the assistance of Ali Bey, which resulted in the Greeks having to evacuate Tasli to gather their dispersed armies. Preparations were being made in Aydin and the public was putting pressure on the Greeks, but these were all scattered battles. No organized program had been made yet. The Aydin front could be established only by the end of June.

Mustafa Kemal's Dismissal

From Amasya, Mustafa Kemal went to Erzurum. There he received a messenger who gave him written orders from the Caliph to return to Constantinople. He refused to obey the order and resigned. When Sultan Vehideddin got this news, he gnashed his teeth in a fit of rage and frustration and, trembling, ordered that Mustafa Kemal be dismissed.

Mustafa Kemal took off his medals and uniform, and went into the countryside, giving speeches and inciting rebellion. He faced the following difficulties:

1. All of Anatolia, to which he had to bring a rebellion, was obsequious and submissive to the Caliph. And the Caliph was a staunch opponent of Mustafa Kemal.
2. All of Anatolia was on fire. Not just the men, even the women had formed their own armies, but there wasn't concentrated unity. Various committees and associations had been established throughout the country. How could there be an authoritative conversation until all these disparate organizations were brought together under a central command in a constitutional and democratic form? And this was a very difficult task. Mutual rivalries were also at work and it was not easy for all of them to gather at

    a central platform. That needed a lot of deliberation and a mastery of strategizing.

3. The matter of procurement of capital, military equipment, and provisions was no less difficult. The trusted Allied powers were willing to assist Greece. But the iron-willed Mustafa Kemal was not one to lose morale. The time had come when he had the responsibilities of discharging the duties of not just a General, but of a statesman too, and to start working then on forming a new government.

Mustafa Kamal started patrolling the villages in plain uniform and giving speeches. In this struggle, his clothes would get tattered. He had to go without food and walk for miles, but there was no problem that he considered difficult. Respecting the feelings of the Muslim inhabitants of Anatolia, he declared himself the Caliph's deputy and said that the Caliph had been imprisoned by the British. "What I say is the voice of the Caliph," he would say. Other than that, he had no choice.

After the end of the war, while being interviewed by Ahmed Emin Effendi, editor of the Constantinople daily *Waqt*, Mustafa Kemal said:

> *"When the terms of ceasefire were signed between Turkey and the Allies, I was in Aleppo. When I returned to Constantinople, I found everyone sad and weary of life. The immediate problems of Turkey had rendered people of every class hopeless. The leaders were jittery. There was a moral turmoil in the nation. I felt that only a system that was helped by the nation itself could cope with the situation. Without that, there was no recourse for the people of Anatolia to be made aware of the*

dangers of partition of Turkey and effective assistance taken from them. That is why there was a need to go into the communities and work alongside the people. The purpose of this work could only have been Anatolia; it was impossible to work in Constantinople. Fortunately, I was made the army's Inspector General and sent to Samsun. I departed from Constantinople the same day that Greeks landed in Smyrna.

"My strategy was to unite the many organizations that had been established in the country for the purpose of national resistance and establish one strong system, and then, to complete the purpose of that system, to help with the resistance and achieve freedom for the country, make use of the army."

Representatives from all corners of Anatolia assembled in Sivas. This was truly a gathering of national representatives. An organization representing all of Anatolia with one voice was established there and Mustafa Kemal was elected president of this national organization. Now Mustafa Kemal had earned the right to speak on behalf of the whole nation of Anatolia. Thus, this modern people's government was established as a competitor of Constantinople.

Meanwhile in Constantinople, in August 1919, Damat Ferid Pasha had the pronouncement made from the Caliphate that Mustafa Kemal was a rebel, there should be no differences among them by joining in the resistance, and the Sultan of the time should be obeyed. He also ordered that Mustafa Kemal be arrested and brought to Constantinople. In this way, Damat Ferid Pasha hoped that the Muslims of Anatolia, who were loyal to the Caliph, would separate from Mustafa Kemal.

In a second attack, Damat Ferid Pasha tried to persuade the Kurdish chiefs to fight against Kemal Pasha and, for that purpose, the English plotted to bribe those chiefs with a large sum of money. Mustafa Kemal gave a befitting response to both those attacks.

The first thing Mustafa Kemal did was to pass a protest resolution at the Sivas Conference. It was Anatolia's first united voice and was full of heartfelt enthusiasm and determination. At the same time, it demanded the dismissal of Damat Ferid Pasha. He then sent the following message to the people of Istanbul (which was another name for Constantinople):

> *"O' people of Istanbul, join in the patriotic duty so that we have the right to object to Ferid Pasha's ministry. If we remain silent, the world will ask us why this nation did not make timely use of its right to dissent against its government. Our Prophet had declared that the rulers that will rule over you will be as you are."*

The newspapers of Istanbul published this message and it exploded like a bomb. Prayers were held in mosques and passionate youth started to secretly leave Constantinople and go to Anatolia to join Mustafa Kemal. The English started being murdered in Constantinople.

A few days later, Mustafa Kemal dropped a second bomb, the explosion of which was more deadly than the first. He sent a document to the ambassadors of England, France, America, Italy, Germany, Sweden, and Denmark, which had the seal of the Sivas Conference on it. There was a proclamation in it that Damat Ferid Pasha was a traitor to the nation, his government was a puppet of the British, and its decisions were illegitimate.

Mustafa Kemal declared his conference to be the legitimate parliament of the nation which was composed of the representatives of the people. No decision was legitimate and acceptable till it had the signatures of the true representatives of the people.

The Sultan again made a proclamation that his authority should be obeyed and differences should not be created among the people, but the psychological front that had been set up by Mustafa Kemal against Damat Ferid Pasha was hard to bring down. The English realized that Damat Ferid Pasha had become unpopular to such an extent that as long as he stayed, Anatolia would not be under their control. As a result, Ferid Pasha was ousted and Ali Riza was appointed Prime Minister in his place. Ali Riza immediately convened the Turkish Parliament, in which the assembled flatterers exaggeratedly praised the Caliph and heaped curses on Mustafa Kemal. But in Anatolia, Mustafa Kemal's sword had already come out of the scabbard and verbal reproach was no answer to it.

Mustafa Kemal declared Ankara to be the capital. Ankara was appropriate for him for two reasons. One was that Ankara was far away from the coast, and defensive measures could be better carried out from there. Second, the Turks had a very emotional attachment to Ankara. It was from where the Turks had set out to rule over three continents, seven rivers and three oceans for centuries and display their glory and magnificence.

Relations with Bolsheviks

Now there was the question of arms. How could there be war without arms? The Allied countries were enemies of Turkey, and Germany and its allies had lost the war and were half dead. Mustafa Kemal was running around, trying his best to procure arms from somewhere. He was using his innate intelligence to try and take advantage of the weaknesses and mutual rivalries of the countries of the world. Consequently, he approached Russia as well. In the northern region of Russia, the Bolsheviks were already dominant over the Mensheviks, but in the southern region, Denikin was still fighting the Bolsheviks. Stalin wielded a lot of power in Russia, but the actual leader was Lenin. Under the leadership of Stalin and Lenin, the Bolsheviks were constantly up to something, which frightened the English.

There was open enmity between Bolsheviks and the English. The English occupied Constantinople and were secretly helping Denikin, who was still holding on to his influence in southern Russia. Not knowing the source of that help, Mustafa Kemal turned toward the Bolsheviks, who in turn did not show any stinginess in supplying arms and other goods.

Passion of the Anatolian Turks

The pen is exhausted writing about the passion of the Turks of Anatolia. They gave it their all. The youth all joined the army. The women and the old got into other support work. Just as a doctor fights to save the life of a patient with terminal illness, the Muslims of Anatolia were ready to sacrifice everything, and Mustafa Kemal was one expert doctor.

The fame of this excitement and tumult among the Anatolian Turks reverberated around the world and it ignited a blaze of passion in the Muslim world. The stories of Greek terror and barbarism, which appeared in pro-justice European language newspapers, were like gasoline on this fire. The atrocities by the Greeks were so grievous that they even drew a verbal protest from the Ottoman Shaykh al-Islam. Turks from all parts of the nation were risking their lives and rushing to Anatolia. Many officers resigned from the army and left Constantinople for Anatolia to join Mustafa Kemal's army. Everyone had realized that this was a life-and-death battle.

Now, to gather proof of the representation of his party, Mustafa Kemal threw a challenge to the Muslim Caliph. The Caliph felt helpless. He didn't know what to do. In the end, he appealed to his foreign masters, but there was a rift between the Allied countries around splitting up the spoils of war and they were not willing to take any significant steps toward squashing nationalist movements. There were, although, news reports from Reuters that military and naval officers were anticipating that the time had come for the fate that was to befall Turkey based on Mustafa Kemal's movement in Anatolia, and were asking for forces and supplies to act upon that threat. During that time, Mustafa Kemal turned the English out of Ozkoy and the French out of Marash and Araxa in southern Anatolia.

In this way, the period of 1919-early 1920 ended. During all this time, news from Anatolia and stories of Greek atrocities awoke the conscience of the Islamic world, and severe criticism of the Allied countries started from all around. Besides Egypt, Afghanistan and African countries, revolutionary cries started coming from even the Arab nations. India was already a house of fireworks and was passionately marching toward its destination of independence under the leadership of Mahatma Gandhi.

The English propaganda machine had also picked up speed. It fanned the rumor that Mustafa Kemal was an enemy of the Caliphate. Obviously, this rumor was very dangerous for the people of Anatolia. In June 1920, the esteemed English language daily of London, The Times, published the news that Mustafa Kemal had given Cemal Pasha, the successor to the late Prince Shaukat Effendi who had recently gone to Anatolia as a senior office of the III Army Corps, the title 'Grand Sultan' and Mustafa Kemal had become the Prime Minister. Other appointments reported were former Foreign Minister Ahmet Saydam as Minister of War, Ferid Bey as Minister of Home Affairs and Sheikh Sunussi as the Shaykh al-Islam.

The Times also reported that the Bolshevik activities had become very advanced, that Mustafa Kemal had become a Bolshevik, and that he had renounced Islam. It also wrote that the wandering nationalists Abbas Hilmy Pasha, Shaikh Abd al-Aziz, and Ferid Pasha had united and were creating trouble in West Asia and Egypt with the help of the Bolsheviks.

There was one befitting response to all this, that sermons on behalf of Sultan Vehideddin were read regularly in the mosques of Anatolia.

Around that time, the Caliph had ordered the arrest of the Shaykh al-Islam and had him sent to Malta for refusing to issue illegitimate religious decrees. Zaid al-Abid Abdullah was appointed Shaykh al-Islam and Grand Mufti. In April 1920, the Grand Mufti issued the following decree in favor of the new ministry of Damat Ferid Pasha:

"According to Islam's canonical law, Sharia, it is justifiable that those people who have gotten together

and conspired to deceive the subjects of His Majesty be uprooted, since these two have started recruiting for their armies, and levying taxes on the people to fund their army and procure supplies. They have attacked some location in the Sultanate and murdered loyal subjects. Gen. HY [name indecipherable] has cut off communications with the Caliphate as well as with other parts of the Sultanate. They have removed religious officers for no reason and have installed their well-wishers in their place. They have stopped the administrative order of the government, and by removing the capital from the rest of the country, they have left a black mark on the authority of the Caliphate. They have spread lies to cause discontent among the people. Although they have been given orders to disperse, they refuse to desist. Why should all the Muslims of the Ottoman Sultanate not rally around Caliph Vehideddin? If the soldiers of the Caliph are unfaithful and favor separatism, they will be worthy of punishment, not only in this world but in the next world too. Those soldiers of the Caliph who kill the rebels, would they not be worthy of being called Ghazis, one who fights against infidels? And those soldiers who are killed, would they not be worthy of being called Martyrs? Those soldiers who are given orders by the King to fight and they refuse to obey the orders, would they not be worthy of getting the punishment prescribed in the Sharia? The answers to all these questions are in the affirmative. This decree bears the signature of Zaid al-Abid Abdullah."

On May 13, 1920, at the insistence of Damat Ferid Pasha, Shaykh al-Islam issued a second decree, which was worded as follows.

Summary of the Decree of Shaykh al-Islam in the New Council of Advisors to the Sultanate of Damat Ferid Pasha

"Is it legitimate according to Sharia and possible that those persons be removed and finished who have formed a gang by mutual consensus to deceive the great subjects of the nation, who have started roguery and taxing people under the pretext of feeding and arming them. They have attacked various parts of the Sultanate and committed atrocities, murdered well-wishing citizens, cutoff passage between the Caliph's General Staff Headquarters and other parts of the Sulatanate, dismissed decent, God-fearing administrators from their jobs and appointed their followers instead, who are obstructing the execution of the orders of the administrators of the Sultanate, who have sullied the name of the Caliph by causing a rift between the house of the Caliphate and other parts of the country, and who have created tensions by spreading lies and rumors. And who, despite being given orders to cease and desist, do not relent from their actions. Is it not the duty of the aggregate of Muslims in the Sultanate to come to the assistance of Caliph Vehideddin?

"If the soldiers of the Caliph desert the Caliphate and join them, would they not be worthy of punishment, not only in this world but in the next world too? Those soldiers of the Caliph who kill such rebels, would they not be worthy of being Ghazi, and those who are killed, Martyrs? Those who are a hindrance to the orders of their King to fight, would such people not be deserving of the punishment

as laid out for them in Sharia? The answers to all these questions are in the affirmative."

On reading these decrees carefully, the power of Mustafa Kemal, the anxiety of Constantinople, and the treasonous attitude of the Caliph and his supporters are obvious.

Mustafa Kemal had established a connection with the Bolsheviks. To uproot it, Shaykh al-Islam issued a third decree, which was as follows.

Decree in Accordance with Islam by Shaykh al-Islam of Constantinople

"Those in whose hands is the destiny of the nations of the world are considering the issue of Bolshevism. In such a situation, it is the duty of the one who is the Islamic leader of a big part of mankind, and is a mirror of their thoughts, to express and declare his point of view to the Muslims, even to the whole world. Whatever may be the real and fundamental principles of Bolshevism... but the truth of the matter is that actually and practically it is detrimental to the society and civilization of mankind and to the personal and property rights of the servants of God. And therefore it is impossible that the principles of Bolshevism and the principles of Islam can be considered consistent and compatible. From the advent of Islam till today, it has always cursed and condemned attacks on life and property, theft, murder, plunder, adultery, and compensation for ugly deeds. Our holy books have not only condemned these crimes but have also set the legal guidelines for the punishment and repentance for them. The most important requirement of Islam is peace and

order, and welfare of mankind. And that is why Islam prohibits killing and wrath, and with great emphasis guarantees the property rights of individuals and nations. Consequently, it is the order of Sharia that every person has the right to a full possession of their properties, and they can gift or transfer it in their lifetime or will it after their death. Islam does not consider extravagance to be permissible and in order to prevent loss of wealth to wastefulness, so that the poor are not disfavored, requires that some of the wealth be distributed among relatives and some among the poor. The interests of Islam demand that all its power and influence be spent opposing Bolshevism, which is a danger to culture, justice, and rights of the servants of God."

Mustafa Kemal's position suddenly fell in Anatolia and the people there started becoming victims of ambivalence. But fate was adamant about protecting this ironman. On May 20, 1920 the last peace treaty concerning Turkey was published and was signed on behalf of the Muslim Caliph by Tevfik Bey on the same day. This was a dreadful event. Mustafa Kemal immediately fired his first shot. In a thunderous speech in front of the National Assembly in Ankara, he held Damat Ferid Pasha responsible for all these calamities and had a resolution passed declaring him a traitor. Now, in all of Anatolia, the slogan that "Damat Ferid Pasha was a traitor" gained popularity. And public opinion turned around. The people understood that the Caliph could not have signed such a humiliating peace treaty and that this was all the mischief and selling out of Damat Ferid Pasha. Mustafa Kemal was unanimously deemed the leader of the Turks. The publication of the treaty of Sevres and Constantinople's signature on it proved to be a grand

and magnificent gong summoning the congregation to divine service. The conditions of the Treaty of Sevres were so strict that on reading them, even Sultan Vehideddin's face turned red, but he kept only his interest in mind. On the one hand was his conscience that was inciting him to shred this treaty to pieces, and on the other hand was this shiny object in his mind which was a life of rest and ease with the title of 'Muslim Caliph,' a decent pension, and immense wealth. In the end, the self triumphed over conscience and he put his signature to the death warrant of Turkey. Now it became abundantly clear to the Turks of Anatolia what the designs of the Allied countries were for Turkey and what the position of the Caliph was, and they decided that only their unity and their swords could help them. Anatolia was now ready to end in blood and ashes for its survival and Mustafa Kemal was their last beacon of hope.

▍**Greek Attack**

On May 20, 1920 the Treaty of Sevres was signed and in June 1920, at the Inter-Allied Conference in Boulogne, a resolution was passed that to suppress the movement of Anatolia's liberals, the Greek front should be moved in. As a result, on June 24, 1920 Greeks attacked Anatolia. The Turkish liberals resisted them, but the Greeks kept winning. In India, reports of the defeat of Turkish liberals were constantly published by Reuters and The Times, and sadness and anger rose among the Muslims. The mosques used to be packed with people offering prayers. Supplications started being read. During the evening *Maghrib* prayers, the supplication *Dua-e-Qunoot* started to be recited. The British government was held responsible for all of these misfortunes, which advanced the non-cooperation movement. Muslims of Afghanistan, Egypt, Africa, and the rest of the world started raising their voices high in protest, but the truth was that Mustafa Kemal never wanted to fight a decisive battle against the Greek army anywhere. He wanted them to come far from their homeland and deep into Anatolia for him to give a befitting response. He would keep the Greek army occupied while effectively retreating continuously.

In the meantime, the attitude of Italy and France changed. They wanted the Treaty of Sevres to be amended. This was the success of Mustafa Kemal's propaganda machinery. He had established relationships with many countries. On November 28, the Prime Minister of France, Foreign Minister of Italy, and Mr. Lloyd George convened a meeting in London to discuss the new situation in the East, and tried to decide what amendments should be made to the Treaty of Sevres. But, at the insistence of Greece, this conference was postponed. In the meantime, Constantine I had become the King of Greece. He arrived in Athens against the wishes of the Allied. He once again decided to wage war. Prior to that, during the lull in war, Greek forces remained entrenched in the territories they had occupied and Mustafa Kemal was busy with his preparations. Constantin I started his onslaught in early January 1921. Mustafa Kemal now decided to resist the Greek attack and a battle was fought for three days and three nights at İnönü, in the end even resorting to swords and bayonets. The result was that the Greeks had to retreat. There was a wave of celebration in Anatolia at this first victory and led to anxiety among the Allied. In recognition of his performance in this battle, Ismet Pasha came to be known as Ismet İnönü, as he was the hero of this victory.

On January 22, 1921 a press conference was convened to state that amendments should be made to the Treaty of Sevres. The second major announcement was that a second peace conference will be held in London where representatives of the government in Ankara shall also be invited. This was a grand victory for Mustafa Kemal. The second peace conference was convened in London on February 21, 1921, in which significant amendments were made to the Treaty of Sevres. But these amendments were insufficient and unacceptable to the liberals of Turkey. However, before they could respond, the Greeks rejected those proposals.

Second Greek Attack

After a lot of planning, Greece initiated a second attack. This attack was carried out with the intent to capture Baghdad Railway. The Turks kept retreating. Their purpose was to draw the Greeks closer to their front. When that finally happened, the Turks went on the offensive, handing the Greeks a massive defeat. This battle went on from March 27 - March 31, 1921. The fighting went on day and night. A European newspaper wrote that the Greeks retreated so quickly that the Turks got tired of chasing them. Fawzi Pasha described this battle in a speech, and slogans of congratulations and joy were raised.

Third Greek Attack

On June 8, 1921, after intense reorganization and planning, Greek forces embarked on a third attack. In the beginning, the Turks allowed them these incursions, but on August 23, 1921 Mustafa Kemal decided to enter a decisive battle, and responded with all his might. This battle went on for 13 days with much bloodshed, and eventually the Turks handed the Greeks a resounding defeat and pushed them far back. After that, in a speech to the Turkish Parliament, Mustafa Kemal said:

> *"God Almighty held the hands of the Parliament, and in the face of that, the Greek forces suffered a terrible defeat. Till our demands are fully met and the world respects all our rights, our hands will not let go of our weapons."*

After that, Mustafa Kemal remained silent for six months. During this time, Greek forces were occupying one bank of the Sakarya River and forces of the liberal Turks were assembled on the other side. Mustafa Kemal sent his delegations to various countries. He had also said in his speech to the Parliament:

> *"We are not infatuated with war. We desire peace and security. We adopted all the peaceful means and resources to acquire our rights, but the world opposed our good intentions with meaningless threats and kept treating us as irreligious tribes. For that reason, the whole world should be aware that the citizens of Turkey, their government, and their great parliament cannot tolerate this humiliation and until, like the rest of the civilized nations, their freedom and independence is respected, they will not lay down their arms. This is our determined decision and the world should become familiar with it. We are friends of Russia only because it has recognized and respected our rights* [Russia was the first one to recognize the government in Ankara]. *And we will always remain Russia's friends because even today we can trust them and will continue to do so in the*

future. And when the Allied governments too recognize our national independence, we will be ready to extend our hands and shake their hands too."

This speech reverberated in capitals around the world and awed them. Mustafa Kemal had raised an entire nation from ashes and given it life, and created a parliament and a government whose age may then have been only a year or two but appeared to be of solid construction.

The Turkish delegations presented their country's demands wherever they went and said that the Turks will never give up their demands at any cost or deviate even an inch from the people's charter, even if the last brave soldier of Anatolia gets martyred fighting.

When a delegation reached London and met with the British Prime Minister Mr. Lloyd George, on Lloyd George's asking, they stated their full demand as Anatolia along with Smyrna, Thrace, Constantinople, and Adrianople. Lloyd George asked what their argument was for it. The delegation replied there was no argument, just that their nation was not willing to accept anything less than that. Lloyd George said the Indian delegation had come recently as well, and they had given a lot of arguments, while the Turks were making all these demands without giving an argument for them. The delegation said that their argument was that their nation was not willing to accept anything less than that. Lloyd George got up saying it was time for his tennis game and he was unnecessarily wasting his time. The delegation came out of that meeting and sent a single codeword telegram to Mustafa Kemal: "Attack." If you compare this with the delegation of Mohammad Ali, you will understand how much difference there is between a slave's petition and a braveheart warrior's challenge.

Results of Turkish Delegations

Mustafa Kemal was becoming effective in statesmanship and tactical planning just as he had found success in the battlefield. He had already brought Russia to his side when in October 1921, an alliance was formed between the Turks and the French which ended the state of war between their two countries. Cilicia was handed over to Turkey.

There was a treaty with Italy as well in which they made a pledge to assist Turkey for the return of Anatolia, Smyrna, and Thrace. Now, except for Britain, no one remained on the side of the Greeks. But Britain's presence on the side of Greece was no small matter. At the time, Britain was the leader of all nations.

Mustafa Kemal established relations with Russia, exchanged messages with Lenin over telegram, brought a Russian delegation to Ankara and signed a substantive alliance treaty with them, and established relations with all the democracies in Central Asia. In the same way, he signed a treaty with Poland. He made a friendly alliance with the Caucasus. An influential delegation from the Caucasus, which included representatives from other Central Asian republics, came to Ankara and a treaty of friendship was signed. Similarly, friendly relations were established with Bukhara, Iran, Ukraine, etc., and everyone recognized the government in Ankara. All this was the result of Mustafa Kemal's friendships.

The effect of the optimistic work of Mustafa Kemal was gaining prominence. First, he had united the nation to form an independent democratic government. Second, he had defeated Greece in the battlefield. The English were being pressured by other members of the Allied countries, and they could not entirely ignore that. Conferences were being convened for this purpose. The Paris Conference started on March 22, 1922 in which representatives of Ankara also participated. This conference ended on March 28 and some amendments to the Treaty of Sevres were made in it, but there was no consequence of this conference because Greece could not agree to retreat from Anatolia, which was the Turk's condition for progress. After that, the second conference was to be held on September 22 at the suggestion of Italy when the stone-splitting swords of the liberals of Turkey settled the matter completely.

The way it transpired was that the Greeks dreamt of occupying Constantinople. They announced that the upcoming coronation of the King of Greece would be held in the church of Hagia Sophia with the status of a Byzantine Emperor. The Greeks were telling the public that the twelfth Emperor of the Byzantine order, the Great Constantine, was about to take the throne of Constantinople. All these yarns were being spun in Constantinople while in Ankara it was time for Mustafa Kemal to strike the final blow There is an interesting story about how that came about. Britain had numerous operatives who would become friends of those people that it wanted to finish. A few such people went to Ankara to assess the strength of Mustafa Kemal, and observed everything under the garb of friendship. On their return, they reported that Mustafa Kemal was very feeble and he did not have the strength to repel the Greeks, although the fact of the matter was, as was later acknowledged in news reports and statements, that Mustafa Kemal had hidden his forces so deep in the folds of the mountains that these 'friends' of Turkey could not have seen them even from airplanes.

On August 21, 1922, Mustafa Kemal launched his full-scale offensive and, in the blink of an eye, occupied parts of Afyonkarahisar Province. He pushed further into the province and, on August 23, 1922, occupied two more towns. On August 26, his forces attacked the city of Afyonkarahisar, the capital of the province. Mustafa Kemal himself was commanding this attack. The fort there was considered impenetrable, but Turkish cannons blew it to smithereens. On August 27, 1922 Mustafa Kemal's forces entered Afyonkarahisar and the Greek forces fled, abandoning their possessions, supplies, and weapons. Mustafa Kemal's other forces that had come after conquering Diyarbakir and Ozkoy assembled there. Diyarbakir, Ozkoy, and Afyonkarahisar are situated on a triangle, 40-45 miles from each other. Mustafa Kemal had orchestrated his attack on the three cities simultaneously, and his forces had run through them bringing down any resistance and had assembled at a place nearby. Mustafa Kemal was riding his horse. Seated in the saddle, he bowed his head in accordance with the *Sunnah*, the practices of Prophet Muhammad as recounted in Islamic traditions, and gave the following speech in front of the assembled army:

> *"Soldiers! You have performed a golden deed in the defense and freedom of the nation and the grace of the Almighty was with you. But work still remains. When my horse stands on the seashore, and on one side is the*

sea and the other our nation, and the Greeks have either drowned or have been pushed away from our land, and not one Greek remains on the soil of Anatolia, then your work will be done."

In this war, approximately 20,000 Greeks were killed and 61,000 were taken prisoners. The war booty netted the Turks 700 field-cannons, 2000 machine guns, 11 planes, and 950 motorcars. In one of his speeches, Mustafa Kemal said that the enemy's deficit was more than 100,000 men, while Turkey's never exceeded 10,000, and three-fourths of them were the injured ones.

There was an incident from around the same time, when 44 Greek Generals were meeting to discuss war matters, and Mustafa Kemal surrounded the place and arrested them all. The newspapers had a field day making fun of the Greeks.

After that, on August 28, Mustafa Kemal attacked Altıntaş and Dumlupinar, and between August 30 and September 1, captured the Geyre-Altıntaş-Dumlupinar and Geyre-Kudos-Kutahiya triangles. And then he attacked all over, and on September 9, leading a contingent of Turkish horsemen, Captain Fawzi Bek entered Smyrna and Lt. Nureddin Pasha was appointed Governor of Smyrna. On September 14, Mustafa Kemal himself, with much splendor and glory, joy and happiness, came to Smyrna and stood in front of his army and a glorious crowd. In the Battle of Geyre, the Turks had captured the Greek General Trikoupis and on September 7, after capturing other areas, the Turkish forces reached Akdeniz (White Sea). Mustafa Kemal's dream had come true. On one side was the sea and on the other, his country with no sign of a Greek in southern Anatolia.

Wherever the Turkish liberals entered victoriously with their conquering armies, be it Afyonkarahisar, Ozkoy, Smyrna, or any other place, the citizens came out and welcomed them with a flood of tears.

War with France

The Turkish forces had to fight France as well and they dominated everywhere. Finally, in February 1921, when Ankara's Foreign Minister Bekir Sami Bey was going to take part in the London Conference, he stopped by Paris on the way and met French statesmen there, and the foundation for peace was laid right away. On September 30, 1921 Henri Franklin-Bouillon reached Ankara and completed the peace agreement between Turkey and France, and on October 20, 1921 it was signed by both parties. By virtue of this agreement, Adana province was returned to the Turks, on November 29, 1921 Turkish forces entered the capital, Adana city, and on December 1, 1921 Turks took the rein of the government in their control.

Lausanne Conference

At a time when all this commotion was going on, I was the editor of the daily *Zamindar* published from Lahore. I remember well that until Mustafa Kemal hadn't fought the decisive battle at Sakarya River and pushed the Greeks across the sea, the English had given him the name 'dacoit.' But immediately after the victory at Sakarya, the attitude of the English changed and he became Mustafa Kemal the 'brave soldier.' The English now spread the net of peace and tried to entangle him in it. The idea was to divide Anatolia between Turkey and Greece.

At that time, I wrote a headlining article in the *Zamindar* under the title "Conspiratorial Peace," at which Allama Iqbal had in appreciation, like with a few other articles, invited me to tea and praised the article. Allama Iqbal had a special knack for raising the confidence of youth.

Mustafa Kamal never expressed his desire to avoid peace and always expressed his willingness for it. He would often address the whole world and say that 'we want peace, but for the defense of our country, as long as we are under attack, our hands will be on the grip of our sword.' In other words, Mustafa Kemal was adamant that as long as all of the terms of the people's charter were not met, he would not stop war.

Now that Mustafa Kemal had dominated over Greeks and Armenians, had pressured France and Italy to make peace, and had been victorious in Smyrna, the rest of the areas that remained, such as Bursa etc., came into their possession and the Greeks were completely expelled from Anatolia. The dreams the Greeks had for Smyrna, Thrace, Aydin, and Constantinople were buried under the corpses of the more than 100,000 of their soldiers killed, and lost forever.

When Smyrna was won, it was the last bugle for the complete expulsion of Greeks from Anatolia. This was the same Smyrna which was acquired by deceit and where the barbaric atrocities of the Greeks were carried out. On entering Smyrna, Mustafa Kemal assured its people peace, security, and reconciliation. The terrorized citizens of Smyrna shed tears of joy on seeing their flag, their leader, and their dignity and grandeur returned.

Now Mustafa Kemal was ready to look Britain in the eye and talk to them. The treaty that Turkey had signed with France and the way in which Italy had returned the occupied territories to Turkey was a big blow to Britain. Britain expressed its great surprise at the treaty between Turkey and France. The victory that Mustafa Kemal had achieved in the field of politics and statesmanship was grand in the same way that he had achieved victory in the battlefield.

Amendments to the Treaty of Sevres

Now the time had come for the notorious Treaty of Sevres to be shredded by the sword of Mustafa Kemal and scattered in the air. On November 20, 1922 the Lausanne Peace Conference was convened, and till February 4, 1923 various discussions took place. One of the demands of the Turks was that the English leave Mosul. Britain was represented by Lord Curzon and Turkey by Ismet Pasha. Lord Curzon was an avowed colonialist and an arrogant man. He had been the Viceroy of India as well and his insolence and conceit were well known. Brimming with haughtiness, he tried to convince the Turks that if they were to be given something in this treaty, it would only be to do them a favor. He still had not gauged the character of Ismet İnönü and the iron will and resolve of the Turkish liberals. Ismet was stone deaf. An aide would take down all the speeches in shorthand, and the speeches would be typed up and placed in front of him, which would tell him what was being discussed. But he didn't want anyone to know he was deaf. As a result, he was always smiling during the speeches. News correspondents from all over the world had assembled in Lausanne. They wrote that Ismet's smile was very confusing. Britain was still not refraining from its ill intents. The British wanted to make some syntax changes in the Treaty of Sevres but were adamant on expelling the Turks from Europe. The conditions presented by Britain were totally rejected by Ismet.

On February 4, 1922 the negotiations at the conference were suspended and a mutual exchange of ideas continued. Those who have their hands on the grips of their sword do not make small talk. A period of 15 days went by with these evasions and put-offs. In the end, Lord Curzon tried to impress upon the others that his patience had run out, and he wrote an extremely arrogant and supercilious letter to Ismet Pasha in which he said, "I am the Foreign Minister of the Government of Britain. I do not have time, but I have held the Continental Mail (train) for two hours. In these two hours, the conditions that have been laid down should be accepted, otherwise Turkey's fate is sealed." Ismet Pasha İnönü gave the following reply, which must have been quite unexpected for Lord Curzon:

"I am not just the Foreign Minister in the great government of Turkey but the Commander-in-Chief of its armed forces. I am leaving for the war front and I do not have time. However, I am leaving a clerk of mine behind so that if you would like to send a letter, we will receive it in Ankara."

In this way, on February 20, 1923 Ismet Pasha returned to Ankara waving the flag of Turkey's glory, self-respect, and self-reliance. On his return, the movement to return to the negotiating table was revived by Britain and the parliament of the Turkish people gave the government permission to complete the negotiations. On April 5, 1923 a second conference was arranged, which began on April 23, 1923, on July 16, 1923 the terms of peace were finalized, and on July 24, 1923 the peace treaty was signed.

An important item to note is that by that time, the government in Constantinople had become extinct. All the negotiations had taken place only with the government in Ankara, which had been immediately recognized by Russia and later by almost all the nations. The opening and introductory remarks of the Lausanne Peace treaty are as follows:

> *"The British Empire, France, Italy, Japan, Greece, Romania and The Serb-Croat-Slovene State, of the one part, and Turkey, of the other part; being united in the desire to bring to a final close the state of war which has existed in the East since 1914, being anxious to re-establish the relations of friendship and commerce which are essential to the mutual well-being of their respective peoples, and considering that these relations must be based on respect for the independence and sovereignty of States, have decided to conclude a Treaty for this purpose."*

It is worth noting that Russia and America did not take part in this peace treaty. The reason for Russia not taking part was that the Tzar had been overthrown and the Allied countries did not recognize Communist Russia. America had grown weary of Europe's filthy politics and had disassociated with them. Through this peace treaty, Turkey was able to almost fully complete the people's charter. In putting together its demands, Turkey had shown a lot of prudence and farsightedness and did not demand such things that were impossible to achieve.

Effect of the Khilafat Movement on Turkey's Victory

Britain did not spare any effort, even if it was behind the curtain, to help and supply aid to the Greeks but they did not openly supply arms to them. There were the following reasons for that:

1. After the end of WWI, such differences arose among the members of the Allied countries, and Mustafa Kemal had laid such a net of prudent thinking, that there was a danger that another war would break out in Europe, and Britain did not want to expose its citizens to another war under any circumstances.

2. The attitude taken by Russia was a great enhancement to this danger. Bolshevism was a new theory that had taken life and politics by storm, and its viewpoint was directly opposed to colonialism. Bolsheviks wanted to overturn the Tzar's imperial policies and bring revolution to every country. The English were very afraid of this revolution as it would strike a blow to their very existence.

3. The third and the most important reason was the general rebellion in India. The entire country had stood up against the English. Till then, the Muslims had been their biggest backers, and the Aligarh Movement proved to be a godsend for them. But under Gandhiji's leadership, all of Islamic India had put everything on the line, and in all his speeches, Gandhiji would deem "Khilafat" to be a foundational issue. Gandhiji used to say that the matter of Caliphate was a religious one for the Muslims, the English had unduly interfered in it, and "if our Muslim bothers are distressed, how can we be pleased?" Therefore, the "Khilafat Movement" in India, its loud slogans of alliance, the scenes of Hindu-Muslim unity, the desire to fill the prisons and the wish to face bullets, and this unanimous decision

of the Muslims that the only way to save Islam was to uproot the British from India and break its power, all of these things were very helpful to the Ottoman Turks. The Muslims of India had decided that India needed to be freed from the clutches of the English in any case, whatever happened. Over there, the Western intellectuals had started to fear for and panic about the future of Britain due to these bold moves by the Muslims. Lord Northcliffe, who had been given the title 'Napoleon of Journalism,' and who used to publish seven newspapers from London, railed against the anti-Muslim policies of Lloyd George. His newspapers would spew fire against Lloyd George on a daily basis and their message was that Lloyd George's policies would destroy the colonial power of Britain. He visited the Islamic world and the countries of the East. After his tour, describing the situation, he wrote that wherever he went, from the east to the west, from the north to the south, he found Muslims anxious and restless. He also wrote that with their trousers above their ankles and shirts below their knees, the Muslims were playing with the fire of rebellion. And, most interestingly, he wrote that the limit was the Indian Muslims had started wearing the Gandhian cap. Lord Northcliffe believed that the Gandhian cap was the symbol of rebellion and enmity for the English on the one hand, and of Hindu-Muslim unity on the other. He warned that these Muslims were ready to sacrifice their lives and would raze the British government to the ground.

4. There was another thing that had become a roadblock for the English. The English had prominent influence among the Allied countries, and it was on their indication that the Greeks had landed in Smyrna. And so, their deeds and actions were the responsibility of the English. The Greeks carried out terrible atrocities in Smyrna and Anatolia; incidents of killing and looting, fire and arson, and rape of women were so rampant that the conscience of Europe trembled. Many Western journalists and intellectuals wrote eye-witness accounts of these incidents, which were very brutal, to the extent that the British slave, Caliph Vehideddin's government was even compelled to protest. The civilized world refused to accept these horrors. That is why, when the Ankara government presented the numbers and statistics in front of the League of Nations, the Allied countries were forced to appoint an investigative commission. This commission did an open inquiry and took testimonies. A sample of the testimonies is from a young man of Anatolia who came with a rifle slung over his shoulders, and leaning the rifle in one corner, said this to the commission:

"We were 10 or 15 carefree youths. We had no idea what was going on in the country or Anatolia. We were just happy wandering in the mountains and hunting game. One day, when I returned, I saw that my entire village was burning and the womenfolk were gathered on one side crying. When I went there, my paternal cousin beat me in the face with her shawl and screamed, "Go you shameless one, put on bangles and sit at home." I asked what the Greeks had done to her. She replied, "Don't ask

what they did; if you see a Greek with long teeth, don't let him live." Right there, all of us sat down and took a pledge, then set out with our guns. We jumped through raging fires, swam in fast flowing rivers, penetrated the Greek armies, but I regret that I could not find the long-toothed Greek. If I had found him, even if he had 1000 lives, he would not have been able to leave with even one."

These horrific and brutal events gave the Greeks a black mark in the civilized world, and the Turks naturally deserved the sympathy of the whole world for defending their homeland in these difficult conditions. No propaganda had worked against Mustafa Kemal. A naked reality was exposed. Britain, which claimed to be the guardian and custodian of civilization, could not openly dare to help Greece in such circumstances. However, one should not think that it did not help. British military officers were always on hand to assist in combat operations and schemes and quietly provided supplies and weapons.

On the other hand, India was making a fuss that all this was the doing of the English. There was a rumor in the newspapers that an Englishman, General Harrington, had been spotted near the battlefield. Public rallies and processions, reproaching, protests, and condemnations of the English were abundant. But the English kept denying.

All of India resounded with slogans in support of Kemal Pasha. Processions would go around singing anthems of praises and eulogies for Kemal Pasha, which would be light on poetic sophistication but full of passion and emotion, such as:

Our chief is Kemal Pasha, he is showing us his 'kemal'
(wonders)

One should not think these slogans were raised only by Muslims. Hindu youth and volunteers participated equally, just as they raised the slogan *"Allah-o-Akbar"* in the same voice as Muslims.

12

Second Phase of the Khilafat Movement

Communique from the Bombay Government and Mahatma Gandhi's Sharp Response

The trial of Maulana Mohammad Ali and others started in Karachi on August 19, 1921 and in September 1921, Gandhi said in a message to the Muslims:

"We should fully comply with non-violence but not with helplessness. It is essential that we adhere to the formula that the Ali brothers have stated regarding the rights of the soldiers. And we should invite them to go to prison. We should not think that our movement cannot continue without our best men. If we don't do that, then we are not ready for Swaraj, nor can we heal the wounds of atrocities that have been committed against the Caliphate and the Punjab."

On October 4, 1921 Gandhiji held a meeting of national leaders in Bombay, in which he asked for a manifesto against the actions of the government. The manifesto was as follows:

"Regarding the communique issued by the Government of Bombay on September 15, 1921, which contains the order to put Ali brothers and others on trial, we the

undersigned, in our individual capacities, wish to announce that it is the fundamental right of every citizen, without any hindrance, to decide to stay in or leave any employment, be it civil or military, and to freely express his opinion about that. We the undersigned wish to express our opinion that it is against the national pride of every Indian that, as a civilian and as a national soldier, he should work for such a system that has put India's economic, ethical, and political status at a humiliating bottom and has used the police and army to forcefully crush their steps toward achieving their national rights. For example, during the agitations against the Rowlatt Act and the deployment of soldiers to trample the freedom of Arabs, Egyptians, Turks and citizens of many other countries, who had never hurt India. In our view, it is the duty of every Indian civilian and soldier to cut off their connection to the government and to find some other employment for their sustenance.

This manifesto was signed by 50 leaders, distinguished among them were as follows:

Gandhi, Abul Kalam Azad, Hakim Ajmal Khan, Lajpat Rai, Motilal Nehru, Mrs. Naidu, Abbas Tayabji, NC Kelkar, VJ Patel, MR Jayakar, Jawaharlal Nehru, Gangadhar Rao Deshpande, Umar Sobani, Jamnalal Bajaj, Dr. Ansari, Khaliquzzaman, Abdul Bari, C. Rajagopalachari, Rajendra Prasad, Hasrat Mohani, Dr. Monje, and Jairamdas Daulatram.

On October 5, 1921 the Working Committee of the All-India National Congress approved this manifesto and soon after, hundreds of thousands of people started repeating it from thousands of platforms. The government was rattled by this counter-attack. It was not anticipating this volcanic response from all of India.

Gandhiji emphatically started explaining this manifesto and explaining his philosophy in 'Young India' and in his speeches. He wrote long articles and gave well-grounded speeches. During the latter days of his life, Gandhi used to converse sparingly, but in those days, when he needed to explain his philosophy, he would not shy from lengthy discourses. He even wrote that "my humility is an obstacle in my way or else I would declare from the rooftops that non-cooperation, nonviolence and Swadeshi has just one message that I want to send to the world, which is that the meaning of *Swaraj* is to remove the fear of death. Those who believe in the existence of the soul (and who among the Hindus, Muslims, Christians, and Parsees does not believe that) know that the soul is immortal, and that is why we should remove the fear of death. And if there is no fear of death, then what is the prison that frightens us so much? We are not in the wrong. It is acceptable for us to go to jail or hang from the gallows post because we oppose the cruel laws of the government."

The determination to fight the unfair conviction of the Ali brothers was touching the sky. The nation gave a befitting response to it when, on November 5, 1921, the All-India Congress Working Committee once again ratified Mahatma Gandhi's manifesto dated October 4 1921 and directed the provincial committees to take the responsibility of commencing civil disobedience, which should include the program of non-payment of taxes. However, before participating in civil disobedience, promises would have to be taken to adhere to the total prohibitions and requirements of the Swadeshi movement, which included spinning the *charkha*, and an oath to strictly adhere to non-violence. It was essential for any person who took part in civil disobedience to have full faith in Hindu-Muslim unity and dismiss untouchability. It was also made clear that whoever enters the movement, they or their families will not get any financial assistance. There is a famous incident that when Gandhiji announced this program, some people expressed their concern that the families of volunteers would die of hunger. Gandhiji replied let them die. But then he smiled, and said no one will die of hunger, and that's what happened. How could the people allow those who were sacrificing everything for their nation to die of hunger?

Civil Disobedience in Bardoli

Along with that, Gandhiji gave the directive that nobody should start civil disobedience just yet. He himself would lead civil disobedience in Bardoli, people should observe it and then start civil disobedience in the entire country along those lines. Bardoli is a town in Surat district in the state of Gujarat. He said to the leaders of the nation that he was not asking for any help from anyone other than empathy for his efforts and to be on the guard for any violence that may ensue in their states. "If there is peace and calm in other states, I have no fear, and our efforts shall certainly be crowned with success."

Gandhiji also argued before the nation and Congress that civil disobedience depended on non-violence. Presenting the civil disobedience resolution before the Working Committee, he said:

"Ordinary civil disobedience is like an earthquake, where the government is dismissed and the rule of civil disobedience is established. Where every policeman, every soldier, every government officer is forced to either flee from there or become a soldier of Swaraj. Police stations and all government offices will no longer remain the property of the government and shall come in the control, at the disposal, and in the charge of the people. But for all these things, there is a foundational and essential condition, that people do not resort to debased actions and violence. Disobedience should be so complete that if the government says go right, without hesitation, doubt, and wavering, we should immediately go left. However, opposition to the government should be with determination, but with calmness and composure. Albeit, if this disobedience, instead of being peaceful, is done as an expression of bravery and courage, or pride and arrogance, or by way or ridicule, or anger, or provocation, or revengeful emotions, then in truth and reality, it will become criminal instead of civil. That is why not everyone is suited for civil disobedience."

At the end of his speech, Gandhi said:

"When the flag of Swaraj is raised in Bardoli, the nearby district will follow suit. In that way, district by district, the flag of Swaraj shall fly all over India. But, in any case, as long as this movement is alive, if there is even a little bit of violence anywhere, it will not be expedient to keep the movement going. All of the country should speak with one voice and there should be complete unity and uniformity. If there is violence in any part of the country,

it will give rise to discord in the same way that a single string being out of tune causes the sound of the musical instrument to change."

A few days later, he left for Bardoli by way of Bombay. The entire country waited with bated breath. Gandhiji's promise to get *Swaraj* within a year was getting started.

The Arrival of Prince of Wales

Gandhiji sent a message to his followers in Bombay that he would be going to Bardoli soon to commence civil disobedience there. He wrote that he knew the army had been called there and bullets would be showered, but come what may, he would go to Bardoli. He requested of the people of Bombay just one thing, that whatever happened in Bardoli, they would remain calm and silent.

On November 17, 1921, the heir to the British throne, the Prince of Wales, was to disembark from a ship in Bombay's port. The government had gone out of its way to welcome the esteemed guest. But Congress, Khilafat Committee, and Gandhiji called for a boycott of Prince of Wales. Gandhi had come to Bombay from Ahmedabad that day and he called for a public rally at Chowpatty Maidan. He called upon everyone not to go for the welcoming ceremony for the Prince of Wales and instead come to their rally. The situation was that when the Prince of Wales disembarked from the ship, there was no one there and there was a total strike in all of Bombay. There could not have been a better display of the nation's discontent and rebellion. Hundreds of thousands of people gathered for Mahatma Gandhi's rally but the people could not adhere to non-violence. There were riots in Bombay and surrounding areas. Gandhiji saw with his own eyes that while shouting slogans for his long life, the people burned the cars of Parsees and government officers, damaged government trams, and harassed Parsee women. Someone else would have brushed these incidents under the carpet, but Gandhiji, whose foundational principle was truth, accepted every detail of them and expressed his deep anguish and sadness over it in a statement. In a state of deep despair, he thought about what hopes he had started out with and what had happened. Gandhi was convinced that there was a particular motive behind it, that these riots were orchestrated in a well thought out and professional manner to let the wind out of the sails of this movement. This was a tested technique of the English from the time of the French Revolution.

Gandhi stayed awake till 1 am in that state of sadness, and that same night he decided to postpone his trip to Surat and Bardoli. The next day, armed Parsees, Anglo-Indians, and Jews with crazed passion took to the streets seeking revenge. The Congress leaders were constantly trying to bring peace and tranquility to the people in the city but there were attacks and counter-attacks, and no one knew where the matter would end.

Gandhiji used to wonder what he should do. He couldn't ask those affected by the violence to seek government help. And if he presented himself to the Parsees to do whatever they wanted to him, there would be more bloodshed. After much heart wrenching consideration and discussion, he decided to go on a fast. He said that the only path for him was to appear in front of God and ask Him for more strength so that he could do His work, and that would be possible only when he presented himself to Him as an insignificant speck and stopped eating the food that He had provided. In this way, He would either give him strength or give him death and call him to His fold so that He could make him anew. In this way, Gandhi announced his fast in a long statement, in which he said that God is a purveyor of truth and love. He said that he didn't hate anyone, not even the English; he had just arisen against their system of government, which was illegal. He stated that Hind-Muslim unity was his faith, and until the Hindus and Muslims truly apologize to the Parsees, he couldn't look them in the eye. In the end, he addressed the Muslims:

> *"I want to say one thing to my Muslim brothers. I entered the Khilafat Movement considering it a consecrated matter. I struggled for the cause of Hindu-Muslim unity because without that, India cannot stay alive. And if we treat each other as enemies, then we deny God. I have given myself in care of the Ali brothers because I am confident they are God-fearing people. I confidently believe that in the riots of the last two days, Muslims have taken a great deal of part. I have been extremely shocked by that. I request every Muslim worker to stand up with all their might, realize the duties that their faith has put on them, and work hard to put an end to this violence."*

On November 19, 1921 Gandhiji called his son Devdas back to Bombay and said that he had been brought back for a specific purpose. That purpose was that if in the nearby districts there was violence again, Devdas would be sent to be sacrificed at the hands of the rioters. During this time, the activists used to keep Gandhiji surrounded and would ask him what they should do to end the violence. Gandhiji would reply that he didn't know, but he did feel an inner peace and calm from the fasting. Another result of this fasting was that Gandhiji decided that every Monday till *Swaraj* is achieved, he would keep a 24-hour fast. To him this was a means to purification of the mind, and he believed that it was only through spiritual strength that there would be success.

On November 22, 1921 Gandhiji's fast produced a result. Activists and sympathizers of the non- cooperation movement and its opposers, Hindus, Muslims, Parsees, gathered in unity and agreement, and only then Gandhiji broke his fast.

On November 23, 1921 there was a meeting of the Working Committee in Bombay, and on Gandhiji's proposal, the Bardoli civil disobedience was postponed indefinitely.

Attitude of the Government and Young Blood in the Movement

In Bombay, the complete boycott of the Prince of Wales and the strike caused a lot of anger in the government. The Anglo-Indian community put pressure on the Viceroy to conduct an inquiry, and various harsh orders were issued throughout India. On November 19, 1921 the Bengal Government passed a law against all the voluntary organizations of Congress and Khilafat and issued orders to suppress political gatherings. Punjab, United Provinces, Bihar, and Assam imitated this and issued similar orders. There was a robust protest of this challenge and the orders were openly violated without any reflection or hesitation. UP led the way in harsh and high-handed dealings. In Allahabad, 55 members of the provincial Congress Committee, who were engaged in a passionate debate on a proposal regarding volunteers, were all arrested.

Mr. CR Das, who had been appointed President of the Ahmedabad session of Congress, was arrested in December. Leading political leaders such as Lala Lajpat Rai, Pandit Motilal Nehru, Maulana Abul Kalam Azad, and Jawaharlal Nehru were arrested throughout the country.

The government was responding to non-violence with force and violence. Even wearing *khaddar* or the Gandhian cap was a matter of vexation for the administration and anyone wearing these items was subject to insult and humiliation. Small cases were sent to trial. Police would in jest or for the sake of amusement ask the volunteers to strip or would make them dip in a lake. The records of national colleges were burned and even houses were burned. Properties of the offices of Congress and Khilafat were destroyed. Crops were burned. Possessions and goods were looted and there were even reports that jewelry was being snatched from women and that women were being criminally assaulted.

Pandit Madan Mohan Malviya was very affected by these brutal tactics and met with the Viceroy. He wanted peace between Gandhi and the Viceroy. Since the Viceroy wanted a peaceful and calm welcome for the Prince of Wales when he visited Calcutta, he agreed to have peace talks with Gandhi. But on December 19, 1921 Gandhiji sent the following bold and spirited telegram to Pandit Malviya:

> *"You shouldn't worry at all about the government's harsh response. A conference with the Viceroy is useless until the government expresses its remorse over its actions and agrees to settle three issues: Punjab, Khilafat, and Swaraj."*

After that, Malviyaji met CR Das and Maulana Azad in Presidency Jail, Calcutta. He was of the opinion that if Das and Azad could be persuaded to stop the strike on a few conditions, Gandhi could also be made to agree. But Gandhiji, in a second telegram in reply to Malviyaji's telegram, said that the conditions should be established prior to any meeting. He also wrote that an issue of primary importance is that all the prisoners, including those from the Karachi trial, should be released and a date for the conference should be set in advance. If both these requirements were acceptable, then the strike could be stopped. When Malviyaji showed Gandhiji's telegram to the Viceroy, he was enraged, but still the discussions continued. But Gandhiji had understood the game Lord Reading was playing and eventually sent the following telegram:

> *"I very much regret that I will have to be excused from the covenant you are trying to arrange. Non-cooperation movement can be halted only when there is a successful result of the conference and the decision of the Congress cannot be changed under any condition. "*

Now the English must have realized the courage, bravery, and mind of the man they were dealing with. In this way, the discussions between Malviyaji and the Viceroy were fruitless.

Eye Witness Account

The orders issued by the government to crush the volunteers' movement were met with stiff opposition, an example of which I witnessed firsthand. In those days, I was on the editorial staff of the newspaper *Madina* (Bijnor) and was diligently working in Congress. I had left the University of Allahabad to join the non-cooperation movement, and after staying for a few days with Hasrat Mohani *Saheb* in Kanpur, I came to Bijnor to join *Madina*. The entire vocation was working for Congress. There were rallies almost every day and I would preside over most of them, and would certainly give speeches every day. There were many prominent people there at the time, which included Mahavir Tyagi. Thousands of people would join the rallies every day. Women took out a procession and a few of them were arrested. There was a firestorm in the air. One day I was presiding over a session when a person giving a speech said that an Englishmen had been found drinking the blood of children. This news was false but had become popular, although it had been strongly refuted. When it was said from the podium, I immediately stopped the person giving the speech and asked him to sit down. I said that according to the principles of Gandhiji, our fight was not with the Englishman but with the colonial system of government. The Sub-Inspector of Bijnor was in the audience and he was very impressed with how I handled the situation. The next day he came and praised me and started to rely on me. He would come to meet me often, perhaps to get some secrets.

When the volunteers' movement was declared illegal, he came to me and asked how many volunteers I had. I told him I had no volunteers and he was convinced that nothing would happen. The truth was also like that. There were many workers but none of them were formally volunteers. After he left, we set out and recruited about 150 volunteers. These were joint volunteers for Congress and Khilafat. Having been told that there were no volunteers, the District Magistrate announced that to become a volunteer of Congress or Khilafat was against the law and warned that such volunteers would be arrested. When this announcement was made, many of my fellows had left Bijnor by bus for Najibabad to catch the train to Ahmedabad to attend the Congress session there. There was no railway station in Bijnor at the time. I thought of bringing them back to give a response to this challenge. I was wondering how to get to Najibabad when I found a Muslim taxi driver on the road. I asked him if we could do something for the cause of Khilafat. He immediately agreed to come without any compensation and we left right there and then. When we reached Najibabad station, the train had not yet arrived. We loaded the taxi and returned to Bijnor the same night. I too was a delegate from UP for the Ahmedabad Congress session, but there were still a few days to go. The thought was that the fortunate ones would go to jail, the rest would leave for Ahmedabad. There was a strange scene the next morning. A Muslim volunteer, a man of strong build, with a 'razakar' band around his waist, was selected leader of the volunteers, and before the sun rose, the volunteers assembled outside the police station and started singing:

O' policemen, stop bothering and treating us ill
Stop running your knives over the necks of our brothers

Life is short and moonlit nights are few
Stop making silver over these short days

The Sub-Inspector was rattled out of bed and watched this scene with surprise. In anger and distress, he beat his head with his hands and yelled that Qazi Adeel had deceived him. The 11 volunteers were arrested and sent to jail and another 11 of them were dispatched from the Congress' office. The whole operation was being supervised by Mirza Abdul Latif

Beg, president of the District Congress Committee. After the second and the third groups were arrested, the Sub-Inspector started to say, "Where is Qazi Adeel? Why doesn't he come here?" When I heard that, I grew restless and was eager to join the group of volunteers. Mirza Abdul Latif Beg caught me and locked me in a room. I was enraged and was banging on the door. Mirza Abdul Latif Beg dispatched another group of volunteers, opened the door to the room, and asked me to calm down and talk it over. He said that to run a movement, the strong ones make up the rear so that they can keep the reins in their grip. "All of us will be the last to go to jail. I will go before you do." He was able to convince me. After responding to the government for three days, we left for Ahmedabad. During these three days, the grounds outside the Congress' office would be filled with hundreds of men at all hours. They would shout slogans, put garlands around the necks of the volunteers, and accompany them to the police station. Everyone wanted to become a volunteer.

Provincial Khilafat and Congress Conference in Agra

Before then, in October 1921, the provincial Khilafat conference presided by Abul Kalam Azad and the provincial Congress conference presided by Hasrat Mohani had been held in Agra. I attended this conference as a correspondent of the newspaper *Medina*. I still remember Maulana Azad's speech's first sentence. He said that "while coming here, I didn't see even that much water in river Yamuna as the blood of Muslims that has been spilled in the last 10 years." In his long speech, the Maulana stated his interpretation of the *Al-'Asr* (The Declining Day) chapter of the Quran.

The crux of the chapter was that there are four requirements to complete a job, and when all four requirements are fulfilled, success is inevitable, otherwise there is only loss. Those four requirements are:

1. There should be complete faith in what needs to be done.
2. The job should be done in the way that particular job is done.
3. After the job is done, invite others to do the same.
4. When this is followed and there are difficulties along the way, meet them with steadfastness.

A particular CID Inspector, Ghulam Husain, had been deployed to follow Maulana Azad. He was the best at Urdu shorthand in all of UP and could write 120 words in one minute. He would sit openly in the first row and note down all the speeches. Sometimes Maulana would start speaking even faster than he could write, and he would put his pencil down and fold his hands pleadingly. Maulana would smile and slow down. A camp would be set up for Maulana Azad. Ghulam Husain was given to flattery. One day, when I went to the camp, he was also there and telling Maulana Azad, "My lord, I could not write everything down. How will I answer my bosses?" Wherever he had missed taking down the speech, Maulana filled him in. Shafaatullah Khan, manager of the newspaper *Zamindar*, was also there. I had actually left *Medina* or was about to leave. It had been agreed with Shafaatullah Khan that after attending the Ahmedabad session of Congress, I would come straight to Lahore and take charge of *Zamindar* as its Editor-in-Chief. Maulana Azad was to leave for Fatehpur Sikri that day. Shafaatullah Khan said to him that since Maulana was alone, he would also come along. Maulana replied, "My friend, loneliness, in and of itself, is an accompaniment." Shafaatullah Khan also enjoyed being by himself. He used to ask why people considered solitary confinement a punishment. Shafaatullah Khan narrated another incident regarding Maulana Azad. Shafaatullah Khan asked the Maulana about the holy biography of Prophet Muhammad taken from the Quran that he was going to write. Maulana Azad replied, "My friend! The book has already been compiled and edited completely in my mind; it just needs to be transferred to paper." Unfortunately, we were waiting for this transfer when Maulana Azad was spiritually transferred.

The provincial Congress conference was going on with much pomp and show. Jawaharlal Nehru had also come. Maulana Hasrat Mohani was to arrive in the morning. I had come a day prior. A separate camp had been set up for the president of the conference and there were grand arrangements for reception at the station and a procession to the venue. Flowers and garlands were abundant. Rides had been arranged, the public had been informed, and it was certain that there would be a huge crowd at the station. But Hasrat Mohani, who was simple-hearted, simplicity-loving, and oblivious to formality and fuss, got down from a train at 11 pm and caught a horse-cart to the conference venue. He had a tin suitcase with him which had a pillow, a mat, a change of clothes, a small *lota* (metal pot with a spout and handle), and a sewing kit to mend clothes, which was his constant traveling companion. On getting there, he called out the president of the welcoming committee in his nasal voice. The poor chap was sleeping. He came out to see the Maulana, president of the conference, standing there with his tin suitcase and, not recognizing him, was very annoyed.

When the Maulana alluded to the fact that arrangements should have been made for the president of the conference, he replied the president was to arrive the next morning. Maulana explained to him tenderly that he himself was the president of the conference and was taken to his camp. The next morning, I asked Maulana why he had arrived sooner than the appointed time. The organizers were very disappointed. He dismissed my concerns with a shrug. Maulana had got his presidential address printed in Urdu on bamboo paper. The only argument it presented was that complete independence in India should be without the British government and strictly opposed the dominion status. Regarding the other issues, he said that in his opinion they should be decided by the conference and the president had no role in that. Maulana Hasrat was single-mindedly obsessed with the acquisition of complete independence. A person, who had been in jail for a long time and was a revolutionary, used to say that he had been forced to drink urine in prison. He had composed some crude couplets that weren't even apropos, but whose essence was that "those who want to live in the shadow of Britain are tantamount to accepting to live in the shadow of the devil." Maulana was jumping up and giving an ovation to every couplet as it was being recited. I wondered how one of the greatest poets in India could give an ovation to such crude couplets that weren't even apt. Maulana would take this 'poet' around with him and praise and eulogize him.

All the leaders attended both the conferences. There was a huge crowd in attendance. There were representatives from all districts. On the sponsorship of Maulana Hasrat Mohani, I too got to give a five minute speech at the Congress conference.

In his inaugural address at the Khilafat conference, Maulana Azad said:

"A period of 18 months has gone by. In these 18 months, so many destinations of the Khilafat Movement came in front of us and we got there. On the matters of the Caliphate, Islam's holy places, and India's freedom, which is a duty of Muslims as much as the protection and defense of the Caliphate, I do not think it appropriate to say anything. Silence speaks for itself on these matters, which will get your hearts' attention.

"The Khilafat conference that took place in Meerut was attended by Mahatma Gandhi as well. In that conference, the non-cooperation movement was announced by the Khilafat Committee as an act of defense and a matter of protest. Now that 18 months have passed, it is our foremost duty to move our journey forward, while we take a look at how much of our journey we have completed.

"When you look at these actions, you should place the truth in front of you regarding what was the arena for resistance in the matter of the Caliphate. Was it the arena which was outside of India or was there another arena besides that? The truth is that there were two arenas concerning this matter. The first arena, which was the primary one for your success, was not outside India. It was not the arena of Iraq and Syria, of Asia Minor and Smyrna, where the blood of Muslims has flown. This arena was that of your country and of its victory and defeat. As long as you hadn't conquered that arena, success in the world would not have welcomed you.

"When your movement was merely biding the time of your early life, when there was helplessness and there were thousands of tongues which were chanting the slogans of the Caliphate but there was no agreed to arena in front of you to carry out your actions, those early times have passed for the Khilafat Movement. God's grace and mercy have opened the floodgates and within a few months we conquered the arena. And when the world opened its eyes, it saw that the Khilafat Movement was a cause of national consensus and not something espoused by a limited handful of persons.

The second destination for the movement was that it found a place not just in the hearts of 70 million Muslims but in the hearts of all 320 million Indians. The beauty of the success of Khilafat Movement is that it revived the issue of India with tremendous force, something that the country hadn't found in 40 years. We see that with the Khilafat Movement, the issue of India has come alive with full force."

Maulana Azad applauded Gandhiji for being the biggest friend of the Khilafat Movement from day one. He said that now God Almighty had allowed the flame of the Khilafat Movement to light the lamp of India and this was the second victory for the issue of Caliphate that was achieved in the Indian arena.

Ahmedabad Session of Congress, December 22, 1921

The annual convention of the All-India National Congress was held in Ahmedabad in late December, 1921. I attended as a delegate from UP Congress. The Khilafat Conference was held concurrently.

'Congress City' and 'Khilafat City' had been constructed on a large scale in a large maidan. For open rallies, wall-tents had been erected on both sides encompassing large areas. Outside the tents, lodging arrangements had been made. There was a separate enclosure for exhibitions. There were 2000 *khaddar*-clad volunteers, both boys and girls. These volunteers were mostly recent graduates. Education was very advanced in Ahmedabad. The exhibition area could hold about 40,000 people. The president of the Congress session was CR Das, but he had been arrested. Hakim Ajmal Khan took his place. The president of the welcoming committee was Vallabhbhai Patel. The manner in which the working session was convened can be understood from the fact that Vallabhbhai Patel took only 15 minutes to deliver his welcome address and the presidential address took only 20 minutes.

Earlier, when open rallies did not take place, there would be different rallies taking place outside. There would be 1000 people assembled somewhere, 2000 elsewhere, and leaders of the nation would be giving lectures. In those days, Maulana Azad Subhani was very close to Mahatma Gandhi, and he would often promote Gandhiji's principles. He had also stayed at Gandhiji's ashram.

Both Congress City and Khilafat City had kitchens. There were tea and snack cafes as well. An interesting thing that happened was that when I stepped inside a tea cafe, the cafe manager said they didn't serve Muslims tea there. I just boiled over. I yelled: how could he discriminate between Hindus and Muslims inside Congress City? I told him I would go immediately to Gandhiji and complain. He pleaded with me not to, and eventually served me tea.

The rallies had more than 100,000 people in attendance. From the Congress stage, Gandhi delivered a passionate speech in English, which warmed the hearts of everyone.

Gandhiji delivered a speech from the Khilafat stage as well. He used to be bare chested with his dhoti up to his knees. He entered the Congress enclosure hurriedly, and accidentally brushed a man with his legs. He apologized but to the man it was a blessing.

Since Maulana Hasrat Mohani was my patron, I would go with him everywhere and nobody would stop me. I attended the meetings of the All-India Congress Committee as well. I would sit in a far corner and observe the proceedings. There, Gandhi proposed his objective of *Swaraj* and the non-violent method of achieving it, and that too in words, deeds, and thoughts.

The resolution presented was in English. Maulana Hasrat Mohani proposed amendments in which he replaced *Swaraj* with 'complete independence without the involvement of the British government,' and in words, deeds, and thoughts of methods of achieving it, 'non-violence' was replaced with 'all means necessary.' Maulana Hasrat Mohani delivered a rational and passionate speech and said that if Congress did not accept 'complete independence without the involvement of the British government,' then he would leave the party. But in the next breath he laughed and said he would never do that. Gandhi said that such a person should resign from the party. After Hasrat's speech, the speech that Gandhiji gave is still in my memory:

"If Maulana moves ahead with the goal of complete independence, I will not fall behind. But strength is needed for that. I can plant the Congress flag on Agra Fort even though the governor is a madman like Hitler. But we need strength for that. I don't want to say anything that I will not be able to do or something that I don't have the strength for."

Maulana Hasrat's proposed amendments were rejected by the Subject Committee (or the All-India Congress Committee). The next day, Maulana Hasrat Mohani raised hell. He regularly made fiery speeches in the adjunct small gatherings, saying that if the Muslims had non-violence on their minds, it would mean that he would reject jihad and would leave Islam. Gandhiji wanted to make Muslims followers of Jainism. In a similar rally, Maulana Hasrat was delivering a speech with his walking stick on the table, when Maulana Azad Subhani stood up and asked if Maulana Hasrat would have any objections to the word 'thought' being replaced by the word 'intention'. Maulana Hasrat picked up his walking stick and walked away. Later, in private, he burst with anger at Maulana Azad Subhani, "What need did you have to propose replacing 'thought' with 'intention'?" It had become well known that Gandhiji was uneasy and Maulana Azad Subhani had gotten permission from him to replace thought with intention. A day earlier, Maulana Azad Subhani had arranged a truce between Gandhiji and Maulana Hasrat, and Maulana Hasrat had agreed that for two years he would not resist Gandhiji. But he changed his mind. Maulana Azad Subhani himself told me this and that is what he said to Hasrat as well.

Mr. Muhammad Ali Jinnah

I was standing in a queue outside a gate, waiting for my pass to be checked, when an extremely beautiful woman in a revealing dress came and tried to enter. When the volunteer asked for her pass, she said in English that she was Mrs. Jinnah. The volunteer replied sternly in English that he was bound by his duty to not allow anyone in without a pass. At that moment, Mr. Jinnah himself walked up, dressed in a fine suit. The woman turned to him and said in English, "J, he is asking for my pass and will not let me in." Mr. Jinnah silently handed his pass to her and she went inside, while he took out a notepad, wrote on a piece of paper, and handed it to the volunteer to take to the dais. By that time I had entered the gate. I saw that there was commotion when the note was delivered. Hakim Ajmal Khan himself stood up and accompanied Mr. Jinnah to the dais a short while later. This was his last attendance in Congress. Later he resigned from Congress.

> *Those raised with love and affection cannot be close to their*
> *wealthy friends*
> *Love is the habit of those knaves who can tolerate misery*
> *and woe*

Gandhi called upon the delegates from UP and told them that Hindus with their *langot* wraps and Muslims with their long sleeved kurtas and trousers above their ankles should take to the villages. Maulana Azad Subhani said to Gandhiji that if he was asking for such a big sacrifice, then the objective should be big too, and that he should aim for the goal of complete independence. Gandhiji replied that Maulana thought that to get rid of a big ill, one has to make a big sacrifice, but his conviction was that even to get rid of a small ill, sometimes one has to make a big sacrifice. In this session, addressing everyone, Gandhiji said that Hasrat Mohani had a lot of influence on UP Congress. They could take Hasrat with them or they could take him, but both couldn't come along. Harish Chandra Bajpai, who was later a member of the Rafi Party and became an MLA, stood up and said they were not influenced by Hasrat. Gandhi said to him, "Sit down please. I said the truth, I did not ask for your opinion." At the Ahmedabad Congress, I saw Abbas Tayabji, who's hair was white as snow. Young girls always surrounded him. He took his daughter up on the stage erected nearby from where he sang the anthem.

Indira Gandhi

There were various small rallies on the maidan outside of session hours in which leaders would give speeches. In those rallies, I saw a young girl whose age, by my estimate, must have been six-seven years at the time. Wearing a Gandhian cap, she would be found everywhere, sitting quietly with sobriety. In my BA studies, I majored in psychology, and had learned that it would be cruel to expect a child younger than seven to sit quietly. That is why I was surprised to see this girl's seriousness and sobriety and I felt the need to inquire about her. I found out she was Jawaharlalji's daughter Indira.

Talk of Truce

At the Ahmedabad Congress, there was talk that the Viceroy had asked Gandhiji to agree to a truce. Malviyaji had proposed a round-table conference which was rejected, but Gandhiji said that the time hadn't come yet for a truce because India had not yet faced sufficient difficulties. He also said that there wasn't discipline in the nation yet; he just saw people entering and leaving the conference tent pushing each other.

People attending the Ahmedabad Congress returned home with renewed determination and enthusiasm to work. I left Ahmedabad for Lahore to take charge of the newspaper *Zamindar* as its Editor-in-Chief.

After the Ahmedabad Congress

After the Ahmedabad Congress, the movement picked up speed. Neither did the government tire of arresting people, nor did the people tire of presenting themselves to be arrested. Newspapers were raided, printed material would be confiscated, and the editor, printer, and publisher would be arrested. This was in reality the bloom of the movement. News of the brutal atrocities of the Greeks in Anatolia was coming every day and even the children were certain that Britain was behind it. This had fueled a lot of hatred against the English. To accelerate the work, Congress had given complete administrative authority to Gandhiji in Ahmedabad.

Gandhiji was asked by people, including some known leaders of India and particularly the moderate ones, what he thought about the fact that he had promised a year ago that he would get *Swaraj* within one year. Gandhi published a long and rational answer in 'Young India,' the synopsis of which is that *Swaraj* was certainly not achieved but the mind, which was in shackles, had been freed. He also wrote that *Swaraj* does not mean transformation of the government, but true transformation of the hearts of the people. True spirit of Hindu-Muslim unity should rise, people should spin the *charkha*, and abide by non-violence. Now Gandhiji too started to forcefully write, speak, and demand freedom to counter the government's oppressive policies.

All Parties Conference

The government's violence and oppression became unbearable even for those who were not opposed to the government or supporters of the non-cooperation movement. Hence, Pandit Madan Mohan Malviya and Mr. Jinnah convened an All-Parties Conference in Bombay on January 14, 1922, which was attended by 100 delegates. Proponents of the non-cooperation movement were specially invited. Sir Sankaran Nair was appointed chairman of the conference. At the proposal of NC Kelkar, Mahatma Gandhi was the lone speaker on behalf of the proponents of non-cooperation. At the Founders' Conference, a draft of truce between the government and Congress was created, whose purport was to convene a round table conference where the matters of Punjab, Khilafat, and *Swaraj* would be discussed and settled. Gandhi said that no conversations could be had until such time that all prisoners were released, that the draft proposal did not mention the release of Ali brothers and other prisoners, and it should have, and the violence and oppression of the government should be condemned. On seeing the direction of the conference, the chairman abdicated his chair and left and Sir Visweswaran was appointed chairman in his place. A final decision was made on January 17, 1922. The condemnation of the government's oppression and demand to release prisoners were included as primary conditions in the draft. After this, Gandhi temporarily suspended the non-cooperation movement. Starting January 16, 1922, Jinnah *Saheb* and Malviyaji kept sending telegrams to the Viceroy but no reply was received. Eventually a letter arrived on January 30, 1922, in which the Viceroy expressed his inability to accept those conditions. All these efforts proved fruitless and the movement started again.

Civil Disobedience Again in Bardoli

On January 29, 1922 Vallabhbhai Patel asked for permission to start civil disobedience in Bardoli. In front of 4,000 representatives, 500 of whom were women, Patel *Saheb* delivered a serious and grounded speech and had everyone pledge non-violence. On January 31, 1922 the Working Committee gave permission for a general civil disobedience to start in Bardoli. The population of Bardoli was around 78,000. On February 1, 1922 Mahatma Gandhi gave an ultimatum to the Viceroy that the issues of Punjab, Khilafat, and *Swaraj* must be resolved, otherwise general civil disobedience would commence in Bardoli. On February 6, 1922 the Viceroy issued a communiqué in which he refused to accept the basis for Gandhiji's demands. On February 7, 1922 Gandhiji replied and presented instances of the government's oppression and violence, which had been refuted by the Viceroy, and which were as follows:

1. Firing on unarmed civilians in Calcutta.
2. Brutal treatment of the public by the Civil Guard.
3. Forced dispersion of peaceful rallies in Dhaka and Aligarh.
4. Looting in many villages of Bihar.
5. Severe assault and battery on Congress and Khilafat volunteers at many locations.
6. Burning of Congress and Khilafat documents in their offices in Sonepur.

7. Searches in the offices of Congress and Khilafat late into the nights, and so on.

Gandhi was carrying out all this correspondence from Bardoli, where he was leading the general civil disobedience. Everything was ready and was just waiting for a signal when a dangerous obstacle emerged.

Chauri Chaura Incident

On the morning of February 8, 1922, Gandhi read in the newspaper the details of the Chauri Chaura incident which had taken place on February 5, 1922. The incident took place after a peaceful procession in Chauri Chaura regarding rising prices and liquor sales ended. Later, there was a heated confrontation between some constables and protesters. The constables started firing upon the protestors and when they had fired all their bullets, they ran and took shelter in a police station. The enraged crowd surrounded the police station and set it on fire. When the constables came out of the burning police station, 22 of them were hacked down and thrown into the fire, and they burned to death.

On reading the news, Gandhiji collapsed. The movement was a matter of his honor and to stop it, particularly after he had challenged the Viceroy, was very difficult for him. He thought for a long time and eventually decided that this was the voice of the devil teaching him pride and arrogance.

Gandhi announced that Bardoli's civil disobedience would be put off. In the January 16 edition of 'Young India,' he wrote that God had cautioned him three times. First, during the agitation against Rowlatt Act, many cities resorted to violence and he was humiliated before God. He acknowledged that he had made a colossal mistake then. The second time was in Bombay, and now the third time, in these incidents reported in Chauri Chaura. As a consequence, he announced a five-day fast for self-purification of the mind and as a punishment.

The stoppage of civil disobedience in Bardoli affected Gandhi's colleagues and followers very much. Everyone was uneasy. Jawaharlal wrote letters from prison to Gandhiji protesting his decision. There was disappointment and hopelessness all across the nation. Mohammad Farooq Deewana Gorakhpuri, past editor of *Hamdard* who was known by the name Haji Baghlol, in his signature humorous style, wrote a mock prosecutorial statement suing Mahatma Gandhi. Young and old, supporters and non-supporters, all were anxious, but Gandhiji was content with his position. He would reply to everyone that the movement could proceed only with non-violence and the nation had not yet taken to non-violence. People would say Bardoli was very far from Chauri Chaura, and that it was no fault of Bardoli. Gandhi's answer was that only Bardoli was not India. Starting from Bardoli, this movement had to be taken everywhere. Until and unless the whole country was ready, what would general civil disobedience do in one place?

Gandhiji Arrested

The Independence movement picked up so much speed that the English were stunned and decided to take more aggressive steps to quell it. Mr. Montagu, the Secretary of State for India threatened the country in a heart-rending speech saying that the government still had the means to crush the people and warned them against disloyalty. On February 24,

1922 Gandhiji gave a fitting reply to that, and on March 10, 1922 he was arrested. After being served the arrest warrant, Gandhiji listened to a Hindu hymn, embraced Maulana Hasrat Mohani, who had incidentally come by, and sat in the police car and left for Sabarmati Jail. This strange coincidence was a moment of rapture for Hasrat's strategy. He opposed Gandhiji all his life but had gone to jail in support of all of Gandhi's movements and that day, when the government's policy regarding Gandhiji changed and he was arrested, Hasrat *Saheb* was present there and Gandhiji embraced him before going to jail. This embrace was proof of the fact that both of them had the same purpose. A fire was burning in both their hearts. Shankerlal Banker, publisher of 'Young India,' whom Gandhiji held in high esteem, was also with him. On March 20, 1922 Gandhiji was transferred from Sabarmati Jail to Yerwada Jail and was separated from Banker.

As a result of his arrest, Gandhiji was disbarred from practicing law as a barrister by the Benchers of the Inner Temple of London. In jail, Gandhi was harassed. He was subjected to a full body search every day, although all he wore was a *langot*. His blanket would be examined. The jailer would trample his eating dishes with his foot. He was allowed to write only four letters in a year. The English had abandoned their gentility and had resorted to cowardly vengeance. As a *satyagrahi*, an individual seeker of truth, Gandhi tolerated everything and eventually the jail administrators apologized. They returned his *charkha* and started treating him with respect. That is, the sword of atrocities was broken by the spiritual blow of truth and non-violence.

The English thought that after Gandhiji's arrest, there was no other such leader who could influence the entire nation.

But Congress fulfilled its duties with full preparedness. On June 7, 1922 a meeting of the All-India Congress Committee was held, whose secretary was Rajagopalachari. Pandit Motilal Nehru had been released. He too participated. A committee was formed consisting of Hakim Ajmal Khan, Motilal Nehru, Rajagopalachari, Dr. Ansari, Vallabhbhai Patel, and Kasturi Ranga Iyengar, tasked with preparing a report by September 30, 1922 on how civil disobedience could be revived. The above list of members also suggests that India's leadership was not shorthanded.

In August 1922, the incident of Guru-ka-Bagh occurred. Akali Dal was an armed group of Sikhs. They wanted to dominate over all the temples. One of the temples wasn't willing and the government backed them. An Akali Dal group would go there and would be repulsed and beaten with sticks and they would just raise slogans of '*wahe guru ki jai, wahe guru ki jai.*' This fine display of non-violence strongly promoted Gandhiji's philosophy and newspaper reporters from abroad scrambled to capture photographs and frame the true situation.

On September 30, 1922 the report of the select committee of the All-India Congress Committee was completed and sent to the Congress president, CR Das. The gist of the report was that civil disobedience was unimplementable.

On October 20, 1922 a meeting of the All-India Congress Committee was convened, where it was decided that provincial committees can give permission for individual civil disobedience in their provinces. General civil disobedience was not approved. The reality was that no one other than Gandhiji could have launched it.

In December 1922, the annual session of All-India National Congress was held in Gaya. A proposal was presented there to enter the government-appointed Reform Councils and break them from within. CR Das supported it but said that if the Khilafat Conference opposed it, then the proposal would not be accepted. Rajagopalachari presented a proposal to maintain complete non-cooperation and the Khilafat Conference accepted only the proposal for complete non-cooperation. Rajagopalachari's resolution passed with 1740 votes in favor and 890 votes against. Congress decided to collect Rs. 2.5 million and recruit 50,000 volunteers.

Gandhi and Malviya

At the time that civil disobedience was put off, the top leaders of India had started wavering on their confidence and belief in Gandhiji's scheme of delivering Swaraj within a year. Some people had openly started criticizing while others would mutter under their breath that when all of India became angels, only then would we move toward our destination. When would that happen? Was that even possible? They used to ask what an incident in one corner of India has to do with other corners of the country. No one was confident that there would be a situation that all of India would be calm at the same time, especially when Gandhiji had declared that even if his opponents were responsible for violence, the responsibility would be his since he was the one running the movement. These were the reasons why, just a few days later, Motilal Nehru and CR Das made the program of entering the Reform Councils, and after the arrest of Gandhiji, when it became necessary to impress upon the government that the movement would not be intimidated by their high-handedness, which included arbitrary arrests of its top leaders, Congress gave permission to the provincial committees for individual civil disobedience.

It was after the arrest of Gandhiji that Pandit Madan Mohan Malviya entered the arena and started a tour of all of India. He used to practice his own interpretation of the non-cooperation movement. He used to say the non-cooperation movement did not even include the boycott of courts and schools. It was at this juncture that four political parties appeared in India:

1. Those who were true followers of Gandhiji and had faith in non-cooperation, non-violence, *khaddar*, and Hindu-Muslim unity and who wanted the color and direction of the movement that Gandhiji had adorned to remain unchanged.
2. Those in Congress who were tired of Gandhiji's scheme and wanted to break the ridiculous reforms of 1919 from within by joining the councils. The prominent leaders among them were CR Das, Motilal Nehru, Hakim Ajmal Khan, and others.
3. Independents, including Mr. Muhammad Ali Jinnah, Pandit Madan Mohan Malviya, etc. These people insisted on establishing reconciliation between the Viceroy and Gandhiji
4. Moderates, which included Sir Tej Bahadur Sapru, Mr. Chintamani, Sir Sankaran Nair etc., who wanted to form a government under the shadow of the English and to gradually introduce reforms and progressive legislation.

Pandit Madan Mohan Malviyaji had a great personality and his conscience was pure and without any blemishes. As a true and dignified follower of Hindu religion, being prejudiced or narrow-minded never applied to him. His services had also been great and establishment of Banaras Hindu University was a magnificent example of his great efforts. Gandhi too held him in high regard and cared for him. His thoughts had never been of an extremist nature although he was never inclined to oppose extremism either. His efforts had been limited to reformism.

During Gandhiji's absence, Pandit Malviya's tours and the unique exegesis of the non-cooperation movement did not after all prove to be the threat it had been feared. Gandhiji had captured the hearts and minds of the people.

Entry Into the Reform Councils

On January 1, 1923 CR Das and Motilal Nehru laid the foundation of the Swaraj Party and said that it would be a party within Congress. Its purpose would be to break the Reform Councils from within, and when the party has a majority within Congress, its work would begin. Maulana Hasrat Mohani went to Calcutta and joined Das and Nehru, and newspapers reported it on their front pages under bold headlines.

On May 1, 1923 Maulana Azad became the president of Congress. A special session of Congress had taken place in Delhi in September 1922. Maulana Mohammad Ali had been released earlier and he was in attendance. Entry into Reform Councils had been approved in that meeting.

The CR Das-Motilal Nehru alliance was a success. The Swaraj Party fought the elections. It was in the majority in many provinces and won half the seats at the center.

The Situation in Turkey

In November 1922, Mustafa Kemal declared Turkey a democracy and Sultan Vehideddin was deposed and sent to Malta on an English ship.

I had heard of Adam coming out of the Garden of Eden but
It was very dishonorably that I left your corner of the world

Now Sultan Abdul Majid was appointed Caliph in his place. But a powerless Sultan as a Caliph of the Muslims could not be paired with a democracy. And that is where the debate started in our country in which the great Muslim scholars and leaders participated.

1923: Suspicions and Differing Views in Congress

Gandhiji was still in jail when gradual setbacks appeared for all his initiatives. Hakim Ajmal Khan, CR Das, Motilal Nehru and others had become averse to the conditions laid down by Gandhiji regarding continuance of the civil disobedience movement. They were not in agreement that the spread of civil disobedience should be curtailed due to one incidence of violence in the entire country. In reality, no leader big or small was in agreement with Gandhiji's decision to stop civil disobedience. But then, to spread civil disobedience, and that too general civil disobedience, from district to district was not something that anybody other than Gandhiji could do either.

People started thinking that if violence in any part of the country was going to completely stop the movement in other parts of the country, then the movement was completely untenable, since inciting violence and riots anywhere in the country was no big deal for the government. And otherwise too, for such a big country to be collectively content in one instance was inconceivable. That is why Das and Motilal thought that the reason why the oppressed were not able to get their pleas heard was that there were no appropriate representatives. Heavy taxes were being imposed and the public was in severe distress. Now, instead of waiting for such time that the entire country would be amenable to non-violence, it was better to enter the councils and the central council, get rid of incompetent people, break those reforms from within, and take that path to move forward toward freedom. In this way, non-cooperation, civil disobedience, and even Swadeshi movement, in short all of Gandhi's organizations and instructions were left behind and people embarked on running in elections.

The second tragedy was that Hindu-Muslim unity faced serious setbacks from many directions. Hindu-Muslim riots began in big cities resulting in unity being blown to smithereens. In Agra district, Malkana Rajputs used to live around Agra city. They had converted to Islam a long time ago. In 1923, Arya Samaj decided to make them 'pure' and to convert them back to Hinduism again, and they started to become 'pure' in large numbers. This caused sentiments to flare among Indian Muslims and religious passion rose to maddening levels. Many Tablighi Jamaat, Sunni Islamic missionary organizations exhorting Muslims to be more religiously observant, started resistance all over India, stopping people from becoming 'pure,' and encouraging those who had become 'pure' to return to the glory of Islam. The leader of this 'purity movement' was Swami Shraddhanand, who had given a speech from the pulpit of the Jama Masjid in the early days of the non-cooperation movement. The 'purity drive' caused a lot of resentment among the Muslims and they concluded that the Hindus were not ready under any circumstance to work together with them. The Muslim scholars tried very hard to not make this issue the basis of conflict. Maulana Abul Kalam Azad himself went to Agra and on returning, gave a statement in Lahore which was published in the April 15, 1923 issue of the newspaper *Zamindar*. Maulana stated:

> *"In India, every person and every group has the right to propagate and preach their religion legally and peacefully. The freedom of choice and faith is man's natural right. This freedom too, like many other freedoms, has been lost. Thirteen hundred years ago, the Quran announced this afresh."*

'There is no compulsion in religion. The right direction is henceforth distinct from error. And he who rejecteth false deities and believeth in Allah hath grasped a firm handhold which will never break. And Allah heareth and knoweth all things.'

In this way, Maulana expressed his opinion that as far as the matter of spirituality was concerned, there was no reason for the Muslims to object to this; on the contrary, they should just fulfill their duties. But Maulana also wrote that whatever was happening in Malkana was in the form of a movement, and those who had started this movement had ignored the better interests of the country. People should have abstained from all those things that diverted the country's emotions and attention away from national consensus and joint struggles, and toward some provocative purpose.

This intelligent, intellectual, and unbiased advice was understood neither by Hindus nor by Muslims. In Punjab, Dr. Saifuddin Kitchlew started a movement of "preach and organize" in response, and the country's energy started being spent on this conflict.

I wrote a series of articles in the newspaper *Zamindar* on this topic, in which it was shown how unfamiliar the Muslims were with even the *'kalima,'* the confession and discourse of the Islamic faith. There were places where there was no one to lead the funeral prayers. In such circumstances, it would have been better if a group of scholars would get behind the reform of Muslims, and let the national efforts proceed as they were and let the other groups do as they were doing. The former was a separate constructive effort which should be done from a purely religious perspective. The weekly *Al-Aman*, whose editor Maulana Mazharuddin was my employer, strongly disagreed with this, and a series of articles and responses ensued between the two newspapers. In the end, *Al-Aman* accepted that what I was saying was right. Maulana Zafar Ali Khan had written the following couplet on this issue:

> *The verdict is finally in favor of Adeel*
> *'Al-Aman' too with your judgment agrees*

In Bengal, the violent revolutionary parties, which had become subdued due to Gandhiji, raised their heads and dacoity, looting, and violence became widespread.

In this way, practical deviation from Gandhiji's philosophy had started all around.

Gandhi's Release

In jail, Gandhi came down with appendicitis. He was transferred to Poona's Sassoon Hospital where he underwent an appendectomy. On February 5, 1924 he was released on medical grounds and on March 10, 1924 he went to Juhu to recover. In the first week of April, he took charge of 'Young India' and wrote a series of articles on Hindu-Muslim unity. On June 19, 1924 he wrote up a plan for reorganizing Congress, which was presented at a meeting of the All-India Congress Committee on June 27, 1924. The scene that he witnessed there left him disheartened and on June 30, 1924 he wrote in 'Young India' that he had been defeated and was ashamed. At the end of the Congress Committee meeting, he also said that it broke his heart to see and understand the behavior and direction of the people. Riots had broken out in Amethi, Sambhal, and Gulbarga, and then there was deadly Hindu-Muslim violence in Kohat.

On December 18, 1924 Gandhiji announced a 21-day fast for Hindu-Muslim unity.

Milap Conference

As a result of this violence, a *Milap* (Reconciliation) Conference was organized, which was attended by all the prominent leaders of the country. The conference was presided by Motilal Nehru. There was a section cordoned off with a bamboo fence where all the leaders sat. Behind it was a resting area where the leaders could also hold private discussions. On the other side, the public had permission to enter and seating arrangements had been made. I attended all the sessions of the conference in the company of my friends

Maulana Abdul Haleem and Maulana Mohammad Irfan, who were both working in the office of Jamiat Ulema-e-Hind. Many topics came under discussion at the conference, and after deliberations on all of them, a consensus was reached. In this way, as it were, all the Hindu-Muslim issues were settled.

The day before cow sacrifice was to be discussed, all the recognized leaders gathered at the home of Hakim Ajmal Khan, where it was decided that when this topic came up, all the Muslim leaders would remain silent, and when everyone had spoken, only Mufti Kifayatullah would give a response. But what happened was that as soon as the session started, Maulana Mazharuddin stood up and gave a nonsensical speech. Nobody paid any attention to it since Maulana Mazharuddin had no leadership position in the country. However, Maulana Mohammad Ali broke this rule and said in a speech that even if Hindus raped his wife or mother, he would not fight them. This sentence created a lot of uneasiness among the Muslims. After the session ended, I stayed back for a little while and heard Hakim Ajmal Khan asking Maulana Mohammad Ali that when it had been decided that no one would speak, why did he give a speech? Maulana Mohammad Ali got irritated and replied angrily that he wasn't that dishonorable that Hakim Ajmal Khan should scold him like that. I was shocked at this reply. For the *Asr* prayers, Maulana Hussain Ahmed Madani, along with Maulana Abdul Aleem and Maulana Irfan, went to the mosque near the office of Jamiat Ulema-e-Hind. The mosque was completely deserted. Maulana Madani inquired about the time set for *Asr* prayers, when the two, who were also his disciples, replied that there was no set time and the prayers were held whenever people showed up. Maulana Madani smiled and asked why they were not saying that there was no occasion to offer prayers in congregation. There, Maulana Abdul Aleem also said to Maulana Madani that it was fine that Maulana Mohammad Ali talked about the rape of his wife, but why did he say that about his mother given she was the mother of everyone there? Maulana Madani smiled again and said that they could say that about his wife too, that she was everyone's sister. In other words, he was not provoked to say anything and deflected the issue. This deflection was non-existent in Maulana Mohammad Ali's demeanor.

The conference was conducted with much simplicity and there were no embellishments. The welcome and presidential addresses were short and to the point and the discussions went directly into the matter at hand. The first resolution was regarding the destruction of temples. Immediately someone proposed the amendment that 'mosques' should be added to the temples. There was a heated debate around that but Maulana Abul Kalam Azad got up and, opposing the amendment, said that the truth about the temples had "emerged" (it was the first time that people heard the word "emerged" as a synonym for apparent and it surprised them), the gentleman who had presented the amendment could not produce a single example of a mosque being destroyed, and the amendment was withdrawn.

The biggest dispute was on the day that the matter of cow sacrifice was presented. All the Muslims remained silent. Patel was wearing a *langot*. He said he too was a Hindu and to him the cow was holy and blessed, but if the Muslims didn't believe in that, then what was the reason that they should impose their belief regarding cows on their Muslim brothers. However, if they were to give up cow sacrifice of their own free will and accord, it would be better. After that, Lala Lajpat Rai got up and in a sarcastic tone said that he congratulated Hindus that there had been an addition of one to their faith; Patelji himself had said to him that he was not a Hindu and today he was saying that he was one. Lalaji proposed a complete ban on cow slaughter. Pandit Madan Mohan Malviya gave a speech in such elegant Urdu that we were amazed. He said the middle path was better. Places where cow sacrifice is held currently, the Hindus would not put any hurdles to it nor should there be any legal pressure. But where no cow sacrifice was held currently, the Muslims should not start this practice in those places. After a few more speeches, Mufti Kifayatullah gave a cogent speech and demanded complete freedom for cow sacrifice and lawful slaughtering of cows according to Islamic tenets. Maulana Mohammad Ali said that Muslims should completely stop the slaughter of cows. The arguments did not end. The next day, I heard Pandit Malviyaji saying to Maulana Kifayatullah, "Maulana, please reflect on this a bit. Given the emotions of Hindus regarding cows, we are still ready to allow cow sacrifice where it is the practice today and also agree that there should be no legal hindrances to such practices. If we are ready to bow to such an extent, you should also move a little from your position. After all, what is the difficulty in accepting that this practice not be started where it is not practiced today? All we are saying is that in places where there has been no cow sacrifice till today, only in those places there should be no cow sacrifice in the future of your own free will and accord." First, Mufti *Saheb* stuck to his position but it was ultimately not tenable. Eventually he was persuaded and Pandit Malviya's resolution passed. It is unfortunate that this agreement could not be sustained and perhaps it was the Muslims who first broke it.

CR Das was not present at the conference. A telegram was sent to him in Calcutta and he came with his wife. It is said that on arriving, the first thing he asked was why he had been called. He was told that Gandhiji was going on a fast and hindrances to Hindu-Muslim unity had to be removed. Das replied that Gandhiji was going on a fast at the call of his conscience, that was his personal decision, and he would not change that at anyone's asking. As far as the Hindu-Muslim issue was concerned, he said that he was neither a Hindu nor a Muslim, so why was he needed? He returned to Calcutta on the next train. Similarly, there were debates on other matters of dispute and eventually, all the matters were decided by consensus. But the differences were deep rooted. These debates were only on secondary issues such as playing music in front of mosques, violence and riots, and cow sacrifice, and the apparent unity was short-lived.

Belgaum Khilafat Conference

Khilafat Conference was held in Belgaum on December 24, 1924 and on December 26, 1924, Congress Conference took place at the same location. Mahatma Gandhi presided over the Congress Conference. He had been persuaded to accept the presidency with much difficulty. The Khilafat Conference was presided by Dr. Saifuddin Kitchlew. The Muslim League Conference was held in Bombay on December 30, 1924, where Mr. Jinnah presented a scheme for separate representation for Muslims. This was Mr. Jinnah's first step toward sectarianism. Prior to that, he had stated in support of joint elections that "if Muslims want to enter politics, they should come in through the main door and not through the window."

In Belgaum, a session of the Hindu Mahasabaha took place at the Congress convention on December 27, 1924, presided by Pandit Madan Mohan Malviya. Congress leaders also participated in it. Malviyaji claimed that Hindu Mahasabha was not a sectarian organization.

At last, Gandhiji put a stake in the ground in Belgaum and the Gandhi-Nehru-Das covenant was prepared, whose main tenet was that the entry to Reform Councils should be approved and spinning the *charkha* should be made compulsory for members. Gandhiji bid farewell to the non-cooperation movement and returned to his ashram.

On June 16, 1925 CR Das passed away, an event that was grieved by the entire nation. And on July 16, 1925 Gandhiji gave the charge of the entire Congress in the hands of Pandit Motilal Nehru. As a result, on September 22, 1925, the Swaraj Party became a part of Congress.

This was an interim period that was termed 'Masterly Inactivity' by Gandhiji. His basis for this was that the people had endured many difficulties and deserved some rest. There was no question at all of going back on the path of yearning for self-determination and freedom that Gandhiji had set the nation on. Gandhiji had achieved victory at the Belgaum conference, but with tears in his eyes he had said that nothing could be done without his great companions. Maualana Abul Kalam Azad's eyes were wet too. The stake that Gandhiji had put in the ground gave testimony to his big-hearted and truth-seeking nature, tactical skills, and sincerity. Gandhiji had been seeing with his own eyes that the bugle would sound once again and the vast multitude of his troops would again be called to the rope and the gallows post.

13

The End of the Caliphate

Mustafa Kemal deposed Sultan Vehideddin and appointed Sultan Abdul Majeed as Caliph, declaring Turkey a European-style democracy, separating politics and religion. This took place on November 1, 1922.

On March 3, 1924 Mustafa Kemal Pasha abolished the Caliphate, and Turkey, like other governments and empires, became a secular government. The incident sparked a wave of grief and anger in India and the same Mustafa Kemal, who had thus far been a hero for Muslims, became the target of their ridicule. Some people became so incensed that they started calling him a deviant and even an enemy of Islam. Newspapers run by government loyalists and the stooges of the English had a field day. They exulted and mocked, and ridiculed the movement for achieving nothing.

When Gandhiji was released from jail, people asked him the same questions. Gandhiji took charge of 'Young India' in the first week of April 1924 and at the earliest opportunity wrote a long article on the subject, which is summarized as follows:

If I had been a prophet and I had been given the knowledge of the unseen, and I knew that this would be the fate of the Khilafat Movement, even then I would have participated in it with the same zeal. This is the movement which gave awakening to the nation and I will not let it sleep again.

These golden words of Gandhiji were a complete and efficacious response to the detractors who said that the Muslims had made a drastic error in starting the Khilafat Movement. Gandhiji, whose principle was truth and who never shied from speaking the truth, declared the Khilafat Movement the awakening of the nation.

The passion and excitement of the Muslims was continuing to build. The Khilafat Committees were still functioning, meetings were being held, and efforts were being made to get Mustafa Kemal to change his mind. It took a lot of knowledge and intelligence to comfort oneself. And so, after this great tragedy, Maulana Abul Kalam Azad wrote an article under the title 'The Great News,' which was published as a serial in Bombay's *Khilafat* and Lahore's *Zamindar*. Although this article described the downfall of the Caliphate, it also shed light on a number of issues related to it. As far as the issue of the downfall of the Caliphate was directly concerned, we quote the Maulana:

"What is intended by Islamic Caliphate is actually the government, and the Caliph is the one who is the head of this government...Now we must consider what is meant by the demise of the Caliphate. Is it that the Turkish government has been suspended from now on or the Turkish government will not be a Muslim government from now on? Because only these two situations would mean that the Caliphate has been abolished. It is a fact that Turkey's Muslim government is still in place. They had turned the Turkish government into a system of

democracy, in which, from an Islamic point of view, there was nothing objectionable, and was in fact among those desires for which the reformers of Islam had waited for centuries. But, after that, there should not have been a Caliph separate from the government... If the assembly had not been against the Ottoman dynasty then the president of the republic should have been Abdul Majeed. If it was against that, then whoever was elected president should have been the Caliph. It did not make sense that in Islam a new temple be created for the Pope's spiritual crown and throne. I was released from prison in January last year and the Associated Press asked me if I had said that there was no place in Islam for a Pope. It is necessary to reconsider the matter. However, it is important to note that the Muslims of India did not make any public demonstrations against it because the Turks had just gotten out of the war. Negotiations for peace had not been completed yet. Opponents could take advantage of any opposition. Therefore, it was against their interest to spread agitation among the common people against this issue. There was a need to try to reform the situation internally and establish an Islamic system for the future. Therefore, it was decided that a delegation of the Central Khilafat Committee go to Ankara for this purpose. The first among its aims and objectives was to correct this error. Besides, even at the highest levels in private, the nobles of Ankara have been regularly made aware of this error. Since January 1923, I have sent various letters to some nobles of the Ankara government and I have found out about their treacheries and trends."

In response to a reporter's question as to whether there was no Islamic caliphate in Turkey, Maulana replied:

"I am amazed that even after hearing such a lengthy statement of mine, you have not been able to establish the correct concept of the Islamic Caliphate. The meaning of Caliphate is Islamic Government. As long as there is an independent government in Turkey and it does not deny being a Muslim government, the Islamic Caliphate is also present there because besides that there is no other independent power and Muslim government. Caliphate is not a criminal or illegitimate post to be deposed or suspended. It is a fact, i.e. the existence of an Islamic government. How can we deny the existence of this fact unless it is non-existent? However, in this case, our belief would be that the present Caliphate has fallen into the hands of those who have committed a grave error and misguidance and the Caliphate system is no longer valid. And so it is the duty of the whole world to try to amend and correct it."

Today, fifty years later, when we read this statement, it is clear that in extreme despair, Maulana was either consoling himself or trying to ameliorate the despair of the Indian Muslim community. The arguments given by Maulana do not bear a moment's logical analysis. Although the Turks had written in their constitution that the religion of the government would be Islam, simply writing as much could not mean anything. From the mode in which the Turkish government was operating, it was not too difficult to infer that now the government there would no longer be an Islamic government. For example, with one stroke of the pen, the ministries of religious affairs and endowments were dissolved and the endowments section was given in charge of the ministry of finance. And the organization of religious education was given in charge of the ministry of education. The ancient religious madrasas that were established in the mosques of Constantinople and other cities were broken up. Although Ismet Pasha interpreted these matters and Maulana also thought of them as mere reforms, he could not keep himself from saying that he did not have any promising expectations from the ruling party of Turkey for these reforms.

Just because the head of the Turkish government was a Muslim, the government was not necessarily an Islamic government capable of playing the role of the Caliphate, which required the duties of *amr-bil-maa'ruf* and *nahi-'anil-munkar*, commands to do good deeds and prohibition of all actions that were in contravention of Islamic canonical law. It is also strange that, according to Maulana Azad, since there was no other independent Muslim government in the world, the one remaining Turkish government should become the center of the Caliphate for no rhyme or reason. Besides, it was not true that there was no other independent Muslim governments on earth: the sovereign government of Afghanistan had come into being. The purpose was merely a verbal tug-of-war and it only proves that the great global community of Islam was in the throes of despair and failure, and instead of accepting it at once, they were providing for their comfort. One of the major issues that Maulana Azad overlooked was the issue of protection and freedom of holy places. The Arabs had revolted and the Turks were not even demanding domination over the Arabs because of the crisis of their existence. When Maulana Mohammad Ali took a delegation to London, he raised this point repeatedly and strongly demanded that the holy places in Iraq and Arabia be left in the possession of Turkey. Lloyd George's response was that the Arabs wanted internal freedom and if they did not want to live under the control of the Turks then they should not be forced to do so by some law of justice. Maulana Mohammad Ali's answer was that they should be given internal freedom but Turkey should not be deprived of power. Therefore, when he became disillusioned with Lloyd George, he approached the Arab leaders and persuaded them to change their position and remain under Turkish rule with internal independence. No one had the answer to Maulana Mohammad Ali's arguments. His religious zeal, his personality, his method of insistence and his logical arguments dazzled everyone and apparently people used to say that praise be to Allah, we are not against a central Islamic Caliphate. Sometimes the Sharif of Mecca and sometimes Amir Faisal would make announcements in newspapers that they were not seeking the Caliphate, and people would spread this irrelevant news, but they would avoid and circumvent the real issue, i.e. whether they were willing to remain under Turkish rule. Therefore, the question of the establishment of the Caliphate in Turkey did not arise.

Dr. Carl Krueger writes on page 24 of his book 'Kemalist Turkey and the Middle East':

"In November 1922, Turkey abolished the Sultanate and declared itself a sovereign independent nation. The reasons for this were as follows:

1. *Indian Muslim armies fought their fellow Muslims in Syria, Palestine, and especially in Mesopotamia, under the supervision of Christian officers, and not a*

single incident of rebellion or disobedience of orders occurred.

2. *In Tsarist Russia, Muslims were not allowed to join conquering armies, but Kazan Tatars fought on the side of the Russians from the beginning till the end of WWI in the Caucasus campaign against the Turks, for whom it was a battle of life and death. Here too there were no incidents of rebellion or disobedience of orders.*

3. *The Arabs, the largest segment of the Ottoman Empire's population, had been harassing the Turks since before the outbreak of WWI and had been fighting alongside the Allied countries against the Turks. If the rule of the Caliphate had been enforced, Syria, Palestine, Mesopotamia, and other Arab countries would not have been snatched from them so easily.*

4. *The matter of the Caliphate had been relegated to an idea. No one remained who believed in it. Only those who were taking advantage of it believed in it. That is why, naturally, Mustafa Kemal decided to end the Sultanate and the Caliphate."*

One More Attempt to Revive the Islamic Caliphate

After the fall of the Caliphate, Khilafat Committees remained active in India and the schemes persisted to advise the Ankara government, to send a delegation there, and ask them to revive the Caliphate. They also thought that Mustafa Kemal himself should be made the Caliph of the Muslims, but these were all dreams which could neither become reality nor did.

The British did not establish rule over Najd and Hijaz under the pressure of the public opinion of the Islamic world.

The success of this movement was due to the Khilafat Movement of India and it was a real distinction of the Khilafat Movement's service to Islam.

In 1924, Prince Abdul Aziz of Najd invaded the Hijaz and captured Taif and Mecca. The families of Prince Abdul Aziz of Najd and Sharif of Mecca had a long-standing animosity toward each other. Now, why would Prince Abdul Aziz not take advantage of the general weariness that had arisen against the Sharif of Mecca? And immediately or within a few days, the tombs of all the elders were demolished along with the mausoleums; even the mausoleum of Hazrat Khadijatul Kubra was not spared. The shrine of Hazrat Abdullah Ibn Abbas was also demolished. Everyone was pleased with the belittling of the traitor Sharif Hussein, and now Maulana Mohammad Ali hoped that a divine government would be established in Hijaz on the advice of the Islamic world and that it would be declared the center of the Caliphate. And since all the holy places were there, this notion seemed appropriate. This hope was also established because Sultan Abdul Aziz made the announcement that he had no desire to rule, and that after the departure of Sharif Hussein, Muslims would be free to choose whomever they want as their Amir. The Muslim leaders of our country, who were very diligent in advising other Islamic Empires, advised Prince Abdul Aziz to establish a divine caliphate in Hijaz and put together a democratic government there.

Shah Moinuddin Ahmed writes[29]:

> "*After the capture of Hijaz by Sultan Abdul Aziz, the news spread that the Najdi forces had carried out a*

---

29 *Hayat Syed Sulaiman*, pp23

massacre in Taif and the tomb of Hazrat Abdullah Ibn Abbas had been demolished. There was word that atrocities had been committed in Mecca as well and observers there feared losses from the conquering forces. Ordinary Muslims were already skeptical of some of the Najd's beliefs, so the news raised further concerns. The Khilafat Committee called for the protection of the shrines, their respect, and the establishment of peace by sending telegrams to Sultan Abdul Aziz, Sharif Ali, League of Nations, Britain, and other powers."

It should be noted that Sharif Hussein had resigned in favor of his son Sharif Ali, who had gone to Jeddah and established residence there.

Shah Moinuddin Ahmed states further[29]:

"Sharif Ali replied that he himself wanted peace and order in Hijaz and that he had come from Mecca to Jeddah merely to save the holy shrines from bloodshed. And he wished that someone would intervene and make peace between the two. Sultan Abdul Aziz had stated his intention to purify the Hijaz from Sultan Sharif Hussein and his descendants. He replied that it was not his intention to occupy Mecca but to save its citizens from oppression and unbearable taxes, revive Islamic jurisprudence in revelation and epiphany, and fulfillment of divine work. All the Muslims of the world have a connection to Mecca and that is why the policies affecting it will be decided according to the wishes of the Islamic world. He stated that a conference of the representatives of the world's Muslims will be convened in Mecca and their opinion shall be taken on all those

matters, which would secure the House of God (Ka'ba of Mecca) from sins and endeavors of personal purposes."

All it took was this announcement for the lover of Islam and a loyalist of the Divine Caliphate Maulana Mohammad Ali to be beside himself with excitement and come out in support of Sultan Abdul Aziz. All his sympathizers in this support were those who had non-imitative views but the Barelvi gentlemen, Hazrat Khwaja Hasan Nizami, heads of monasteries, and his own spiritual guide and mentor, Hazrat Maulana Abdul Bari, all turned against him. Maulana Hasrat Mohani joined Maulana Abdul Bari to set up a strong front against Maulana Mohammad Ali. Now it was Maulana Mohammad Ali and this world-full of opposition. If he had a little control over his tongue and pen, things would not have gotten so bad, but that was his nature. A fierce battle ensued and Maulana Mohammad Ali was given the title 'Wahhabi.' When the news of the demolition of the domes came, all of India became a place of mourning. In Lucknow, Shia gentlemen performed *zanjeeri maatam*, the mourning ritual involving self-flagellation with chains. In the end, the government had to implement section 144 of the Indian Penal Code (unlawful assembly). Safi Lakhnavi wrote:

Medina and Mecca were demolished by the ill-natured Najdis
Even the infidels would not have done what these Islamists did

Maulana Abdul Majid Badayuni, who was a prominent Indian scholar and among the leaders of the Khilafat Movement, used to tell the story of how Sultan Ibn Saud broke the stone flour mill of Hazrat Fatima, daughter of Prophet Muhammad. What idolatry was being committed with this stone mill? And if people were kissing it out of affection, how was that a strike against the monotheism of Islam? Even if it was, they could have sold it to Germany for Rs 10 million, what was the need to break it? Maulana Syed Sulaiman Nadvi, who was considered among the established and broadminded scholars, gave a speech in front of Ibn Saud, which will give an idea of the depth of emotions. He said:

"Religiously, the status of tombs and monuments are different. Hadith and Islamic jurisprudence contain explicit words of prohibition for the building of tombs, but they contain no such prohibition when it comes to the construction and protection of monuments, i.e. sacred places which have a special relationship with Hazrat Prophet Muhammad or his venerable Companions. Albeit, if some ignorant Muslims come to these monuments and commit acts that are against Sharia, then, like other such acts, it is the duty of the government to post watchmen or police officers who would prevent visitors from doing that."

Maulana Mohammad Ali's excuse was that these domes were demolished in the absence of Sultan Abdul Aziz and he was not aware of it. Now the discussion on these issues began.

1. Is it permissible to build domes on tombs?
2. If it is not permissible but they were built, is it permissible to demolish them?
3. And if they are demolished, is it permissible to build them back again?

In the scattered volumes of *Maarif* ('Knowledge'), Allama Syed Sulaiman Nadvi wrote:

"The result of the cooling down of the past national movements is that there is a hot market for sectarian

strife and riots, especially against Muslims, as if the wars of Najd and Hijaz were happening in India. If the fight there is with swords and rifles, the clashes here are of throat and tongue, and hand and pen. There, if the issues have a political and nationalist status, here they are about religion and faith. But alas, I wish our nation could know what its significance is in the eyes of those in whose support we are stirring up emotions through religious arguments and reasons."

The Khilafat Committee sent a delegation led by Allama Syed Sulaiman Nadvi, whose members were Maulana Abdul Majid Badayuni and Maulana Abdul Qadir Qasuri. Thus the delegation represented the whole of India. But Sharif Ali rejected the suggestion of the Khilafat Committee that an Islamic democratic government be established in Hijaz based on the opinion of the Islamic world, did not allow the delegation to proceed further, and the delegation returned.

The battles of Najd and Hijaz were raging and heated debates were going on in India when suddenly an authentic newspaper reporter gave the news that Sultan Abdul Aziz had bombarded the Holy Shrine (Prophet Muhammad's tomb) in Medina. Now such a commotion arose that it was not even to the liking of Maulana Mohammad Ali. He said that the real situation should be assessed by the delegation that was present there, but who was listening. Eventually it was discovered that it was not the Holy Shrine but some other tomb that had been shelled somewhere else in Medina during the war, but all this research was done later. Opposition to Sultan Ibn Saud increased during this period, to the extent that a group, in which Barelvis and *Sajjada-Nashin* of all the *Khanqah*, spiritual caretakers of the tombs of saints, were prominent, took the side of the traitor Sharif Hussein. Anyway, this group could not become very influential, but Maulana Abdul Bari, who carried a lot of weight in all of India, entered the fray. With him were Maulana Hasrat Mohani, Maulana Abdul Majid Badayuni, Maulana Nisar Ahmad Kanpuri, and others. On the other side were Maulana Mohammad Ali, Zafar-ul-Malik, Chaudhuri Khaliquzzaman, etc. Both groups were centered in Lucknow. Consequently, under the patronage of Maulana Abdul Bari, the *Anjuman Khuddam-al-Harmain* (Society of the Servants of the Holy Places) was formed. Sheikh Mushir Husain Qidwai and Syed Jalib Dehelvi also participated in this society. Of course, the members of Firangi Mahal, who by themselves carried a lot of importance, also took part. They held a grand meeting at the Rifa-e-Aam and cursed Sultan Ibn Abbas to their hearts' content. And later, when Maulana Mohammad Ali wanted to hold a meeting there, he was unsuccessful, and the audience refused to hear his speech on two occasions at two different meetings. Good Lord! This was the same Mohammad Ali that crowds would greet effusively and light lamps in honor of. How well Maulana Abul Kalam Azad has said, addressing the Muslim community:

> *"As fast as you come in, you run away as fast. So, there is no value in your compliments nor weight in your insults. You have neither a heart nor a mind. You have doubts that you consider thoughts and there are risks that you call intentions."*

The result of these conflicts and arguments was that in Awadh province, two Khilafat Committees were established.

When the Khilafat Committee sent a telegram to Sultan Abdul Aziz, he replied that no harm shall come to the tombs and monuments. Their intent was not to establish their government in Hijaz but to get salvation for the people of Hijaz from the atrocities of Sharif Hussein. After the capture of Hijaz, they intended to form a system of government on the advice of the Islamic world and for this purpose they had issued invitations. A delegation went from India with a proposal to coalesce an Islamic conference.

Debates and talks continued. Finally, when Abdul Aziz had conquered the Hijaz by 1925, the people of India suddenly came to know through a telegram sent from Cairo dated January 10, 1926 that Ibn Saud had declared the establishment of the Kingdom of Hijaz and Najd, even though, on October 24, 1924, Ibn Saud had replied to the proposal of the Khilafat Committee that the final decision was in the hands of the Islamic world. In any case, even then, Sultan Abdul Aziz issued invitations to Egypt, Beirut, Syria, Palestine, Sudan, Asir, Najd, Yemen, Russia, Turkey, Afghanistan, Java and India. In India, invitations were received by three parties: Jamiat Ulema-e-Hind, Khilafat Committee, and Ahl-e-Hadees Conference. The Jamiat Ulema-e-Hind delegation was formed under the leadership of Mufti Kifayatullah and its members were Maulana Shabbir Ahmad Usmani, Maulana Ahmad Saeed, and Maulana Abdul Aleem. The head of the Khilafat Committee delegation was Maulana Syed Sulaiman Nadvi and its members were Maulana Mohammad Ali, Maulana Shaukat Ali and Shoaib Qureshi.

The members of these delegations reached Jeddah in May 1926 and left for Medina the next day. They met the Sultan on the 27th. As was his habit, Maulana Mohammad Ali gave a strong, bold and emotional speech but it became clear that Abdul Aziz had become the Sultan of the Kingdom of Hijaz and Najd and there would be no change of any kind in it. On May 30, Maulana Syed Sulaiman Nadvi, Mufti Kifayatullah, Maulana Muhammad Ali and Maulana Shaukat Ali met the Sultan again and said that they had been made promises regarding the tombs in Medina that no actions would be taken about them without the decision of the Islamic conferences. But these promises were violated, and against the sentiments of the Islamic world and without consulting them, the tombs were demolished. The Sultan said in reply that if they had not demolished the tombs, their nation would have become rebellious, and their demand was not against the Sharia. The Sultan also said, "What you said is true and from the heart, and that is what I want. But the difficulty is that you are not familiar with our nation. Their fanatical tribes threatened that they had sacrificed their lives and property in Jihad for the abolition of polytheism and establishment of Quran and Sunnah, and therefore these buildings should be demolished as soon as possible, otherwise they shall demolish them themselves. We had two options after this threat, to stop them with force or give them permission to demolish the tombs. In the first case, there was a fear of civil war, and in the second case, there would be sedition and mischief, which would have caused trouble to the people of Medina, they would have been traumatized, and other communities would have faced trauma as well. Their demand was not against Islamic law either, but was in accordance with the command of God and His Messenger and the Book and Sunnah. Therefore, I asked the Chief Justice to go out of his way to do what was according to the order of God and his Prophet. There should be no disagreement on that."

This statement of the Sultan was completely different and completely contradictory to his earlier statement that this was done in his absence and without his knowledge and information, and on which Maulana Mohammad Ali had based his position.

Maulana Mohammad Ali's heart was on fire. He had come there with high hopes. His desire was that a democratic Islamic government be established there and the tombs and domes restored, but the scene there was that:

> *To visit your street, I deeply wished*
> *So, I left here after taking a bath with blood*

Seeing that he would be unsuccessful in both of his objectives, he boiled over. To abstain from telling the truth was not in his habit. And that is why he had to endure all his life. Maulana Mohammad Ali said to the Sultan, "The Islamic world had high expectations of you and wanted to see you in a position much more glorious than that of the Sultan of the Kingdom of Hijaz. Why did the Sultan settle for such a low position and why did he settle for that end?" Then he read the following Urdu couplet:

> *From infinity, accomplishment rests on endurance*
> *In the eyes is that raindrop that could not become a pearl*

He went on to say that the raindrop is content to become a pearl in an oyster or even an ornament around the neck of a dancer in Paris, but they want the Sultan to become that drop of water that becomes a teardrop in the eyes of a Muslim and falls on the Holy Shrine of the Prophet Muhammad. Maulana Syed Sulaiman Nadvi again made prominent the distinction between tombs and monuments and with references to the Hadith, made clear the necessity of establishment and preservation of monuments. This speech was so scholarly, proficient, and full of wisdom, that no one had a response to it. The Sultan said that he was not a religious scholar and that this matter should be presented to the Council of Scholars.

Consequently, on May 31, 1926 the Council of Scholars was convened. Allama Rasheed Raza Misri delivered a speech in praise and eulogy of the Sultan, and the same trend continued from all sides. Nobody noticed the series of religious and scholarly debates that Allama Syed Sulaiman Nadvi had initiated. There was no response or engagement with it. As the famous saying goes, nothing succeeds like success. The Sultan didn't care about anyone after making the government. But Maulana Mohammad Ali could not tolerate the insult of ignoring it. He got very agitated and gave a forceful speech. He said:

> *"We appeal in the name of the Book and Sunnah that you reject monarchy in favor of democracy and instead of the practices of Caesar and Cyrus, you revive the practices of Farooq and Siddiq."*

How strange and how brave this heady slogan was. Maulana Abdul Aleem and Mufti Kifayatullah delivered speeches on tolerance with other sects. These speeches infuriated the Sultan and the Chief Justice. And the nature of the matter became clear to everyone, but still from time to time meetings like this continued. There were speeches. Some proposals were accepted, which were useful in any case, but the real objective of establishment of the Caliphate and a democratic government failed. The defeated and demoralized delegation came back at the end of July 1926. This last attempt of Maulana Muhammad Ali, for which he endured the taunt and ridicule of friends and strangers alike, was ruined and there was now no possibility of establishing a Caliphate in the world. But the Khilafat Committee remained. Enthusiasm had already waned, and there was no excitement at the Khilafat Conference held in Kanpur at the end of December 1925. People seemed wilted, whereas before that there was even a display of lights. People thought:

What remains now for which to grieve for the rivals?

At that time, the people there had decided to focus on reformative work and most of them had turned to education. The establishment of Jamia Millia Islamia was enough for a kind of consolation. Now everyone felt that the Muslims needed a mental revolution, only then something big could be done. Therefore, it was decided to establish schools of study and night madrasas in even the smallest of Muslim villages. The conference ended with that small sense of achievement, but later nobody gave it even the smallest attention nor did anyone pay any attention to its requisites, requirements, means, and resources. It was just a golden proposal which had been accepted in a state of extreme hopelessness and had been inserted just to give peace of mind to the heart of paper, that's all.

Lucknow Khilafat Conference

This was the state of affairs in December 1925. When the failed Khilafat delegation returned in July 1926, no one had any scheme to act on. But the devoted Khilafatists were still holding onto their principles and wanted to keep the movement alive. A very effective and true picture of this scene has been depicted by Maulana Abdul Majid Daryabadi, which needs no critique after having been quoted in parts several times. This was 1927. Maulana states[30]:

"Who asks about the poor Khilafatists anymore? All the passion had died between 1921 and 1923. The remaining effects gave company between 1924 and 1925. Now, there is neither a Khilafat Conference anywhere nor do any members of the Khilafat Committees remain. It was nothing but a sweet dream that the Muslims saw and have long since forgotten. Poor Shaukat Ali sat in Bombay embracing the central Khilafat Committee to his chest...In any case, toward the end of 1926, the central Khilafat Committee decided to hold a session of the Khilafat Conference one more time, and this time a session of distinguished Islamic scholars be added to it as an appendix. It was decided that Seth Haroon would preside over the Khilafat Conference and Hakim Ajmal Khan over the session of Islamic scholars. The venue of the conference was selected by lottery to be Lucknow and the dates were decided to be at the end of February 1927. I cannot forget the comment of an old lady in Wazirganj when she saw a procession of our volunteers take to the street in horse-carts and on foot, blowing horns and beating drums. She said, "Take that! Khilafat marches again." The concept of Khilafat had faded from the people's hearts. Now that they heard the

---

30 "Mohammad Ali" Vol I, pp 395

name again, it was as if they instantly remembered a forgotten dream."

Abdul Majid Daryabadi was the president of the Awadh Khilafat Committee and was made chairman of the welcoming committee of this conference. Let us read his statement again.

"The grooms of the wedding party were still these two brothers (the Ali brothers). The Khilafat Movement was now in the last throes of its life. The Caliphate itself had ended at the hands of Mustafa Kemal. In India, the garland on the living corpse of the Khilafat Committee were these two brothers. As it happened, neither the president-elect of the Khilafat Conference nor that of the session of Islamic scholars could make it to the conference. Seth Saheb was represented by Maulvi Haji Shafi Daudi Muzzaffarpuri. Hakim Ajmal Khan's place was taken by Dr. Ansari. Now I will enter here my entire welcoming committee address. This will bring to the fore an overview of the issues of the time."

(Excerpts of Abdul Majid Daryabadi's welcome address at the conference are reproduced below)

"Today, in a belittling and heartless tone, we are asked what has the Khilafat Committee done till now? We are asked the question, but should we give the answer? If you want the answer, ask the hallways and the walls of the English courts, ask the registers of the police, ask the gates and entrances of the jailhouses, ask the handcuffs made of iron, ask the heavy fetters and the chains normally reserved for dacoits and murderers. Take the answer from Egypt, from Palestine, from Hijaz, from

Turkey, from Afghanistan, from Java, from every free and semi-free Islamic country, from the entire Islamic world, and if even that does not satisfy you, hear it from the tongues of the holy angels of Allah, and hear them mention to each other that when the time came for trials and tribulations, when it was the hour that the Islamic Caliphate was in danger, when the question of the life and death of Islam was presented, and in the name of Allah and the message of His last Prophet, and in respect of His Sharia, the people who gave up their belongings, sacrificed their honor and their fame, offered up their comfort and luxury, who saw their worlds ruined and destroyed, who put their lives on the line and yelled "I'm ready," in their desire to put on fetters, their taste for irons and manacles, their appetite for hunger and nakedness, their wish to climb to the gallows post, their seeking out the bullet to their chest, who left the dead bodies of their comrades on the battlefield without funeral rites and burials, those puppets of ashes who were slaves, Muslim slaves of India, those helpless followers of the Messenger of God of a helpless India, the servants who were inhabitants of this same house of oppression, they were Khilafat itself. It is possible that a person who forgets quickly, or is cunning, a person who is unsettled by patience and endurance, may have forgotten these incidents by now or has intentionally forgotten them, but in the leaves of the book of the times, on the grains of sand on the face of this earth, on every page of the Books revealed to prophets, till the time that the dedication of Prophet Abraham, the sacrifice of Prophet Ishmael, and the martyrdom of Hazrat Ali are recorded, till that time the humble and small efforts of those famous chiefs and the lowly soldiers, servants of Islamic Caliphate and the flag bearers of the Khilafat Movement cannot be erased from the face of the earth."

In the end, Maulana Abdul Majid Daryabadi talked about two tasks for the Khilafat Committee:

1. *"Today, the Khilafat Committee has to succeed the Righteous Caliphate to the best of its ability and strength, because the whole world of Islam comes under its spread. In India as well as outside India. But its real and central relationship is naturally with the true center of Islam...If a calamity strikes India, it will certainly be our calamity. The misery of our brothers in Turkey, Egypt, Afghanistan, or Morocco will also be our misery. But, God forbid, if this center of Islam, this right path of religion, this center of faith is harmed in the slightest, it will not be a shock to our body, but our lives will be in danger, our souls will be trampled, our faith will be attacked...Hundreds and thousands of Indians, Afghans, Egyptians, Turks and others are devoted to our faith. They give offerings to every nook and corner of this Holy Land. Even if Carlyle counts on every grain of this Land of the Beloved to be included in his frivolities by saying that "the British nation can accept the loss of the British Empire but will not give up Shakespeare," then surely a Muslim does not fall into the category of ignorant people by stating this devotional belief about the land of Hijaz. But if it is ignorance, then thousands of wisdoms have been sacrificed over it, and if it is madness, then thousands of rationalities have been based on this madness.*

"Today, on the horizon of this Land of Light...clouds of dictatorship and tyranny have gathered and the first and foremost duty of the servants of the Caliphate should be to rid this cloud through legitimate and proper measures and to hand over the land of Ka'ba, the direction toward which the Muslims face for prayers, to the people of Ka'ba. It is the duty of the people of the nation to decide what these legitimate and proper measures are and why they should be adopted.

2. *"Along with this service to the land of Hijaz, there is a vast arena of work in our own country. The difficulty is that on one side, we are engaged through conferences in the service to Hijaz and along with that, on the other side, we need to keep all kinds of educational, organizational, social, political, and religious efforts going in our country. At every location, we need to make arrangements for the right education and upbringing of the children. Arrange for employment for the unemployed, have them open shops, and promote charkha and khaddar."*

After writing this much, perhaps Maulana realized that there were other societies already engaged in this work, and hence wrote that the Khilafat Committee was neither anyone's guardian nor adversary, and therefore a hand of collaboration should be stretched toward Muslim and non-Muslim societies.

The motive for all of this was that Maulana Mohammad Ali wanted to keep the Khilafat Committee alive and still wanted to endeavor to establish a democratic Islamic empire or, in other words, establish a Divine Caliphate. Maulana Mohammad Ali did not realize that even if Sultan Ibn Saud had agreed, the Hijaz would not have been able to carry the burden of the

Divine Caliphate. The Islamic governments had disintegrated. This conference was the last sputtering flame of the candle. After that, although the Khilafat Committee remained in name and its name was still heard in some places, in reality, the work of the Khilafat Committee was over and could not be revived again. But generous-hearted people would say this about the founders and the activists of the Khilafat Committee:

They laid the foundation for good rituals of agonizing in blood and ashes
May the Lord shower mercies on these pure souls and good natured lovers

One Last Question

We have written earlier that Mahatma Gandhi, who was a religious man and called himself a *Sanatan Dharmi*, a believer in an 'eternal' or absolute set of duties incumbent on all Hindus, Pandit Madan Mohan Malviya, who was a recognized leader of the Hindus of India and a very religious man, Jagadguru Shankaracharya, Arya Samaj Leader Swami Shraddhanand, and other all-India leaders such as Motilal Nehru, CR Das, and Lala Lajpat Rai, etc. gave their total support to the Muslims for the survival of the Caliphate. This is a great proof of the fact that the establishment of the Caliphate could not have done any harm to anyone's patriotic emotions.

The Khilafat Movement and extra-territorial patriotism are two different things. Nationalism toward a foreign nation has elements of aggressive disposition and temperament, and its foundation is material, while the Khilafat Movement was purely a construct of religion, faith, and spirituality, and did not clash with patriotism in the slightest.

If the demands of the time did not render the hundred years of hard work of the British fruitless, then at least it did not let it bear full fruit. Turkey did lose its great empire. Arab lands were torn to pieces. We also saw that the Arabs who rebelled against Turkey were bound in chains of slavery. And Syria, etc., were subjugated to Europe under such humiliating conditions that it taught them the art of civilization and self-management. But today, we also see that they are all free.

Just a few days after the establishment of law and order, protests and demonstrations broke out in the Arab world and France was about to leave empty handed, which prompted Iqbal to write the following couplets:

The eternal skeptic has departed from the border of Syria
Shelving away all the rules and etiquette of the tavern

If such, how much is this the occasion for admonition
The blue sky changes its color in a moment

Lord Curzon is certainly concerned about remedies
In the belly of obedience has started unequaled convulsion

Sir Aga Khan is demanding the delegation from India
Is this the digestive for devouring Iraq and Palestine

Rewards and Impressions of the Khilafat Movement

What the Khilafat Movement gave to India and Indian Muslims has been realized in different places, but it seems appropriate to give a summary of the total in a numbered list so that the topic can be treated comprehensively and intelligently. This has been detailed below.

1. Khilafat Movement freed all the citizens of India, whatever religion or faith they belonged to, whether they were Hindu, Buddhist, Jains, Brahmo Samaji, Sanatan Dharmi, Arya Samaji, Sikh, Christian, Parsee, or Muslims, from the moth's urge to circumambulate the fire of the foreign ruler and taught them to settle in the manifestation of their own nature. For further elucidation of this notion, it is necessary to delve deep into the environment, the general concerns, and the mental and psychological conditions of the people of the time. Today, in view of the heights of intellectual freedom we have reached, it is difficult to understand this abjection. Those were times when every Indian fell prey to the spell of the English that they were far superior to us in their education and culture. In other words, they were civilized and we were uncivilized, and they were only trying to take the world out of ignorance and lack of understanding and take humanity to this elevated status which the White people have already achieved. That is why we were persuaded to benefit from these teachers of civilization. Every one of us was ashamed to call ourselves Indian and felt pride in being deemed subjects of the British Crown. This feeling was across the board with no exceptions. Muslim League was certainly no exception, but Sir Syed particularly fell prey to it. His Aligarh Movement has been mentioned in detail earlier. Anyone who has studied Sir Syed's writings cannot help but feel that he considered

the British very polite and noble and the Indians uncivilized and uncouth. For instance, he used to praise the English for the knives and forks at their tables and considered the Indian way of eating at a *dastarkhwan*, a cloth spread where people ate with their hands, worthy of condemnation and ridicule. The method of using a toothpick, the practice of washing hands and face in a basin, and the style of rinsing the mouth have been ridiculed in various ways. The undue shame and embarrassment that the English have of meeting someone, that they do not address any stranger until someone introduces them, is contrasted with the verbose nature and informality of the Indians and fun is made of them that they even ask strangers if they eat eggs on Wednesdays. The same is true of letter writing. If an Englishman is unfamiliar with the addressee, he will simply write "Dear Sir." But Indians waste a lot of time on titles and etiquette. Etc. etc. In this book too, you may have noticed that there is a feeling everywhere and in every gathering that we are the subjects of Britain. As if to say that it is a settled fact and nothing to be ashamed about. The English had spread their net so wide and our people had fallen prey to such inferiority complex that if the government gave the title of 'Raja' to anyone, the person would sit on a throne with a sword as if he was really an absolute ruler, and his elderly relatives (paternal uncles, etc.) would appear before him respectfully and address him as 'Maharaja.' To put such a flaw in the minds is to contrive very effectively.

2. The demands being made by the moderate leaders of Congress were about a few rights. They were not about liberty from British slavery. Even that was looked upon with great trepidation at that time. When Maulana Hasrat raised the slogan of complete independence, a case was brought against him in a court of English judges at the Bombay High Court. This jute cloth clad dervish who feared no one but God, self-aware and truthful, was not frightened at all and argued in his own defense. He did not even retain a lawyer. The English judge pronounced the judgment that merely preaching an idea was not a crime, and since the accused did not commit any act that would have led to complete independence being established, he is being exonerated. But perhaps this was the lone exception. Lokmanya Tilak certainly said, "Swaraj is my birthright," and he was certainly an extremist, but he was always in the minority in Congress.

3. Khilafat Movement left the Aligarh Movement behind. It shredded the concept of being a subject of Britain. It taught the people to be Indian and be proud of it, washed the turbidity of the heart, and raised high and lofty ideals of self-respect and self-confidence. Khilafat Movement had sowed the seeds for all that and had matured into a tenacious tree. It taught how to look into the eyes of others and talk, took us out of slavery, and let us stand tall in the valley of complete independence. The arena of the Khilafat Movement prepared us for that. Thanks to this movement, our destination was identified. This blessing of realization of one's existence is a gift of the Khilafat Movement.

Individual sacrifices and the wish to give it all up for freedom was not entirely missing. What I mean to say is that the awakening melody of the republic was born in the Khilafat Movement, and there were two reasons for that.

a. The defeat of the Turks in World War I and the Islamophobia of the Allied countries gave the Muslims a sense that the end times were approaching and the Muslims of India came to realize that their existence as a nation in the world, which had the power of defense, was in danger. This also led to the conclusion that the means for protection of the holy places was about to be lost. God knows what would happen after that. So the Muslims decided to fight the last trench battle and set the battlefield against the British with great enthusiasm.

b. In Gandhiji, Khilafat Movement found a dervish-like great man of action, a great leader who was a straight talker, righteous, courageous, determined, and committed. Fiery speakers like Maulana Mohammad Ali, Maulana Abul Kalam Azad, Maulana Azad Subhani, Maulana Ahmad Saeed, Maulana Abdul Majid Badayuni, Maulana Syed Mohammad Fakhir Allahabadi, etc., and scholars like Maulana Abdul Bari Firangi Mahali, Allama Syed Sulaiman Nadvi, Maulana Abul Wafa Sanaullah Amritsari, Mufti Kifayatullah, Dr. Mukhtar Ahmad Ansari, Hakeem Ajmal Khan, and all Muslim and non-Muslim leaders of India came with Gandhiji without any exception and the Khilafat Movement turned into the Indian independence movement. Gandhiji himself wrote in Young India of April 1924:

"This is the Khilafat Movement which has awakened the nation and I will not let it sleep again."

And it so happened that this great man kept the nation awake until the sun of freedom rose.

Patriotic Spirit

The Khilafat Movement created a great sense of patriotism among the Muslims. They felt that they were a great power and, if they used this power, they could uproot Britain and throw them out of India. But at the same time they felt that to use this power, it was necessary to create an alliance and consensus with all the other parties of the country. Just as the migration movement failed, so did the Muslims in India intensify their sense of love for their country and nation.

Eyes longed to see the vision of Hindu-Muslim unity that came to the fore during the Khilafat Movement. The independence movement had captured the hearts and minds of the people. Now there was just one emotion at work, to drive the English out of India, and the entire nation filled with volunteers in tattered clothes, uncovered heads, and bare feet. People left their work and came out in pursuit of independence. Three slogans were heard from the voices of both Hindus and Muslims: *Allah-o-Akbar, Mahatma Gandhi ki jai* (long live Mahatma Gandhi), and *Maulana Mohammad Ali ki jai* (long live Maulana Mohammad Ali). Hindu and Muslim students set out from schools and colleges and started working shoulder to shoulder. It was like a wave of a river that was rising and falling in unison, without a trace of confrontation or hate.

Patriotism also requires that people love the things made in their homeland. The complete answer to the monopoly of the British with their foreign goods, and especially cloth, was given by *khaddar*, *charkha*, and *swadeshi*. Bonfires were made of imported clothes and songs were written in condemnation of imposing these goods. Slogans of "Down, down. Keep off, keep off," were shouted and India was on its way to becoming self-sufficient in its clothes. The Khilafat Movement had given a practical lesson to the common man within India to walk towards the goal of complete freedom with determination and perseverance in the face of difficulties and hardships of the path. We moved forward and we stumbled, and mistakes were made by our leaders, but the sounds of the bells of the moving caravan were not silenced. And this spirit was born from the Khilafat Movement.

The poets warmed the blood with their compositions. Shibli Nomani did not survive this path of the nation but his poems remained to refresh the zeal for freedom.

When the sun starts to set on the government, how long will its traces last
How long will the smoke rise from the extinguished lamps of the gathering
If heavens and sky tatter the cloaks of the empire
How long will the shreds of the garment fly in the sky

Someone ask these masters of human culture
How long these atrocities, how long this doom?

> *How long these reprisals for the victory of Ayyubi?*
> *How long will you show us the scenes of the Crusades?*

Maulana Zafar Ali Khan was a great leader and also a great journalist, but above all he was a poet. When one of India's most distinguished and renowned scholars Maulana Dawood Ghaznavi was arrested, as a manifestation of truth and just to have fun, he refused to go to jail and return on his own feet. Two constables would carry him back and forth on their shoulders. Zafar Ali Khan could not have found any better material than this. He stated:

> *When the police gave Hazrat Dawood a shoulder to sit on*
> *His friends asked with a smile, what is going on?*

> *Why are you riding on the shoulders of the government?*
> *This certainly is a novel ride for the Hazrat!*

> *On hearing this he stated, 'I am a scholar of religion'*
> *And scholars are much revered in the government*

> *Why should I not rejoice, as today under my thighs*
> *Are the donkeys on which Prophet Jesus himself rode*

In Lahore, there was a statue of Sir John Lawrence that the public wanted to tear down. British Army soldiers used to guard the monument. In the meantime, Hindus and Muslims jointly built a mosque and a temple on municipality grounds. Muslims had the temple made and Hindus the mosque. The government had both the mosque and the temple demolished. Look at Zafar Ali Khan's sarcasm:

One day I stated this to the government
O' the one that I don't dare speak to

O' the one, whose lands are petrified with dread
And whose skies don't have the courage to breathe freely

We hear there is respect for law in your times
The traditions of the bygone era are not ashamed

Then why did His Honor demolish the house of Lord itself
Why did His Honor not take down just the idol itself

Guilty is this idol, as is the Lord to blame
Their ways too are not without fault

My question was avoided with such a lame excuse
When the government could not make up a reply

English savagery is free of prejudice impurity
It is not an idol-breaker like Mahmud Ghaznavi

Allama Iqbal was not writing anything on this movement, so Zafar Ali Khan also wrote a poem on him.

So, the articles on Khilafat have not been trampled upon

Although Muslim League was not opposed to the movement, it was a party of Nawabs, Taluqdars, and capitalists. Its members were not taking any practical part in it and the reality was that the Khilafat Committee had suspended the membership of Muslim League. In 1922, it was rumored that Sir Aga Khan was coming to India to arrange reconciliation and he would use Muslim League for that end. Zafar Ali Khan immediately said:

> *We hear that Sir Aga at Curzon's hint*
> *The house of darkness, India, will inhabit*
>
> *The League that turns on its side once a year*
> *This time he will be showing it the right way*
>
> *They will make Khusro let go of Shirin over here*
> *Let Shirin be inclined to entreaty over there*
>
> *Tell Sir Aga that Islam's children*
> *From their own God will seek assistance*
>
> *To London they will absolutely not go to beg*
> *They will give up this accustomed habit today*
>
> *The verdict that comes from the court of Islam*
> *The English shall that verdict grant*

Maulana Hasrat Mohani was a political man to the core. The biggest purpose of his life was the acquisition of complete freedom. His poetry was full of enmity with the English and spirit of militant action.

> *The drill of poetry goes on as does the flour mill*
> *A one way window is this temperament of Hasrat*
>
> *We can even turn the soul into a beautiful face*
> *If we want we can turn into a garden the jail*

The gathering of rivals does appear a little drab
Let's see how long this wine and its accompaniments last

The times of oppressive slavery for Hasrat and Azad
By way of hatred and enmity, let's see how long they last

After Gandhi, Hasrat too was arrested and locked up in Sabarmati Jail. There he wrote an ode:

Do you remember any of that bygone era
O' enemy and friends sincere

There is something about my optimistic thoughts
These actions your tyranny surmounts

For Hasrat the lover's home
Never did favorable become

A witty poet writing under the nom de plume *Ahmaq Phaphundvi* ('Fungused Dunce') sent his humorous poems to *Zamindar*. Ghulam Rasool Mehr, who was a joint-editor with me at the newspaper, was of the opinion that this poet should be promoted. He would publish *Ahmaq*'s poems after revising them a bit. Gradually, his poems started appearing in *Zamindar* regularly and with time, his compositions became rather sophisticated. In the end, he had become quite an acclaimed humorous poet. He wrote a lot of prose too and went to jail as well. He has since passed away. I still remember a verse of his:

Jailhouse has the pleasure of the in-laws' home, Ahmaq

Poor quality rhyming verses were so rampant that they cannot be counted. Every person would show their temperament's frolics. When a person wanted to object to Amir Faisal during a speech in Hyderabad, he said, "Amir Faisal, who is a *fazool* (useless) man."

Enmity with the English

There is a verse in the Bible that says, 'Love your enemies.' Mahatma Gandhi had lofty ideals of thoughts, ideas, and principles, and used to say that he didn't have any enmity with the English; what he did have is only opposition to their system of governance, which was diabolical. But with the awakening masses, such lofty ideals could not prevail. It was inevitable that to get freedom from these foreign rulers, hatred for those that were at the helm of this diabolical regime would arise. Whether anyone wanted it or not, one gist of the Khilafat Movement was this enmity with the English. Shaykh al-Hind Maulana Mahmud Hasan was at the forefront of this sentiment and all those who worked with him in the Khilafat Movement were his followers in this regard. All kinds of stories and incidents were related to incite this enmity.

Gandhi used to talk about spirituality, morality, virtuous character, forgiveness and grace and would do it from the bottom of his heart. His belief was strong in this matter. He would go to the extent of saying that if someone deceives you, trust him, and if he deceives you again, trust him again. The one who deceives you is at a loss, and the one who is being deceived has everything to gain. And Gandhiji's education was not ineffective either.

India was saved from the bloodshed that accompanied revolutions in France, Russia, and China. The result was that peasants didn't kill the landlords and laborers didn't shed the blood of capitalists, as happened in other countries. Khilafat

Movement lifted that curtain that was over the tongues and the Muslims came out in the open. The message that the Khilafat Movement promulgated became the foundation of Hindu-Muslim unity and the citadel of future struggles was built on this foundation, which led us to complete freedom. Under Gandhiji's leadership, Muslims adopted the path of non-violence and they were convinced that they would be able to turn the English out through Hindu-Muslim unity and the path of *swadeshi, khaddar,* and *charkha*. Gandhiji's scheme was, which Maulana Mohammad Ali would repeatedly affirm, that if we expel the English from India, its colonial empire would collapse and other countries would be free as well. The English would then be confined to their tiny island, which was smaller than UP and where nothing except potatoes grew. In this way, the intense harm that the English caused to Islamic countries would be avenged too. Maulana Mohammad Ali would say repeatedly that the *charkha* was like a cannon whose cannonball lands right on the heart of Britain. The result was that the Muslims came to the forefront of the Independence movement and all of India woke up. This was the biggest effect of the Khilafat Movement, i.e. Khilafat Movement ended to give all of India a movement to take the country to independence.

Simplicity and Self-Awareness

It is a well-known principle of psychology that every human being is affected by their appearance. That is why there is a saying in English that 'a tailor makes a man respectable,' i.e. if you dress a man well, he will start saying and doing civilized things. The result of India's enslavement was weariness with all its traditions. That included the way they dressed. Dressing like the English, speaking English, and imitating the English in everything was considered a distinction. It was the miracle of Gandhiji's extreme intelligence, and his thoughtfulness and statesmanship, that he gave prevalence to *swadeshi*, *khaddar*, and *charkha*, and in one motion, the fortress of Westernism crumbled.

Among the Muslims, imitation of the English, receiving conferred titles by them, and emulating them in dress and appearance were more pronounced. Beyond the education given by Gandhiji, the Muslims of India, who had had previously expressed their emotions wholeheartedly during the wars in the Balkans and Tirablus-al-Gharb, and were now witnessing the collapse of the grand empire of Turkey and the holy places falling into the control of alien powers, were compelled to think that all these were merely the result of their misdeeds and evil deeds. That is why they had now bowed their heads to divine commandments and the first thing that was noticed about them was that almost all of them had gotten rid of English style haircuts, started wearing kurta, pajama, and a Gandhian cap, a cloth bag hung over their shoulders, and started living the simplest life.

Simplicity of attire is one of the characteristics of Islam. Muslims had adopted this simplicity from a religious point of view. This prompted emotions of lofty thoughts, strong beliefs, and a righteousness in the intellect. When Muslims took to wearing the Gandhian cap, the English stooges, who invoked Islam everywhere merely in support of the English, immediately started questioning if this was allowed from a religious point of view. Answers were given, but the most befitting reply was that the Muslim scholars themselves started wearing the Gandhian cap.

The New Era

Khilafat Movement gave way to that new age that was going to disassemble the old system of beliefs and values of life and was going to bring a system of modern ideas and thoughts. An epoch when Indians were going to step out of the darkness of tyrannical and colonial feudalism and slavery, and into the beam of light of freedom, justice, equality, and self-development. Allama Iqbal's sharp-sightedness predicted this.

Asia's time-honored cloak grows ragged and wears out
From upstart lands her young men borrow their finery

Today, Asia and Africa have awakened from their dreams and numerous independent nations have emerged. Europe's colonialism, its arrogance, dominating culture, the force of its power and strength, its privilege to rule over the Black population of the world - in other words, all those traits that were in fact disasters and calamities, but wore the false garbs of civility and service - are no more. Britain was once proud that the sun never set on its empire. Today they have only their tiny nation. Suffice it to say that the Khilafat Movement was that first step that opened the eyes of Asia and Africa, and they saw what they were unaware about till then.

The glitter of the western culture dazzles the eyes
But it's the craftsmanship of small diamonds that aren't real

The wizardry of deliberation cannot fortify
The culture of the world that is based on wealth

It would be ungrateful of me not to mention Mahatma Gandhi again. The message of the new era that the Khilafat Movement brought with it was given the cloak of practical action and promoted by this self-aware and dervish-like man, who, along with his deliberate thought and instincts, was the very personification of honesty, truth, courage, bravery, love of mankind, and resoluteness. His leadership achieved those things that were in the slogans of the Khilafat Movement. It is also true that if the Khilafat Movement had not received the leadership of this great man, there would neither have been a Khilafat Movement nor its wide-ranging effects, and perhaps the country of India would not have achieved complete independence in the time frame that it did.